全国英语专业博雅系列教材/总主编　丁建新

博雅阅读·精读 4

主　　编　洪　丹
副 主 编　周传进

参编人员　罗巾如　莫利娜　胡　琨
　　　　　梁　凌　陈　珍　何湘君　罗　琴

·广州·

版权所有　翻印必究

图书在版编目（CIP）数据

博雅阅读·精读·4/洪丹主编；周传进副主编．—广州：中山大学出版社，2016.1

（全国英语专业博雅系列教材/丁建新　总主编）

ISBN 978-7-306-05387-9

Ⅰ.①博… Ⅱ.①洪… ②周… Ⅲ.①英语—阅读教学—高等学校—教材 Ⅳ.①H319.4

中国版本图书馆 CIP 数据核字（2015）第 180828 号

出版人：	徐　劲
策划编辑：	熊锡源
责任编辑：	熊锡源
封面设计：	曾　斌
责任校对：	刘学谦
责任技编：	黄少伟
出版发行：	中山大学出版社
电　　话：	编辑部 020-84111996，84113349，84111997，84110779
	发行部 020-84111998，84111981，84111160
地　　址：	广州市新港西路135号
邮　　编：	510275　　传　真：020-84036565
网　　址：	http://www.zsup.com.cn　　E-mail: zdcbs@mail.sysu.edu.cn
印　刷　者：	广州中大印刷有限公司
规　　格：	787mm×1092mm　1/16　16.75印张　410千字
版次印次：	2016年1月第1版　2016年1月第1次印刷
印　　数：	1～3000册　　定　价：39.00元

如发现本书因印装质量影响阅读，请与出版社发行部联系调换

英语专业博雅系列教材编委会

总主编 丁建新（中山大学）

编 委 会

李洪儒（黑龙江大学）
司显柱（北京交通大学）
赵彦春（天津外国语大学）
田海龙（天津外国语大学）
夏慧言（天津科技大学）
李会民（河南科技学院）
刘承宇（西南大学）
施　旭（浙江大学）
辛　斌（南京师范大学）
杨信彰（厦门大学）
徐畅贤（湖南城市学院）
李玉英（江西师范大学）
李发根（江西师范大学）
肖坤学（广州大学）
宫　齐（暨南大学）
张广奎（广东财经大学）
温宾利（广东外语外贸大学）
杜金榜（广东外语外贸大学）
阮　炜（深圳大学）
张晓红（深圳大学）

博雅之辩（代序）

大学精神陷入前所未有的危机，许多人在寻找出路。

我们的坚持是，提倡博雅教育（Liberal Education）。因为大凡提倡什么，关键在于审视问题的症结何在，对症下药。而当下之困局，根源在于功利，在于忘掉了教育之根本。

博雅教育之理念，可以追溯至古罗马人提倡的"七艺"：文法、修辞、辩证法、音乐、算术、几何、天文学。其目的在于培养人格完美的自由思考者。在中国教育史上，博雅的思想，古已有之。中国儒家教育的传统，强调以培养学生人格为核心。儒家"六艺"，礼、乐、射、御、书、数，体现的正是我们所讲的博雅理念。"学识广博，生活高雅"，在这一点上，中国与西方，现代与传统，并无二致。

在古罗马，博雅教育在于培育自由的人格与社会精英。在启蒙时代，博雅教育意指解放思想，破除成见。"什么都知道一点，有些事情知道得多一点"，这是19世纪英国的思想家约翰·斯图亚特·密尔（John Stuart Mill）对博雅的诠释。同一时期，另外一位思想家，曾任都柏林大学校长的约翰·亨利·纽曼（John Henry Newman）在《大学理念》一书中，也曾这样表述博雅的培养目标："如果必须给大学课程一个实际目标，那么，我说它就是训练社会的良好成员。它的艺术是社会生活的艺术，它的目的是对世界的适应……大学训练旨在提高社会的精神格调，培养公众的智慧，纯洁一个民族的趣味"。

博雅教育包括科学与人文，目标在于培养人的自由和理性的精神，而不是迎合市场与风俗。教育的目标在于让学生学会尊重人类生活固有的内在价值：生命的价值、尊严的价值、求知的价值、爱的价值、相互尊重的价值、自我超越的价值、创新的价值。提倡博雅教育，就是要担当这些价值守护者的角色。博雅教育对于我们来说，是一种素质教育、人文教育。人文教育关心人类的终极目标，不是以"有用"为标准。它不是"万金油"，也无关乎"风花雪月"。

在美国，专注于博雅教育的大学称为"文理学院"，拒绝职业性的教育。在中国香港，以博雅教育为宗旨的就有岭南大学，提倡"全人教育"；在台湾大学，博雅教育是大学教育的基础，课程涉及文学与艺术、历史思维、世界文明、道德与哲学、公民意识与社会分析、量化分析与数学素养、物质科学、生命科学等八大领域。在欧洲,博雅教育历史中的七大范畴被分为"三道"(初级)与"四道"(高级)。前者包括语法、修辞与辩证法,后者包括算术、几何、天文与音乐。在中国大陆的中山大学,许多有识之士也提倡博雅之理念,让最好的教授开设通识课程,涉及现代学科之环境、生物、地理等各门。同时设立"博雅学院",学拉丁,读古典,开风气之先。

外语作为一门人文性很强的学科,尤其有必要落实博雅之理念。对于我们来说,最好的"应用型"教育在于博雅。早在20世纪20~40年代,在水木清华的外文系,吴宓先生提倡"语""文"并重,"中""西"兼修,教学上提倡自主学习与互动研究。在《西洋文学系学程总则》中,吴宓明确了"博雅之士"的培养目标:

> 本系课程编写的目的为使学生:(甲)成为博雅之士;(乙)了解西洋文明之精神;(丙)熟读西方文学之名著、谙悉西方思想之潮流,因而在国内教授英、德、法各国语言文字及文学,足以胜任愉快;(丁)创造今日之中国文学;(戊)汇通东西方之精神而互为介绍传布。

博雅之于我们,不仅仅是理念,更重要的是课程体系,是教材,是教法,是实践,是反应试教育,是将通识与专业熔于一炉。基于这样的理念,我们编写了这套丛书。希望通过这样的教育,让我们的学生知道人之为人是有他内在的生活意义,告诉我们的学生去求知,去阅读,去思考,去创造,去理解世界,去适应社会,去爱,去相互尊重,去审美,去找回精神的家园。

无需辩驳,也不怕非议。这是我们的坚守。

中山大学外国语学院　教授、博士生导师
中山大学语言研究所　所长
丁建新
2013年春天

前　言

《博雅阅读·精读》是供英语专业本科学生或水平相当的英语学习者使用的一套教材。本教材共4册，每册12个单元，每单元由A、B两篇课文组成，每篇课文后附有文章注释，以帮助学习者更好地理解文章内涵。文章A（Text A）为主课文，包括"读前"活动（Pre-reading Questions）、正文（Text）及课后练习（Exercises）组成。文章B（Text B）为副课文，是主课文A在主题、语言技能等方面的延伸。

本教材的编写是在本"博雅教育"系列教材的总的指导思想下完成的。从材料的选取，到练习的设计，都力争做到以文载物，与时俱进。在推进学生的英语语言综合能力培养的过程中，融入东西方文化经典的内涵，使学生在学习过程中得到良好的人文、科学思想的全面熏陶和发展。围绕这一思想，选题尽可能地做到博观取约、务实去华，并最终确定了"母爱与成长、人生态度、情感故事、历史文化、旅游地理、家庭生活、时代科技、历史人物"等几方面主题。

课后习题的设计旨在提高学生的阅读能力及语言技能，并进一步培养学生独立分析问题、解决问题的能力。其中，"课文理解（Text Comprehension/Understanding the Text/Comprehension Questions）"以阅读为主线，引导学生通过对课后问题的思考，培养其阅读理解与分析语篇的能力及文化意识。"词汇和结构（Vocabulary and Structure）""语法（Grammar）""翻译（Translation）"通过词汇、语法及翻译等练习，引导学生逐步提高自身的语言基本功、语言敏感性等。一年级设计了"语法巩固（Grammar Consolidation）"部分，旨在较系统地巩固复习英语语法知识（多数在中学已学过），考虑到来自不同地域的学生的水平差异，基本上通过以练习代巩固的形式进行，侧重于一些语法难点项目的练习，为进一步开展大学阶段的英语教学夯实语法基础。二年级重点培养学生的释义（Paraphrase）、翻译以及写作能力，并且给出了一些topic让学生自由讨论，培养他们独立思考和辩证思考的能力。每个单元后还有与主题相关的"引语（Quotation）和"拓展阅读推荐书目（Further Readings）"，在于开阔学生视野，引发新的思考。

在编写上，我们尽量做到：
（1）充分考虑学习者的英语基础，所选文章难易适中、文字规范、长度合理。

（2）结合本套教材的博雅主题，注重文章选取时博雅精神的体现，既考虑文章本身的知识性、可读性，也考虑文章文化精神的体现。

（3）符合英语专业教学大纲及我国培养创新型英语专业人才的要求。

（4）在编排模式上，结合语言习得及外语教学的相关理论，注意体现学生在课堂上的主体地位。

（5）理论联系实际，注重学习效果的实用性。

（6）注重教材编排的系统性及科学性。

编写过程中，外籍专家 Jeffery 和 Norma 给予了审阅和帮助，在此我们致以衷心的感谢。受编者经验与水平限制，本教材难免有疏漏之处。望广大师生读者批评指教，以利今后修订完善。

编 者

2013 年

Contents

Unit 1 ·· 1
    Text A Live and Learn, Why We Have College ···································· 2
    Text B The Complete Collection of Lies That High School Told Me ·········· 15

Unit 2 ·· 21
    Text A The Trying Twenties ··· 22
    Text B Cure Yourself of Unhappiness ·· 34

Unit 3 ·· 40
    Text A The Joy Luck Club (Excerpt) ·· 41
    Text B A Defining Gap: Seniors for Romney, Millennials for Obama ········ 53

Unit 4 ·· 59
    Text A News in the Television Schedule ·· 60
    Text B How to Establish Your Professional Network Through Social Media
              ·· 72

Unit 5 ·· 75
    Text A The World Turns Gray ·· 76
    Text B Oil's New World Order ·· 88

Unit 6 ·· 93
    Text A Is Technology a Threat to Liberal Society? ····························· 94
    Text B Modern Science and Technology and the Challenges of
              Third World Countries ·· 105

Unit 7 ·· 111
   Text A   Digital Photography Does Not Exist? ····································· 112
   Text B   THE iPHONE: Three Revolutionary Products in One ················ 124

Unit 8 ·· 129
   Text A   ChildFund International ··· 130
   Text B   Stop Telling Rich Folks to Give More to Charity ······················ 144

Unit 9 ·· 151
   Text A   The Story Behind the Amazing Success of Black Athletes ·········· 152
   Text B   Why the Story of Muhammad Ali's Rebellion Matters Today ········ 172

Unit 10 ·· 183
   Text A   Body Politics ··· 184
   Text B   The Moral Causes of Europe's Predicament ···························· 199

Unit 11 ·· 205
   Text A   Beauty ·· 206
   Text B   Give Her a Pattern ·· 218

Unit 12 ·· 223
   Text A   Plato ·· 224
   Text B   Who Was Socrates? ··· 237

Phrase List ·· 243

Vocabulary List ··· 248

Unit 1

More and more Americans are going to college, but how many of them are actually learning anything?

Pre-reading Questions:

1. Is your college life like what you had imagined before your entrance? If not, what are the differences?

2. Have you ever thought why we need to go to college, to help us become more competitive in job-hunting or to learn things that will make us a whole person well-adjusted to the society? Or do you hold any other opinions?

3. Should we have tests at college? Why or why not?

Text A
Live and Learn, Why We Have College

Louis Menand

1 My first job as a professor was at an Ivy League university. The students were happy to be taught, and we, their teachers, were happy to be teaching them. Whatever portion of their time and energy was being eaten up by social commitments — which may have been huge, but about which I was ignorant — they seemed earnestly and unproblematically engaged with the academic experience. If I was naïve about this, they were gracious enough not to disabuse me. None of us ever questioned the importance of what we were doing.

2 At a certain appointed hour, the university decided to make its way in the world without me, and we parted company. I was assured that there were no hard feelings. I was fortunate to get a position in a public university system, at a college with an overworked faculty, an army of part-time instructors, and sixteen thousand students. Many of these students were the first in their families to attend college, and any distractions they had were not social. Many of them worked, and some had complicated family responsibilities.

3 I didn't regard this as my business any more than I had the social lives of my Ivy League students. I assigned my new students the same readings I had assigned the old ones. I understood that the new students would not be as well prepared, but, out of faith or ego, I thought that I could tell them what they needed to know, and open up the texts for them. Soon after I started teaching there, someone raised his hand and asked, about a text I had assigned, "Why did we have to buy this book?"

4 I got the question in that form only once, but I heard it a number of times in the unmonetized form of "Why did we have to read this book?" I could see that this was not only a perfectly legitimate question; it was a very interesting question. The students were asking me to justify the return on investment in a college education. I just had never been called upon to think about this before. It wasn't part of my training. We took the value of the business we were in for granted.

5 I could have said, "You are reading these books because you're in college, and these are the kinds of books that people in college read." If you hold a certain theory of education, that answer is not as circular as it sounds. The theory goes like this: In any group of people, it's easy to determine who is the fastest or the strongest or even the best-looking. But picking out the most intelligent person is difficult, because intelligence involves many attributes that can't be captured in a one-time assessment,

like an I. Q. test. There is no intellectual equivalent of the hundred-yard dash. An intelligent person is open-minded, an outside-the-box thinker, an effective communicator, is prudent, self-critical, consistent, and so on. These are not qualities readily subject to measurement.

6　Society needs a mechanism for sorting out its more intelligent members from its less intelligent ones, just as a track team needs a mechanism (such as a stopwatch) for sorting out the faster athletes from the slower ones. Society wants to identify intelligent people early on so that it can funnel them into careers that maximize their talents. It wants to get the most out of its human resources. College is a process that is sufficiently multifaceted and fine-grained to do this.

7　College is, essentially, a four-year intelligence test. Students have to demonstrate intellectual ability over time and across a range of subjects. If they're sloppy or inflexible or obnoxious — no matter how smart they might be in the I. Q. Sense — those negatives will get picked up in their grades. As an added service, college also sorts people according to aptitude. It separates the math types from the poetry types. At the end of the process, graduates get a score, the G. P. A. , that professional schools and employers can trust as a measure of intellectual capacity and productive potential. It's important, therefore, that everyone is taking more or less the same test.

8　I could have answered the question in a different way. I could have said, "You're reading these books because they teach you things about the world and yourself that, if you do not learn them in college, you are unlikely to learn anywhere else. " This reflects a different theory of college, a theory that runs like this: In a society that encourages its members to pursue the career paths that promise the greatest personal or financial rewards, people will, given a choice, learn only what they need to know for success. They will have no incentive to acquire the knowledge and skills important for life as an informed citizen, or as a reflective and culturally literate human being. College exposes future citizens to material that enlightens and empowers them, whatever careers they end up choosing.

9　In performing this function, college also socializes. It takes people with disparate backgrounds and beliefs and brings them into line with mainstream norms of reason and taste. Independence of mind is tolerated in college, and even honored, but students have to master the accepted ways of doing things before they are permitted to deviate. Ideally, we want everyone to go to college, because college gets everyone on the same page. It's a way of producing a society of like-minded grownups.

10　If you like the first theory, then it doesn't matter which courses students take, or even what is taught in them, as long as they're rigorous enough for the sorting mechanism to do its work. All that matters is the grades. If you prefer the second theory, then you might consider grades a useful instrument of positive or negative reinforcement, but the only thing that matters is what students actually learn. There is stuff that every adult ought to know, and college is the best delivery system for getting that stuff into people's heads.

11   A lot of confusion is caused by the fact that since 1945 American higher education has been committed to both theories. The system is designed to be both meritocratic (Theory 1) and democratic (Theory 2). Professional schools and employers depend on colleges to sort out each cohort as it passes into the workforce, and elected officials talk about the importance of college for everyone. We want higher education to be available to all Americans, but we also want people to deserve the grades they receive.

12   It wasn't always like this. Before 1945, élite private colleges like Harvard and Yale were largely in the business of reproducing a privileged social class. Between 1906 and 1932, four hundred and five boys from Groton applied to Harvard. Four hundred and two were accepted. In 1932, Yale received thirteen hundred and thirty applications, and it admitted nine hundred and fifty-nine — an acceptance rate of seventy-two per cent. Almost a third of those who enrolled were sons of Yale graduates.

13   In 1948, through the exertions of people like James Bryant Conant, the president of Harvard, the Educational Testing Service went into business, and standardized testing (the S. A. T. and the A. C. T.) soon became the virtually universal method for picking out the most intelligent students in the high-school population, regardless of their family background, and getting them into the higher-education system. Conant regarded higher education as a limited social resource, and he wanted to make more strait the gate. Testing insured that only people who deserved to go to college did. The fact that Daddy went no longer sufficed. In 1940, the acceptance rate at Harvard was eighty-five per cent. By 1970, it was twenty per cent. Last year, thirty-five thousand students applied to Harvard, and the acceptance rate was six per cent.

14   Almost all the élite colleges saw a jump in applications this year, partly because they now recruit much more aggressively internationally, and acceptance rates were correspondingly lower. Columbia, Yale, and Stanford admitted less than eight per cent of their applicants. This degree of selectivity is radical. To put it in some perspective: the acceptance rate at Cambridge is twenty-one per cent, and at Oxford eighteen per cent.

15   But, as private colleges became more selective, public colleges became more accommodating. Proportionally, the growth in higher education since 1945 has been overwhelmingly in the public sector. In 1950, there were about 1.14 million students in public colleges and universities and about the same number in private ones. Today, public colleges enroll almost fifteen million students, private colleges fewer than six million.

16   There is now a seat for virtually anyone with a high-school diploma who wants to attend college. The City University of New York (my old employer) has two hundred

and twenty-eight thousand undergraduates — more than four times as many as the entire Ivy League. The big enchilada of public higher education, the State of California, has ten university campuses, twenty-three state-college campuses, a hundred and twelve community-college campuses, and more than 3.3 million students. Six per cent of the American population is currently enrolled in college or graduate school. In Great Britain and France, the figure is about three per cent.

17 If you are a Theory 1 person, you worry that, with so many Americans going to college, the bachelor's degree is losing its meaning, and soon it will no longer operate as a reliable marker of productive potential. Increasing public investment in higher education with the goal of college for everyone — in effect, taxpayer-subsidized social promotion — is thwarting the operation of the sorting mechanism. Education is about selection, not inclusion.

18 If you are friendly toward Theory 2, on the other hand, you worry that the competition for slots in top-tier colleges is warping educational priorities. You see academic tulip mania: students and their parents are overvaluing a commodity for which there are cheap and plentiful substitutes. The sticker price at Princeton or Stanford, including room and board, is upward of fifty thousand dollars a year. Public colleges are much less expensive — the average tuition is $7,605 — and there are also many less selective private colleges where you can get a good education, and a lot more faculty face time, without having to spend every minute of high school sucking up to your teachers and reformatting your résumé. Education is about personal and intellectual growth, not about winning some race to the top.

19 It would be nice to conclude that, despite these anxieties, and given the somewhat contradictory goals that have been set for it, the American higher-education system is doing what Americans want it to do. College is broadly accessible: sixty-eight per cent of high-school graduates now go on to college (in 1980, only forty-nine per cent did), and employers continue to reward the credential, which means that there is still some selection going on. In 2008, the average income for someone with an advanced degree (master's, professional, or doctoral) was $83,144; for someone with a bachelor's degree, it was $58,613; for someone with only a high-school education, it was $31,283.

Notes

1. About the author.

Louis Menand has been contributing to *The New Yorker* since 1991. Menand is the author and editor of several books. His book *The Metaphysical Club*, was awarded the 2002 Pulitzer Prize for History and the Francis Parkman Prize from the Society of American Historians. He was an associate editor at *The New Republic* from 1986 to

1987, and was a contributing editor at *The New York Review of Books* from 1994 to 2001.

Menand is the Anne T. and Robert M. Bass Professor of English and American Literature and Language at Harvard University. He has also taught at the Graduate Center of the City University of New York, Princeton, Columbia, and the University of Virginia School of Law.

2. My first job as a professor was at an **Ivy League** university. (Para. 1)

The Ivy League is an athletic conference composed of sports teams from eight private institutions of higher education in the Northeastern United States. The conference name is also commonly used to refer to those eight schools as a group. The eight institutions are Brown University, Columbia University, Cornell University, Dartmouth College, Harvard University, Princeton University, the University of Pennsylvania, and Yale University. The term Ivy League also has connotations of academic excellence, selectivity in admissions, and social elitism.

3. An intelligent person is open-minded, an **outside-the-box thinker**, ... (Para. 5)

Thinking outside the box (also thinking out of the box or thinking beyond the box) is to think differently, unconventionally, or from a new perspective. This phrase often refers to novel or creative thinking. To think outside the box is to look further and to try not thinking of the obvious things, but to try thinking beyond them.

4. Ideally, we want everyone to go to college, because college gets everyone **on the same page**. (Para. 9)

In business meetings and college classes people often make copies of a single report and hand a copy to each person at the meeting. While they discuss the different points in the report, each person needs to be reading from the same page ("on the same page"). Everyone is "on the same page" when they are all following along and understanding the basic idea that the group is sharing. "On the same page" has a further meaning of people being in basic understanding and agreement on something. Example: "Before we make any decisions today, I'd like to make sure that everyone is on the same page."

5. ...the **Educational Testing Service** went into business, ... (Para. 13)

Educational Testing Service (ETS), founded in 1947, is the world's largest private nonprofit educational testing and assessment organization. It is presently headquartered near Princeton, New Jersey. ETS develops various standardized tests primarily in the United States for K—12 and higher education, and it also administers international tests including the TOEFL (Test of English as a Foreign Language), TOEIC (Test of English for International Communication), GRE (Graduate Record Examinations) General and Subject Tests, and The Praxis test Series — in more than 180 countries, and at over 9,000 locations worldwide.

6. ...and standardized testing (the **S. A. T.** and the **A. C. T.**) soon became the virtually universal method... (Para. 13)

The SAT is a standardized test for college admissions in the United States. The SAT is owned, published, and developed by the College Board, a nonprofit organization in the United States. The test is intended to assess a student's readiness for college. It was first introduced in 1926, and its name and scoring have changed several times. It was first called the Scholastic Aptitude Test, then the Scholastic Assessment Test.

The ACT (originally an abbreviation of American College Testing) is a standardized test for high school achievement and college admissions in the United States. It was first administered in November 1959 by Everett Franklin Lindquist as a competitor to the College Board's Scholastic Aptitude Test, now the SAT Reasoning Test. The ACT has historically consisted of four tests: English, Mathematics, Reading, and Science Reasoning.

7. To **put it in some perspective**, the acceptance rate at Cambridge is twenty-one per cent, and at Oxford eighteen per cent. (Para. 14)

If you put something into perspective you show that you realize or make others realize the importance/significance of the thing you are referring to. Alternatively, it means you put the thing into its correct place (or make it clear for you and others). e. g.

1) You know that we have done a good research. We ask you to do a favor for us and put it into perspective when you talk to the stakeholders. (to show the significance of our work)

2) Let's put it into perspective: 100 years ago the frequency of skin cancer was way lower than what it is now. (to give a clear idea of what has happened)

8. You see academic **tulip mania**: students and their parents are overvaluing a commodity for which there are cheap and plentiful substitutes. (Para. 18)

Tulip mania or tulipomania was a period in the Dutch Golden Age during which contract prices for bulbs of the recently introduced tulip reached extraordinarily high levels and then suddenly collapsed. The term "tulip mania" is now often used metaphorically to refer to any large economic bubble (when asset prices deviate from intrinsic values).

Glossary

accommodating [ə'kɒmədeɪtɪŋ]	a.	helpful and obliging
aptitude ['æptɪtjuːd]	n.	an inherent ability, as for learning
attribute [ə'trɪbjuːt]	n.	a quality or characteristic inherent in or ascribed to someone or something
cohort ['kəʊhɔːt]	n.	a group or band of people
commitment [kə'mɪtmənt]	n.	the state of being bound emotionally or

	intellectually to a course of action or to another person or persons
credential [krɪˈdenʃəl] n.	that which entitles one to confidence, credit, or authority
deviate [ˈdiːvɪeɪt] v.	to turn aside from a course or way
disabuse [dɪsəˈbjuːz] v.	to make someone realize that they were wrong to believe something
disparate [ˈdɪspərət] a.	fundamentally distinct or different in kind; entirely dissimilar
ego [ˈiːgəʊ; ˈe-] n.	your sense of your own value and importance
élite [eɪˈliːt] n.	a group or class of persons or a member of such a group or class, enjoying superior intellectual, social, or economic status
enchilada [entʃəˈlɑːdə] n.	(from Spanish) A tortilla rolled and stuffed usually with a mixture containing meat or cheese and served with a sauce spiced with chili
equivalent [ɪˈkwɪvələnt] a.	equal, as in value, force, or meaning
exertion [ɪgˈzɜːʃn] n.	great physical or mental effort
funnel [ˈfʌnəl] n.	something resembling this utensil in shape
v.	(to cause) to move through or as if through a funnel
grain [greɪn] v.	to cause to form into grains
incentive [ɪnˈsentɪv] n.	something, such as the fear of punishment or the expectation of reward, that induces action or motivates effort
legitimate [lɪˈdʒɪtɪmət] a.	lawful; reasonable
literate [ˈlɪtərət] a.	able to read and write
mechanism [ˈmekənɪz(ə)m] n.	an instrument or a process, physical or mental, by which something is done or comes in to being
meritocracy [merɪˈtɒkrəsɪ] a.	a system in which the talented are chosen and moved ahead on the basis of their achievement
monetize [ˈmʌnɪtaɪz] v.	to coin into money
obnoxious [əbˈnɒkʃəs] a.	extremely unpleasant, especially in a way that offends people
prudent [ˈpruːdənt] a.	wise in handling practical matters; exercising good judgment or common sense
reflective [rɪˈflektɪv] a.	of, relating to, produced by, or resulting from reflection
reinforce [riːɪnˈfɔːs] v.	to give more force or effectiveness to; strengthen

rigorous [ˈrɪgərəs] a.	thorough and careful; strict or severe
sloppy [ˈslɒpɪ] a.	that shows a lack of care, thought or effort
stopwatch [ˈstɒpwɒtʃ] n.	a watch that can be instantly started and stopped by pushing a button and used to measure an exact duration of time
subject [ˈsʌbdʒɪkt] a.	being in a position or in circumstances that place one under the power or authority of another or others
subsidize [ˈsʌbsɪdaɪz] v.	to give money to sb or an organization to help pay for sth; to give a subsidy
suffice [səˈfaɪs] v.	to meet present needs or requirements; be sufficient
thwart [θwɔːt] v.	to prevent the occurrence, realization, or attainment
undergraduate [ˌʌndəˈgrædjuət] n.	a college or university student who has not yet received a bachelor's or similar degree
warp [wɔːp] v.	to turn or twist (wood, for example) out of shape

Comprehension Questions

Answer the following questions after reading the text.

1. Is intelligence as easy to be measured as athletic ability?
2. Why should students take almost the same tests at college according to the first theory?
3. What is the function of college according to the second theory?
4. Does going to college mean that you can act in whatever ways you want without knowing what the accepted ways are?
5. Which of the two theories have been applied to American higher education since 1945?
6. Which part of American higher education has higher acceptance rates, private or public colleges?
7. Do people who believe in the meritocratic theory hope that colleges enroll more students?
8. Do people who believe in the democratic theory feel it necessary to participate in fierce competitions to be enrolled in the top-tier colleges?
9. Is American higher education system losing the function of selection while the acceptance rate increases?

Exercises

I Vocabulary

Section A Paraphrase the sentences chosen from the text.

1. Whatever portion of their time and energy was being eaten up by social commitments — which may have been huge, but about which I was ignorant — they seemed earnestly and unproblematically engaged with the academic experience.
2. Society needs a mechanism for sorting out its more intelligent members from its less intelligent ones, just as a track team needs a mechanism (such as a stopwatch) for sorting out the faster athletes from the slower ones.
3. They will have no incentive to acquire the knowledge and skills important for life as an informed citizen, or as a reflective and culturally literate human being.
4. Independence of mind is tolerated in college, and even honored, but students have to master the accepted ways of doing things before they are permitted to deviate.
5. It would be nice to conclude that, despite these anxieties, and given the somewhat contradictory goals that have been set for it, the American higher-education system is doing what Americans want it to do.

Section B There are ten sentences in this section. Beneath each sentence there are four words or phrases marked A, B, C and D. Choose one word or phrase that best completes the sentence.

1. Patience is one of the most important _____ in a teacher.
   A. attributes   B. viewpoints   C. characters   D. drawbacks
2. The occurrence left him with a badly bruised _____.
   A. self   B. ego   C. himself   D. mind
3. Achieving success at this level requires a(n) _____ of time and energy.
   A. engagement   B. involvement   C. commitment   D. endowment
4. Another _____ pass like that might lose them the whole match.
   A. swift   B. straight   C. slight   D. sloppy
5. Breathing such polluted air is the _____ of smoking ten cigarettes a day.
   A. equivalent   B. same   C. more   D. similar
6. Bonus payments provide a(n) _____ to work harder.
   A. stimulus   B. incentive   C. obstacle   D. hindrance
7. When she's in a bad mood she's _____ to everyone.
   A. benign   B. faithful   C. obnoxious   D. benevolent
8. The two cultures were so utterly _____ that she found it hard to adapt from one to the other.
   A. similar   B. identical   C. resemble   D. disparate
9. I suppose I shouldn't be laughing about death — perhaps I've got a _____ sense of humor!

A. warped B. normal C. common D. natural
10. One example will _____ to illustrate the point.
A. supply B. suffice C. sacrifice D. sustain

Section C Use the proper form of the following words given in the brackets to fill in the blanks.

1. I intend to challenge the _____ of his claim. (legitimate)
2. "As a responsible nation India feels it will be _____ to use such weapons," it added. (prudent)
3. He put silver foil around the fire to increase heat _____. (reflective)
4. At least he was able to sign his name, and bluff people into believing he was not _____ _____ when collecting dole or wages. (literate)
5. Any _____ from the party's faith is seen as betrayal. (deviate)
6. The country's press is _____ controlled. (rigorous)
7. The harbour walls need urgent _____. (reinforce)
8. It was thought that he'd committed the crime but there wasn't _____ evidence to convict him. (suffice)
9. The company received a substantial government _____. (subsidize)
10. It was the first time in his life that he had _____ himself to a woman. (commitment)

Section D Use the proper form of the following phrases to fill in the blanks.

| deviate from | disabuse sb. of | accommodate sb. with | exert pressure on |
| reflect off | commit oneself to | have aptitude for | be subject to |

1. To burn one's bridges is to _____ an irreversible course.
2. He thought that all women liked children, but she soon _____ that idea.
3. Travel arrangements _____ confirmation by State Tourist Organizations.
4. Students who _____ computing may continue to diplomas in computer applications or Geographical Information Systems.
5. Why does light _____ a silvered surface but scatter off a painted wall?
6. The bus had to _____ its usual route because of a road closure.
7. Some managers _____ their staff to work extra hours without being paid.
8. We always try to _____ our clients _____ financial assistance if necessary.

II Grammar

Choose the best answer to complete the following sentence from the respective four choices.

1. He left orders that nothing _____ touched until the police arrived here.
   A. should be B. ought to be C. must be D. would be
2. The physicist has made a discovery, _____ of great importance to the progress of

science and technology.
   A. I think which is   B. that I think is
   C. which I think is   D. which I think it is
3. _____, he is ready to accept suggestions from different sources.
   A. Instead of his contributions   B. For all his notable contributions
   C. His making notable contributions   D. However his notable contributions
4. The team can handle whatever _____.
   A. that needs handling   B. which needs handling
   C. it needs handling   D. needs to be handled
5. Come and see me whenever _____.
   A. you are convenient   B. you will be convenient
   C. it is convenient to you   D. it will be convenient to you
6. I have never been to London, but that is the city _____.
   A. where I like to visit most   B. I'd most like to visit
   C. which I like to visit mostly   D. where I'd like most to visit
7. I was to have made a speech if _____.
   A. I was not called away   B. nobody would have called me away
   C. I had not been called away D. nobody called me away
8. I felt that I was not yet _____ to travel abroad.
   A. too strong   B. strong enough   C. so strong   D. enough strong
9. John is _____ hardworking than his sister, but he failed in the exam.
   A. no less   B. no more   C. not less   D. no so
10. The children prefer camping in the mountains _____ an indoor activity.
    A. to   B. than   C. for   D. with
11. If there were no subjunctive mood, English _____ much easier for Chinese students to learn.
    A. would be   B. could have been C. will be   D. would have been
12. Had Alexander been more careful on the math exam, he _____ much better results now.
    A. would get   B. could have got   C. must get   D. would have getting
13. If only the patient _____ the treatment of using the antibiotics, he might still be alive now.
    A. should have received   B. received
    C. had received   D. were receiving
14. He would have finished his learning of writing, but he _____ to quit and find a job to support his family.
    A. has had   B. has   C. would have   D. had
15. If you explained the situation to your tutor, he _____ able to advise you much better than I can.

A. would be
B. will have been
C. could have been
D. were

III Cloze

Decide which of the choices given below would best complete the passage if inserted in the corresponding blanks. Mark the best choice for each blank.

High school seniors who (1) _____ on the complicated road of applying to an academic institution learn quickly that the majority of academic institutions require that students (2) _____ a college application essay along with their application. Some universities even require more than one report; however additional reports might be optional. The good news is that the university consideration process is generally completed while students still have the (3) _____ of having their high school instructors, counselors, and (4) _____ available to (5) _____ their college application essays. No student is expected to go it alone.

College application essays are generally creations that ask (6) _____ students to explore a particular event in their lives, a goal they would like to achieve, or the reason they would like to study at the university they are applying to. Some universities will direct the college application essay by giving applicants the topic (7) _____ which they are to write. But, even a topic such as "how I spent my summer vacation" invites more thought for a college application than it did for a high school freshman.

When a college application essay invites students to write about their summer vacation, the university wants more than (8) _____ an itinerary of what the student actually did during his or her summer vacation. The student who fails to delve properly into the subject matter is likely to have his or her application summarily (9) _____. What the university wants to know is what the student did during their summer vacation that mattered, not literally the activities they participated in. Of course, there is the rare student who can make a trip to Disneyland read like well-written literature, but, for the most part, the university is looking for something that sets the student apart from the thousands of other submissions that university recruiters will have to sift (10) _____.

Many learners pay (11) _____ attention to the university consideration article. They are (12) _____ that it is merely a way for university recruiters to make sure that they can read, write, and follow instructions. And, in a way, they are right. It goes without (13) _____ that the student who (14) _____ to pay attention to spelling, grammar, and punctuation is not likely to have his or her college application (15) _____ in the "accepted" pile.

However, the college application essay is more about differentiation than (16) _____. The universities that student's apply to are (17) _____ to receive applications from thousands of (18) _____ applicants every year. There has to be some way to evaluate students (19) _____ qualifications other than grade point average and extracurricular activities. The student who finds a way to use his or her college application essay to make himself or herself (20) _____ in the eyes of the educational institution recruiters is the student who is most likely to receive acceptance letters to one or more of the universities of his or her choice.

1. A. begin   B. start   C. commence   D. embark
2. A. admit   B. remit   C. submit   D. receive
3. A. disadvantage B. advantage   C. drawback   D. feature
4. A. mentors   B. parents   C. friends   D. fellow students
5. A. critique   B. comment   C. reject   D. return
6. A. respective   B. prospective   C. retrospective   D. inspective
7. A. at   B. in   C. on   D. to
8. A. mere   B. rather   C. just only   D. merely
9. A. rejected   B. reject   C. projected   D. project
10. A. in   B. through   C. out   D. Down
11. A. little   B. a little   C. few   D. a few
12. A. convincing   B. convinced   C. believing   D. believed
13. A. say   B. said   C. saying   D. to be said
14. A. succeeds   B. tries   C. attempts   D. fails
15. A. landed   B. landing   C. to be landed   D. land
16. A. something   B. anything   C. anything else   D. something else
17. A. likely   B. bound   C. happy   D. upset
18. A. qualified   B. qualifying   C. competed   D. competing
19. A. on   B. in   C. at   D. by
20. A. stand by   B. stand out   C. step up   D. step out

IV Translation

Section A Translate the following Chinese sentences into English.

1. 约1000万美金援助通过政府机构注入到这个国家。(funnel)
2. 这些住房项目是由政府资助的。(subsidize)
3. 苏格兰人宣称詹姆士·斯图尔特是英国王位的合法继承人。(legitimate)
4. 当公共交通花费昂贵的时候，人们几乎没有任何动力愿意将自己的车留在家里。(incentive)
5. 这次获奖大大增强了她的自信心。(ego)
6. 我必须消除你的傲气。(disabuse)
7. 这份工作要求你具备团队合作能力等个人品质。(attribute)
8. 在正式信函中出现拼写错误，往往显得非常马虎。(sloppy)
9. 由于用力骑车上山，她又热又喘不过气来。(exertion)
10. 不能酒后驾车这个事要时不时地对你强调一下。(reinforce)

Section B Translate the following English paragraph into Chinese.

　　I'd compare college tuition to paying for a personal trainer at an athletic club. We professors play the roles of trainers, giving people access to the equipment (books, labs, our expertise) and after that, it is our job to be demanding. We need to make sure that our students are exerting themselves. We need to praise them when they deserve it and to tell them honestly when they have it in them to work harder.

　　Most importantly, we need to let them know how to judge for themselves how they're coming along. The great thing about working out at a gym is that if you put in effort, you get very obvious results. The same should be true of college. A professor's job is to teach students how to see their minds growing in the same way they can see their muscles grow when they look in a mirror.

V Topic for Discussion

　　Based on the two kinds of function of college distinguished by the author in this essay, what kind of function do you think your university or college performs for the society? Find examples to prove your viewpoint.

VI Written Work

　　Write a short essay of about 200 words on either of the topics.

　　It seems that there's a tendency that universities are enrolling an increasing number of students in many major countries of the world. Under the current situation, do you think higher education should be meritocratic or democratic? In turn, what kind of life should college students lead according to this function of higher education?

Text B
The Complete Collection of Lies That High School Told Me

Emily Grier

　　1 I'm always amazed by the crazy college myths that students fall for: If you get hit by a bus on campus, you get free tuition (because college would be so much fun in a full body cast), if your roommate dies, you get straight As for the semester (not to mention a single room), and (my personal favorite) the college you attend will determine the rest of your life…no pressure or anything. Really, who believes some of this stuff?

　　2 …Okay, I did. Which got me thinking: how many ridiculous things did I go through high school (and my freshman year of college) believing to be true? Whether

these myths live on in order to scare incoming freshmen or entertain high school guidance counselors in their free time, this is the complete collection of lies that high school told me:

Picking a college is the biggest decision of your life.

3 Let's be honest: Although it completely seems true during your senior year of high school, picking a college probably isn't the biggest decision you will ever make in your lifetime (kickin' in the front seat or sittin' in the back seat? ...now there's a big decision). It took me basically an entire year away at school before I finally realized this. Meeting people who didn't end up at their first choice schools (and were convinced their lives were over because of it), will eventually convince you otherwise. For anyone who didn't get into their dream school, you'll probably figure out (if you haven't already) that you're where you're meant to be.

Your major will be your life path.

4 Yeah, the major you check-off on your college app is your new life path...and I'm Lady Gaga. While most students don't believe that what they initially select will be their major for the rest of college, most students do assume that picking their major will be the second most important decision they will ever make (falling just behind the college you pick). That is A LOT of pressure. I can barely decide between Peachy Paterno and Death By Chocolate ice cream at The Penn State Creamery, let alone what I want to do with the rest of my life.

5 One thing I've learned from talking to people is this: your major may have nothing to do with your job some day. While it probably will be connected in some way, earning a degree in finance, for example, doesn't necessarily mean that you will be working on Wall Street. Most people tend to fall into their careers, and that's half the fun of it. While choosing a major is in fact an important decision, it's not the most important — and it will in no way be the determining factor of the rest of your life.

Attending a prestigious college = A perfect life.

6 I spent the better part of my junior and senior years of high school obsessing over which college I was going to attend. This was mainly because I associated attending a school with an impressive name with being automatically assured of a perfect life. Looking back on it now, I realize that my thinking was beyond shallow. Yes, prestigious colleges are an honor to attend, there is no denying that. However, attending a college with a well-respected name by no means guarantees you anything, let alone the ideal life. Just like a college degree does not equal a high paying job, a high-status school does not mean that the best things in life will fall into your lap. What matters more is being a self-motivated, ambitious person. At the end of the day, the name stamped on the top of your degree will never be able to do that for you.

College is SO much harder than high school.

7 This lie is courtesy of just about every high school teacher on the planet. But

really, it's not their fault for telling us this. I mean, how many things can you really threaten high school students with? They can't tell us to sit in the naughty corner if we talk over them in class, but they can tell us "you'll need to know this stuff for your super hard college classes" and suddenly we'll pay attention. In my experience, college and high school are a fairly similar academic challenge. True, one's opinion of college's level of difficulty will vary from school to school and from class to class. But the shared difference is this: college is all you. YOU are responsible for keeping track of due dates, YOU are required to manage your time in a smart way, YOU are the only one watching out for your academic well-being. College isn't harder than high school. It's just...self-directed.

Once you choose a school, you're stuck there forever.

8   The one thing that nobody ever mentions when you're initially picking a school is that you can always change your mind. Choosing a college isn't like getting a tattoo on your face... it's by no means permanent. Sure, it's no walk in the park to transfer, but you can always correct your mistake if you felt you made one. Think of it like this: If you make a wrong turn while driving, you reroute yourself, right? Nobody in their right mind would tell you to stay on the wrong road only to get yourself even more lost. For some reason, there seems to be a sort of stigma attached to transferring schools— like if you transfer, you failed. But if you really think you'd be happier somewhere else, then it's always an option that's worth considering.

Study, sleep, party: Choose two of the three.

9   I cannot even begin to tell you how many times I heard this phrase before arriving at college. And really, what kind of philosophy is "study, sleep, party: Choose two of the three"? You can have it all. I'm not saying that you can sleep through classes, party all night every night, and still get A's for the semester... because life just doesn't work like that — at least not without an easy schedule and a lot of energy drinks. But, college seems to be really good at inadvertently teaching time management. While you can be the student that picks two of the three, you can also be the student that studies a little bit every day (so you don't have to cram for exams the night before), actually sleeps normal hours (like, you know, when it's dark out), and still has time to have fun with friends (Rebecca Black would be more than happy to highlight the importance of *Friday* for you).

Participate in EVERYTHING.

10   Remember that girl at the Activity Fair whose name was on like EVERY club sign-up sheet... that was probably me. In less than 20 minutes, I managed to jot my name down for any club that had potential to interest me (or free candy). All through high school, it was drilled into my head that in order to succeed, you have your hand in everything: student council, sports, community service clubs, etc. Luckily, college is different: Nobody expects you to do it all. Instead of stretching yourself too thin, it's

important to stay involved in major related clubs and anything that interests you... which means that you don't need to be president of nine clubs in order to feel like you accomplished something.

College is exactly four years.

11 Nowadays college can be anywhere from three to five years. Depending on who you are, this could be positive or negative. On one hand, college is awesome. Who wouldn't want to spend an extra year dodging the real world and finishing up those last minute credits? On the other hand, you run the risk of watching friends graduate and move-on, leaving you all alone on campus. The fact is: everyone is different. This is not new information, I know, *Sesame Street* beat me to it. But how many credits you need to graduate, if you already had credits from AP classes, whether or not you choose to study abroad, etc. are all things that will impact the length of your education. Even though most of us tend to think that we have four years at school, it could in fact be more (or less).

These are the best years of your life.

12 Don't get me wrong, Asher Roth and I LOVE college. But this is as good as it gets... really? That either means that college is super awesome or the rest of my life is going to be super dismal... take your pick. As soon as the over-thirty crowd starts throwing around phrases like "these are the best years of your life", I panic (who wouldn't?). If the next three years are all I have to look forward to in life, wow. Just, wow.

13 I think what people actually mean is not that these are the only good years, but your four years in college are unique from the rest of your life. Think about it: You have the next four years to focus on yourself, where you want to go in life, and (more importantly) how you want to get there. Typically after college, you enter the real world, only to be graced with a career, bills, spouses, children, mortgages, etc. Suddenly, there is a lot more to worry about then which frat you got invited to this weekend. For anyone who ever told you that college is "the best time of your life", they're really just trying to say "enjoy where you're at because it will never be like this again". Which, when you think about it, is pretty sage advice.

14 And while these probably aren't the best years of your life, I think we can all agree that they're definitely the best years yet.

Emily Grier is a rising sophomore at Penn State University. She is a staff writer for **Valley** *magazine, Penn State's life and style magazine, and is also a contributing writer for* **Her Campus.**

Notes

1. ... if your roommate dies, you get **straight As** for the semester (not to mention

a single room), ... (Para. 1)

Straight A means achieving or showing the highest grade or superior accomplishment, esp. scholastically.

2. I can barely decide between Peachy Paterno and Death By Chocolate ice cream at **The Penn State** Creamery ... (Para. 4)

The Pennsylvania State University (commonly referred to as Penn State or PSU) is a public, state-related research university with campuses and facilities in Pennsylvania.

3. ... **let alone** what I want to do with the rest of my life. (Para. 4)

to say nothing of; not to mention — used especially to emphasize the improbability of a contrasting example. E. g. He would never walk again let alone play golf.

4. **fall into your lap** (Para. 6): **drop/fall into your lap** or **land in your lap** (*informal*): If something good drops/falls into your lap or lands in your lap, it comes to you suddenly in an unexpected way even though you did not try to get it. E. g. This wonderful new job just fell into my lap when I was least expecting it!

5. **At the end of the day**, the name stamped on the top of your degree will never be able to do that for you. (Para. 6)

(*informal*) when all things are considered; in the end. E. g. It was a difficult decision, but at the end of the day, we knew we made the right choice.

6. Sure, **it's no walk in the park to transfer**, but you can always correct your mistake if you felt you made one. (Para. 8)

"Walk in the park" means something easy or pleasant, especially by comparison to something.

7. **Rebecca Black** would be more than happy to highlight the importance of *Friday* for you. (Para. 9)

Rebecca Black (born June 21, 1997) is an American pop singer and dancer who gained extensive media attention with the 2011 single *Friday*.

8. This is not new information, I know, **Sesame Street** beat me to it. (Para. 11)

Sesame Street is a long-running American children's television series created by Joan Ganz Cooney and Lloyd Morrisett. The program is known for its educational content, and creativity communicated through the use of Jim Henson's Muppets, animation, short films, humor, and cultural references. The series premiered on stations on November 10, 1969 to positive reviews, some controversy, and high ratings.

9. ...if you already had credits from **AP classes** ... (Para. 11)

The Advanced Placement (AP) is a program created by the College Boardoffering college-level curriculum and examinations to high school students. Colleges often grant placement and credit to students who obtain high scores on the examinations. The AP curriculum for the various subjects is created for the College Board by a panel of experts and college-level educators in each subject.

10. Don't get me wrong, **Asher Roth** and I LOVE college. (Para. 12)

Asher Paul Roth (born August 11, 1985) is an American rapper from Morrisville, Pennsylvania. *I Love College* is the debut single by American rapper Asher Roth, from his debut album *Asleep in the Bread Aisle*. The song was released on January 13, 2009.

11. Suddenly, there is a lot more to worry about then which **frat** you got invited to this weekend. (Para. 13)

A fraternity (Latin *frater*: "brother") is a brotherhood, although the term sometimes connotes a distinct or formal organization and sometimes a secret society. A fraternity (or fraternal organization) is an organized society of men associated together in an environment of companionship and brotherhood; dedicated to the intellectual, physical, and social development of its members.

Questions for Discussion

In this article, the author tells us the lies people believed about college in high school. Now, as sophomores, what are the rumors about life of seniors spread among college students that you have ever heard of? Do you hold them to be true or not? What are your expectations of your own life in the next two years at college?

Memorable Quotes

1. A University should be a place of light, of liberty, and of learning.
 — Benjamin Disraeli
2. I learned three important things in college — to use a library, to memorize quickly and visually, to drop asleep at any time given a horizontal surface and fifteen minutes.
 — Agnes DeMille
3. No man should escape our universities without knowing how little he knows.
 — J. Robert Oppenheimer
4. The purpose of primary education is the development of your weak characteristics; the purpose of university education, the development of your strong.
 — Nevin Fenneman
5. Standardization is the fertilizer of college education. A little may be useful, but flowers do not grow in pure manure.
 — Martin H. Fischer

Further Readings

1. John Henry Newman, *The Idea of a University*
2. Cal Newport, *How to Win at College*

Unit 2

Pre-reading Questions

1. Which stage do you think is the most defining one in the several stages of human growth?

2. To what extent do you agree with the statement that "Lazy youth makes lousy age"?

3. What does life mean to young people in their twenties?

Text A

The Trying Twenties

Gail Sheehy

1   The Trying Twenties confront us with the question of how to take hold in the adult world. Incandescent with our energies, having outgrown the family and the formlessness of our transiting years, we are impatient to pour ourselves into the exactly right form — our own way of living in the world. Or while looking for it, we want to try out some provisional form. For now we are not only trying to prove ourselves competent in the larger society but intensely aware of being on trial.

2   Graduate student is a safe and familiar form for those who can afford it. Working toward a degree is something young people already know how to do. It postpones having to prove oneself in the bigger, bullying arena. Very few Americans had such a privilege before World War II; they reached the jumping-off point by the tender age of 16 or 18 or 20 and had to make their move ready or not. But today, a quarter of a century is often spent before an individual is expected or expects himself to fix his life's course. Or more. Given the permissiveness to experiment, the prolonged schooling available, and the moratoria allowed, it is not unusual for an adventurer to be nearly 30 before firmly setting a course.

3   Today, the seven-year spread of this stage seems commonly to be from the ages of 22 to 28.

4   The tasks of this period are as enormous as they are exhilarating: To shape a dream, that vision of one's own possibilities in the world that will generate energy, aliveness, and hope. To prepare for a lifework. To find a mentor if possible. And to form the capacity for intimacy without losing in the process whatever constancy of self we have thus far assembled. The first test structure must be erected around the life we choose to try.

5   One young man with vague aspirations of having his own creative enterprise, for instance, wasn't sure if his forte would be photography or cabinetmaking or architecture. There was no sponsor in sight; his parents worked for the telephone company. So he took a job with Ma Bell. He married and together with his wife decided to postpone children indefinitely. Once the structure was set, he could throw all his free-time energies into experimenting within it. Every weekend would find him behind a camera or building bookcases for friends, vigorously testing the various creative streaks that might lead him to a satisfying lifework.

6   Singlehood can be a life structure of the twenties, too. The daughter of an

ego-boosting father, taught to try anything she wished so long as she didn't bail out before reaching the top, decided to become a traveling publicist. That meant being free to move from city to city as better jobs opened up. The structure that best served her purpose was to remain unattached. She shared apartments and lived in women's hotels, having a wonderful time, until at 27 she landed the executive job of her dreams.

7   "I had no feeling of rootlessness because each time I moved, the next job offered a higher status or salary. And in every city I traveled, I would look up old friends from college and meet them for dinner. That gave me a stabilizing influence."

8   At 30 — Shazam! The same woman was suddenly married and pregnant with twins. Surrounded by a totally new and unforeseen life structure, she was pleasantly baffled to find herself content. "I guess I was ready for a family without knowing it."

9   The Trying Twenties is one of the longer and more stable periods, stable, that is, in comparison with the rockier passages that lead to and exit from it. Although each nail driven into our first external life structure is tentative, a tryout, once we have made our commitments we are convinced they are the right ones. The momentum of exploring within the structure generally carries us through the twenties without a major disruption of it.

10   One of the terrifying aspects of the twenties is the conviction that the choices we make are irrevocable. If we choose a graduate school or join a firm, get married or don't marry, move to the suburbs or forego travel abroad, decide against children or against a career, we fear in our marrow that we might have to live with that choice forever. It is largely a false fear. Change is not only possible; some alteration of our original choices is probably inevitable. But since in our twenties we're new at making major life choices, we cannot imagine that possibilities for a better integration will occur to us later on, when some inner growth has taken place.

11   Two pulses, as always, are at work during this period.

12   One is to build a firm, safe structure for the future by making strong commitments, to be set. Yet people who slip into a ready-made form without much self-examination are likely to find themselves following a locked-in pattern.

13   The other urge is to explore and experiment, keeping any structure tentative and therefore easily reversible. Taken to the extreme by people who skip through their twenties from one trial job and one limited personal encounter to another, this becomes the transient pattern.

14   The balance struck between these two impulses makes for differences in the way people pass through this period of provisional adulthood and largely determines the way we feel about ourselves at the end of it.

The Power of Illusions

15   However galvanizing our vision in the early twenties, it is far from being

complete. Even while we are delighted to display our shiny new capacities, secret fears persist that we are not going to get away with it. Somebody is going to discover the imposter.

16 To have seen the vivacious, 24-year-old junior executive at her work in a crack San Francisco public relations firm, one would probably not have guessed the trepidations underneath: "I realized that I had not grown up. I was amazed at how well I functioned at work, when clients would deal with me as an equal, I'd think, 'I got away with it', but the feeling wasn't one of joy. It was terror that eventually they would find out I was just a child. Simply not equipped. The other half of the time, I would have tremendous confidence and arrogance about who I was — a hotshot out there accomplishing all sorts of things and everybody thinking I was so terrific. I was like two people."

17 Many of us are not consciously aware of such fears. With enough surface bravado to fool the people we meet, we fool ourselves as well. But the memory of formlessness is never far beneath. So we hasten to try on life's uniforms and possible partners, in search of the perfect fit.

18 "Perfect" is that person we imbue with the capacity to enliven and support our vision or the person we believe in and want to help. Two centuries ago, a fictional young poet in Germany, torn by his hopeless passion for the "perfect" woman, drank a glass of wine, raised a pistol, and put a bullet through his head. It was a shot heard round the world. The lovelorn dropout who fired it was the hero of Goethe's novel *The Sorrows of Young Werther*, which contributed to the romantic movement that colors our expectations of love to this day. Goethe himself was a poet of 25 when he wrote the story. And like the fictional Werther, he suffered from an infatuation with a married woman, an unreachable woman, whose very mystery invited his fantasies of perfection. Goethe's hero struck such a chord in young people throughout Europe that a wave of suicides followed the book's publication.

19 Today, as then, it's enlightening to speculate on the degree to which a young man invents his romanticized version of the loved woman. She may be seen as the magical chameleon who will be a mother when he needs it and in the next instant the child requiring his protection, as well as the seductress who proves his potency, the soother of anxieties (who shall have none of her own), the guarantor of his immortality through the conversion of his need. And to what degree does the young woman invent the man she marries? She often sees in him possibilities that no one else recognizes and pictures herself within his dreams as the one person who truly understands. Such illusions are stuff of which the twenties are made.

20 "Illusion" is usually thought of as a pejorative, something we should get rid of if we suspect we have it. The illusions of the twenties, however, may be essential to infuse our first commitments with excitements and intensity, and to sustain us in those

commitments long enough to gain us some experience in living.

21   The tasks before us are exciting, conflicting, and sometimes overwhelming, but of one thing most of us are certain in our twenties.

22   Will power will overcome all.

23   Money may be scarce, the loans and laundry endless. The evil bait of selling out may tempt the would-be doctor, writer, social worker. But clearly, or so it seems, we have only to apply our strong minds and sturdy wills to the wheel of life, and sooner or later our destiny will bend under our control.

24   A self-deception? Yes, in large part. But also a most useful *modus operandi* at this stage. For if we didn't believe in the omnipotent force of our intelligence, if we were not convinced that we could will ourselves into being whatever kind of persons we wish to be, it wouldn't make much sense to try. Doubts immobilize. Believing that we are independent and competent enough to master the external tasks constantly fortifies us in our attempts to become so.

One True Course in Life

25   If and when we feel we have made a friend of the real world and are about to fix our course, a tone of optimism and vitality propels us forward in giant steps. We are most brimming with aliveness when we are just about to gain a solid form. This applies throughout life and to the different forms we may take. But upon discovering our very first independent form, we may assume it is the forever one and cling to it obstinately.

26   That is why people in their twenties commonly insist what they are doing is the one true course in life. Any suggestion that we are like our parents raises our hackles. What if we were to find out the truth? That the parental figures, unknowingly internalized as our guardians, provoke the very feelings of safety that allow us to dare all these great firsts of the twenties. They are also the inner dictators that hold us back.

27   To tell such a thing to most 25-year-olds will call forth howls of denial. This is precisely the interior reality from which each of us at this stage is trying to make a break. We are utterly convinced that all our notions spring full blown, as if by magic, from our own unique selves.

28   At all costs, any parts of our personality that might interfere with our chosen "one true course in life" must for the time being be buried. We cannot, will not, dare not know how strongly we are influenced by the deep tugs of the past: by identifications with our parents and the defense mechanisms we learned in childhood. Indeed, if there is a blemish on our behavior or something annoying about the one we love, this is the age when we are certain all that's needed is to have it pointed out.

29   "If there's something about me you don't like, just tell me," says the newlywed anxious to please. "I'll change it." If he or she is not forthcoming with such an offer, the other one is determined to change it for the partner. "He may drink a little

too much now," the bride confides to her friend, "but I'll reform him."

30　Examination of the internal forces acting upon us will resume in the thirties, when we are more stabilized externally. Well into our forties, we will still be dredging up exactly those suppressed parts we are now making every effort to ignore.

Glossary

arrogance ['ærəgəns] n.	pride and self-importance shown in a way that is rude and disrespectful to others
blemish ['blemɪʃ] n.	a stain, mark or fault
bravado [brə'vɑːdəʊ] n.	a display of boldness
brim [brɪm] vi.	be or become full to the top edge of a container
chameleon [kə'miːlɪən] n.	a small long-tongue animal whose color changes according to its background
confront [kən'frʌnt] vt.	deal with (something unpleasant) head on
crack [kræk] a.	(colloq.) first-rate
dropout ['drɒpaʊt] n.	a person who drops out of ordinary society and tries to practice another life style
forte ['fɔːt] n.	a strong point in a person, character or ability
forego [fɔː'gəʊ] vt.	give up; (being willing) not to have (esp. sth. pleasant)
forthcoming [fɔːθ'kʌmɪŋ] a.	ready to help, give information, etc.
fortify ['fɔːtɪfaɪ] vt.	strengthen; give courage to
galvanizing ['gælvənaɪzɪŋ] a.	exiting and active; startling; stimulating
hackles ['hæklz] n.	a feeling of anger and animosity
hotshot ['hɒtʃɒt] n.	(sl.) a highly-successful and aggressive person or thing
howl [haʊl] n.	a long loud cry, as in pain, anger, etc., esp. that made by certain animals, as wolves and dogs
illusion [ɪ'luːʒn] n.	a false idea or belief
imbue [ɪm'bjuː] vt.	become filled with
imposter [ɪm'pɒstə] n.	a person who deceives by pretending to be sb. else
incandescent [ɪnkæn'desnt] a.	glowing or shinning when heated; lively and impressive
infatuation [ɪnfætʃu'eɪʃn] n.	unreasonable, all-absorbing passion or desire
irrevocable [ɪ'revəkəbl] a.	that cannot be changed once started
marrow ['mærəʊ] n.	the soft substance in the hollow parts of bones
mentor ['mentɔː] n.	a person who habitually advises and helps another who knows less than him
modus operandi [məʊdəsɒpə'rændiː] n.	(Latin) mode of operation; method or

		manner of working
moratorium	[mɒrə'tɔːrɪəm] n.	(pl. moratoria) a permissive delay; legal authorization to delay payment or a debt
omnipotent	[ɒm'nɪpətənt] a.	almighty or unlimited in power
obstinately	['ɒbstɪnətlɪ] ad.	unyieldingly; stubbornly
outgrow	[aʊt'grəʊ] vt.	grow too large or too mature for
pejorative	[pɪ'dʒɒrətɪv] a.	a word or phrase showing disapproval or derogatory meaning
potency	['pəʊtnsɪ] n.	power; strength; being capable of having sexual intercourse
provisional	[prə'vɪʒənl] a.	for the present time only, with the strong probability of being changed
seductress	[sɪ'dʌktrəs] n.	a woman who seduces others
soother	['suːðə] n.	a person who comforts or calms others
streak	[striːk] n.	a quality which sometimes appears among different qualities or character
tentative	['tentətɪv] a.	done, said, etc. To test sth. ; hesitant or exploratory; not definite or decisive
transient	['trænzɪənt] a.	lasting for only a short time
trepidation	[trepɪ'deɪʃn] n.	great fear or worry about sth. unpleasant that may happen
tug	[tʌg] n.	a pulling force
vivacious	[vɪ'veɪʃəs] a.	full of life and high spirits

Notes

1. About the author and the text.

Gail Sheehy (1937—) was born in New York and educated at the University of Vermont and Columbia University. She is specialized in the study of adult development. Since 1970, she has published many works, including *Lovesound* (1970), *Hustling: Prostitution in Our Wide Open Society* (1973), *Passages* (1976) and *Character: America's Search for Leadership* (1988).

Gail, in the proper text, describes the difficulties and freedom which the twenties are confronted with when they enter the adult world.

2. So he took a job with **Ma Bell**. (Para. 5)

The colloquial term Ma Bell (as in "Mother Bell") was often used by the general public in the United States to refer to American telephone company, as it held a near complete monopoly over all telephone service in most areas of the country. The company is so named because of the inventor of the telephone: Alexander Bell.

3. At 30 — **Shazam**! The same woman was suddenly married and pregnant with twins. (Para. 8)

Shazam is word which is used by magicians while performing magic tricks. Here it is used to describe an exclamation of shock.

4. The lovelorn dropout who fired it was the hero of **Goethe**'s novel *The Sorrows of Young Werther*, which contributed to the romantic movement that colors our expectations of love to this day. (Para. 18)

Goethe (Johann Wolfgang von Goethe, 1749—1832), is a German poet, novelist, playwright, natural philosopher, diplomat, civil servant. Among his works, *Faust*, *The Sorrows of Young Werther*, *Wilhelm Meister's Apprenticeship*, *Elective Affinities* are the most notable.

The Sorrows of Young Werther is an epistolary and loosely autobiographical novel by Goethe, first published in 1774; a revised edition of the novel was published in 1787. It was an important novel of the Sturm und Drang period in German literature, and influenced the later Romantic literary movement. In the novel, Werther, a young artist of highly sensitive and passionate temperament, falls in love with Charlotte, who is betrothed to Albert. While Albert is absent, Werther has a few weeks' happy life with Charlotte. By the time Albert and Charlotte are married, Werther tears himself away and despair gradually comes over him, and finally he ends his own life.

Comprehension Questions

Answer the following questions after reading the text.

1. Why is it common today for an adventurer to be nearly 30 before firmly setting a course?
2. What life structure of the twenties can we know from the text?
3. Does the author think the choices made in the twenties revocable? How does she argue for her view?
4. Why is will power so significant according to the author?
5. Why do the twenty-something insist what they are doing is the one true course in life?

Exercises

I Vocabulary

Section A Paraphrase the sentences chosen from the text.

1. The Trying Twenties confronts us with the question of how to take hold in the adult world. (Para. 1)
2. Goethe's hero struck such a chord in young people throughout Europe that a wave of

suicides followed the book's publication. (Para. 18)
3. Money may be scarce, the loans and laundry endless. (Para. 23)
4. The evil bait of selling out may tempt the would-be doctor, writer, social worker. (Para. 23)
5. Any suggestion that we are like our parents raises our hackles. (Para. 26)

Section B There are ten sentences in this section. Beneath each sentence there are four words or phrases marked A, B, C and D. Choose one word or phrase that best completes the sentence.

1. The _____ nature of high fashion tells people not follow fashion blindly.
   A. transient   B. transmit   C. transform   D. transparent
2. It was announced that the times were _____ and subject to confirmation.
   A. provided   B. providing   C. provisional   D. occasional
3. The government tended to have a _____ negotiation with those terrorists.
   A. hesitant   B. tentative   C. beginning   D. initiative
4. Before becoming a _____ director, Mark had worked as a film critic for a magazine for many years.
   A. full blown   B. lovelorn   C. grown up   D. rootless
5. The lieutenant general has got such an enormous _____ — I've never met anyone so full of themselves!
   A. humility   B. illusion   C. altruism   D. ego
6. According to a survey of 100 colleges, the _____ rate among students is presently one in five.
   A. alteration   B. impulse   C. dropout   D. denial
7. The company she was working for was failing so she decided to _____, and set up her own business from scratch.
   A. deal out   B. bail out   C. hold out   D. fall out
8. Difficult situation can _____ a person's best qualities.
   A. call on   B. call in   C. call for   D. call forth
9. Please don't be so depressed; I'm sure things will _____ for your business in the coming year.
   A. look up   B. sell out   C. take hold   D. dredge up
10. You could see her face turning red and _____ as she heard him outline his plan.
    A. energy raising   B. voice raising   C. heckles raising   D. heckles rising

Section C Use the proper form of the following words given in the brackets to fill in the blanks.

1. Even though they are _____ rules, they should be observed strictly. (provision)
2. We insisted on payment by a confirmed, _____ letter of credit. (revoke)
3. Why does he choose young Joseph, who's an _____ spoiled brat? (arrogance)

4. He appears to have a unique _____ with bullfighting. (infatuate)
5. For novelist Michèle Roberts, it's all about gender: "The damaged king, who by artistic sleight of hand is Everyman, can be restored to full _____ when he gets his voice back. (potent)
6. Sometimes I even got the illusion and _____ believe that Shanghai should have such flourishing and confusion. (obstinate)
7. Her methods of _____ are subtle. (seduce)
8. The next round of talks is _____ scheduled to begin on October 21st in Washington. (tentative)
9. Opponents say such savings are merely _____ because they expect Congress to put off those provisions. (illusion)
10. Daisy looked at him imploringly, eyes _____ with tears. (brim)

Section D Use the proper form of the following phrases if necessary to fill in the blanks.

| strike a chord | take hold | speculate on | on trial |
| at all costs | confront with | bail out | dredge up |

1. We have to show our great courage and determination to _____ the difficulty and manage to get rid of it.
2. It's really a challenge for the new graduates to _____ in the competitive business world.
3. Partners are _____ of our company under such complex circumstance.
4. When you see something like this, you can't help _____ what happened.
5. For Jeremy Goldkorn, a China media commentator, Hanhan's attitude combined with his writing helps _____ with millions of China's disaffected youth.
6. This is both contagious and deadly and must be avoided _____.
7. He likes _____ unpleasant little facts about the film stars.
8. He is, after all, _____ for his life, for the charge of impiety.

II Grammar
Choose the best answer to complete the following sentence from the respective four choices.

1. He _____ another career but, at the time, he didn't have enough money to attend graduate school.
   A. might have chosen   B. might choose
   C. had to choose   D. must have chosen
2. _____ if I had arrived yesterday without letting you know beforehand?
   A. Would you be surprised   B. Were you surprised
   C. Had you been surprised   D. Would you have been surprised
3. "I don't know. But it's about time _____ on something."

A. I'd decide B. I decided C. I decide D. I'm deciding
4. He left orders that nothing _____ touched until the police arrived here.
   A. should be B. ought to be C. must be D. would be
5. It is highly desirable that a new president _____ for this college.
   A. appointed B. is appointed C. be appointed D. has been appointed
6. He meant _____ you, but he told me that he changed his mind at the last minute.
   A. telephone B. being telephoned
   C. to have telephoned D. to be telephoned
7. A planetarium (天文馆) is a special kind of educational facility _____ the teaching of astronomy.
   A. devoted to B. which devotes C. to devote D. to devote to
8. Realizing that she had no money to buy her husband any birthday present but _____ to disappoint him, she had her long cascading hair — her only treasure — cut and sell it in exchange for a watch chain for her husband.
   A. not wanted B. not wanting C. not to want D. wanting not
9. All flights _____ because of the snowstorm, many passengers could do nothing but take the train.
   A. were canceled B. having been canceled
   C. had been canceled D. have been canceled
10. The meeting was put off because we _____ a meeting without John.
    A. objected having B. were objected to having
    C. objected to have D. objected to having

III Cloze

Decide which of the choices given below would best complete the passage if inserted in the corresponding blanks. Mark the best choice for each blank.

Most worthwhile careers require some kind of specialized training. Ideally, therefore, the choice of a (n) (1) _____ should be made even before the choice of a curriculum in high school. Actually, (2) _____ most persons make several job choices during their working live, partly (3) _____ economic and industrial changes and partly to improve their positions. The "one perfect job" does not exist. Young people should therefore (4) —_____ into a broad flexible training program that will (5) _____ them for a field of (6) _____ rather than for a single job.

Unfortunately many young people, knowing (7) _____ about the occupational world or themselves for that matter, choose their lifework (8) _____ a hit-or-miss basis. Some (9) _____ from job to job. Others (10) _____ to work in which they are unhappy and (11) _____ they are not fitted.

One common mistake is choosing an occupation for (12) _____ real or imagined prestige. Too many high-school students — or their parents for them — choose the professional field, (13) _____ both the relatively small proportion of work vacancies in the professions and the extremely high educational and personal (14) _____. The imagined or real prestige of a profession or a "white-collar" job is (15) _____ good reason for choosing it as a life's wore (16) _____, these occupations are not always well paid. Since a large proportion of jobs are in mechanical and manual work, the majority of young people should give serious (17) _____ to these fields.

Before making an occupational choice, a person should have a general idea of what he wants (18) _____ life and how hard he is willing to work to get it. Some people desire social prestige, others intellectual satisfaction. Some want security; others are willing to take (19) _____ for financial gain. Each occupational choice has its demands as well as its (20) _____.

1. A. academy   B. occupation   C. guidance   D. identification
2. A. therefore   B. so   C. though   D. however
3. A. in case of   B. for   C. because of   D. to
4. A. enter   B. participate   C. involve   D. join
5. A. leave   B. fit   C. require   D. fix
6. A. careers   B. profession   C. prospects   D. work
7. A. few   B. little   C. Much   D. less
8. A. with   B. by   C. on   D. at
9. A. flow   B. wander   C. jump   D. drift
10. A. stick   B. turn   C. adhere   D. subscribe
11. A. to which   B. that   C. for which   D. what
12. A. its   B. their   C. /   D. the
13. A. to have disregarded   B. to disregard
    C. disregarding   D. disregard
14. A. preparations B. Requirements   C. specifications   D. preferences
15. A. such   B. no   C. very   D. so
16. A. Moreover   B. Otherwise   C. Nevertheless   D. Still
17. A. priority   B. regulation   C. assessment   D. consideration
18. A. out of   B. towards   C. for   D. from over
19. A. advantage   B. patience   C. risks   D. turns
20. A. awards   B. rewards   C. prizes   D. bonuses

IV Translation

Section A Translate the following Chinese sentences into English.

1. 当今世界,体育天才往往为了参加职业比赛而放弃上大学,而泰格·伍兹却

选择一边在斯坦福大学学习经济学，一边打业余高尔夫球赛。(forgo)
2. 运动会令你远离感冒发烧。凡是有规律的运动项目的参与者们都较少地被感冒病毒传染。(fortify)
3. 欣赏你平时在生活中通常不注意的小事情，因为你从不曾知道它们会给你的未来带来什么样巨大的不同。(make for)
4. 那些罪犯知道怎样钻制度的空子并逃脱惩罚。(get away with)
5. 学校应该教导学生如何解决问题，并且向他们灌输正确的道德价值观。(imbue...with)
6. 我们不了解所有的情况，妄加推测原因是没有意义的。(speculate on)
7. 看到雪，许多女孩似乎一下子变得兴奋起来。(infuse...with)
8. 经理发脾气时避开他要稳妥些。(raise one's hackles)
9. 她的故事能拨动那些有同样遭遇的女人们的心弦。(strike a chord)
10. 政府认为唯一的解决办法是帮助该国企摆脱困境。(bail out)

Section B Translate the following English paragraph into Chinese.

During college years, young adults are going through an identity crisis and are endeavoring to find out who they are and what their strengths and weaknesses are. They have, of course, plenty of both. It is important to know how people perceive themselves as well as how other people perceive them. According to Piers and Landau, in an article discussing the theories of Erik H. Erickson in International Encyclopedia of Social Science, identity is determined by genetic endowment (what is inherited from parents), shaped by environment, and influenced by chance events. People are influenced by their environment and, in turn, influence their environment. How people see themselves in both roles is unquestionably a part of their identity.

V Topic for Discussion

Nowadays, young people are given little time to enjoy the innocence of childhood before the pressures of the world are thrown upon them. They are highly expected to fulfill ideals that they are made to feel they must live up to. As the twenty-something grapple with the issue of taking hold in the adult world, many problems arise. State your view on the growing pains and happiness of young people.

VI Written Work

Write a short essay of about 200 words on the following topic. You are required to choose a title by yourselves.

Oscar Wilde once said, "Life is far too important to take seriously." How far do you agree with this philosophy?

Text B
Cure Yourself of Unhappiness

Anonymous

1   It seemed as if my wife and I had a lot to be unhappy about. At the age of 12 months, our son, Raun Kahlil, began to withdraw from all human contact and slip behind an apparently impenetrable wall. He was diagnosed as autistic, which is considered the most irreversible of all forms of children's mental illness. "Incurable... Hopeless." There were the underlying message of the books we read and the experts that we consulted throughout the country.

2   His was a classic case of autism. Silent and distant, Raun stared through us as though we were transparent. He rocked back and forth to some internal music. Using his hands with great skills, he would spin every object in sight for hour after hour. He had a self-stimulating smile and moved his fingers in a repetitious motion against his lips. There was a lack of language development.... no words, no sounds, no pointing gestures. No calling or crying for food. No eye contact. The pushing away... the deafening silence... the aloneness.

3   Committing ourselves to being open to see anyone, go anywhere, we consumed every book available on autism and journeyed to different cities to consult with various experts.

4   What became increasingly clear was that most programs for the autistic were little more than experiments. And the ratio of children reached was depressing. Perhaps only a few of one hundred were helped. What was considered "success" often mean that a child learned to perform minimal functions on a very primitive level.

5   The more we viewed and understood the nature of these treatments, the more alienated we became to what was obviously a disapproving perspective on these children. For us, Raun was a beautiful human being with his own very special qualities and dignity. His eyes were so intense, so bright and so alive. But who out there was really willing to respect that?

6   Refusing to give up our good feelings, refusing to end the life of the delicate and different child by placing him behind the stone walls of some faceless and indifferent institution (as we were advised to do), we decided to trust ourselves... to design and create our own program for Raun.

7   In approaching our son, we decided there would be no conditions to which he had to conform... there would be no expectations which he had to fulfill... there would be no judgments which designated his behavior as either good or bad.

8   We would respect Raun's dignity, instead of forcing him to adapt and conform to our ideals and behavior. Working with him in a variety of ways, imitating him, holding him, talking to him, reading to him, being with him during his very walking hour (80 hours each week), we met him on his own ground and entered his world with love and acceptance. During this time we were always aware that for whatever reasons, Raun, like all of us, was doing the best he could.

9   By following him and trusting ourselves, we developed an elaborate and intensive program. Improvement was slow, almost imperceptible, at first. We began to train others as teachers to work with Raun, including our two daughters, Bryn, eight years old, and Thea, five years old.

10   Within eight months, this totally withdrawn, self-stimulating, functionally retarded and "hopeless" little boy became a social, highly verbal, affectionate and loving human being displaying intellectual capabilities uncommon for his age.

11   Had we followed the advice of the "experts", our son today would perhaps be sitting alone and forgotten on the cold floor of some nameless hospital. Instead, at the age of four, the child who they said would never speak or communicate sensibly had become a delightful conversationalist, filling our home with the music of his words every day. Affectionate, loving and sensitive in touch, he continues to grow and learn.

12   Some have called the story of the rebirth of our son a miracle. Others consider it a one-in-a-million occurrence. We don't think either explanation is accurate or appropriate. What we did was not the result of any special brilliance or capability. Our energy and understanding was a product of our happiness and inner comfort with ourselves and our child. By clearing away fear and anxieties, we each create the opportunity to function more productively and more effectively.

13   Fortunately, before Raun was even born, both my wife and I had learned to discard a lot of the unhappiness we once believed to be outside of our control. We had learned how to remain happy people when faced by seemingly unhappy situations. We live and teach a philosophy and technique for living we call the Option Process. The Option Process enabled us to help Raun and ourselves. Option can be segmented into several components, each an important aspect of a personal journey toward discarding unhappiness.

14   First, Option is an attitude which we call "To love is to be happy with," an accepting and loving embrace of ourselves and those we love. It is saying: I love you as you are... without judging you or needing you to conform to my wants or fantasies. The story of our feelings toward our son is an example of this attitude in operation.

15   Secondly, Option is a way of understanding ourselves. And the most important understanding one can have about personal unhappiness is that it is learned. For instance, in looking at my own unhappiness, what really astonished me was my increasing awareness that I had learned to be unhappy through the beliefs taught me by

parents, peer groups, teachers, religions, institutions and government.

16   Unhappiness as a mechanism had been so internalized and operated with such consistent regularity that for a long time I never thought to question it in the way that I now do. Being uncomfortable was accepted as a necessary component of my life as well as in the lives of all those around me. It was a way of dealing with myself and my environment. A way of motivating myself and others.

17   For example, I feared lung cancer so that I could force myself to stop smoking. I became anxious about unemployment as a way of pushing myself to be more conscientious and to work harder. I even became gloomy when someone I loved was unhappy in order to show them I cared! I got angry at others to make them move faster.

18   What's more, I had been taught that I "had to" be unhappy sometimes because it is "good" or productive to be unhappy. Our culture supports this notion. Unhappiness is the mark of a "thinking, feeling" man; it is the mark of sensitivity. It is also considered by many to be the only "reasonable" and "human" response to a difficult and problematic society. The expression "happy idiots" is not just a casual comment but a suspicion that happiness and idiocy are almost identical. I adopted these beliefs and many others, never considering or testing their validity in my mind.

19   The more questions I asked of myself the more amazed I was to see how often I used unhappiness as a condition I promised myself if I did not get what I wanted or expected. If my lover or mate was uncaring, I'd be miserable (misery was a proof of my involvement and caring). If I did not reach my goal, I'd be angry with myself for failing. To give my wanting extra importance, I made my happiness conditional on getting. If I didn't get what I said I needed — love, money, security — then I would become unhappy. It's a self-fulfilling prophecy!

20   And yet, I now know it doesn't have to be that way. If my wife and I had been unhappy about our son, we would not have been able to help him. He would not have improved and so we would have become more unhappy. But by accepting and doing — and not judging the situation — we were able to reach an "unreachable" child. People who initially use unhappiness as a whip to push themselves can learn that happy people do not stop moving! And doing something out of happiness does not cause inactivity. On the contrary, it usually increases our mobility and effectiveness. Instead of fighting fears and running from pain, we can see what we want and can move toward it with greater ease.

21   Basically, then, the Option Process uses a loving and accepting attitude toward life. But it is also more than that. Its third component is a tool of self-examination that can help one during seemingly difficult times. We can dispense with a lot of unhappiness by uncovering and discarding the beliefs that fuel it. I have found that by asking oneself a series of simple questions, a lot of the unhappiness a person believes he "should" or "must" feel can be alleviated.

Question No. 1: What are you unhappy about?
Question No. 2: Why are you unhappy about it?
And No. 3: Why do you believe it?

What? That's impossible, you might be thinking. These questions are too simple and I'm so complex. It's too confining. Yes... and maybe no. Yes, it is beautifuly simple in terms of questions; but no, not in terms of its capacity to help us focus and understand ourselves. Like happiness itself, the route to it is simple and uplifting. No one is implying we "should not" feel unhappy or, if we get unhappy, that we "should" suppress it or not vent it; the probe is to identify the underlying belief, and not to judge it. The questions are not indictments or criticisms, only part of a search for the reasons why. Of course these three questions are just a blueprint which we breathe life into by using them. When born out of the attitude of "to love is to be happy with," they become a highly effective and successful technique for exploring and discarding unhappy and self-defeating beliefs. If each of us just changes one self-limiting belief as the result of asking ourselves these questions when we're unhappy, if we discard just one self-defeating notion and the uncomfortable feelings it causes, then that could change our whole lives as we approach previously unhappy situations with a new feeling of comfort. If we are more accepting and less judgmental toward someone we love for even just one day, then we have created endless new possibilities for ourselves.

22 We do not "have to" be unhappy. We can choose to change and delight in our humanness. The walls of unhappiness we have built around ourselves are only monuments to fear. Allowing ourselves to be loving is a joyful pursuit and embracing ourselves and those we love with an accepting attitude is a surprisingly practical, effective and powerful way to deal with our lives.

23 Each time I gaze into the deep and eager eyes of my very verbal and affectionate son, I know that his life is more than a gift. It is a testament to the specialness and creativity in all of us.

Notes

1. His was a classic case of **autism**. (Para. 2)

Autism is a disorder of neural development characterized by impaired social interaction and verbal and non-verbal communication, and by restricted, repetitive or stereotyped behavior. It has long been presumed that there is a common cause at the genetic, cognitive, and neural levels for autism's characteristic triad of symptoms.

2. He rocked back and forth to some internal music. (Para. 2)

Paraphrase: He moved back and forth to the rhythm of the music coming from his mind.

3. Had we followed the advice of the "experts", our son today would perhaps be

sitting alone and forgotten on the cold floor of some nameless hospital. (Para. 11)

Please pay attention to the Subjunctive Mood with "if".

4. Others consider it **a one-in-a-million occurrenc**e. (Para. 12)

A one-in-a-million occurrence means a rare incident or sth that rarely happens.

5. That the parental figures, unknowingly **internalized** as our guardians, provoke the very feelings of safety that allow us to dare all these great firsts of the twenties. (Para. 16)

internalize: adopt and assimilate (an idea or mannerism) into the framework of one's personality

6. I became anxious about unemployment as a way of pushing myself to be more **conscientious** and to work harder. (Para. 17)

Being conscientious means being guided by one's sense of duty.

Questions for Discussion

1. What makes you happy? What is "happiness" according to your own experiences? Discuss in groups.
2. Why do we have more autistic children and autistic adults in the modern society?
3. It is said that those who want the least are the happiest. Is it reasonable to say this?

Memorable Quotes

1. One can choose to go back toward safety or forward toward growth. Growth must be chosen again and again; fear must be overcome again and again.

   — Abraham Maslow

2. There is no such thing as a great talent without great will power.

   — Balzac

3. As fruit needs not only sunshine but cold nights and chilling showers to ripen it, so character needs not only joy but trial and difficulty to mellow it.

   — Hugh Black

4. No one can degrade us except ourselves; that if we are worthy, no influence can defeat us.

   — B. T. Washington

5. Life is a series of experiences, each one of which makes us bigger, even though sometimes it is hard to realize this. For the world was built to develop character, and we must learn that the setbacks and grieves which we endure help us in our marching onward.

   — Henry Ford

Further Readings

1. Jay Meg, *The Defining Decade*
2. J. D. Salinger, *The Catcher in the Rye*
3. Khaled Hosseini, *The Kite Runner*

Unit 3

Pre-reading Questions
1. Does generation gap exist in your own life? Have you ever felt haunted by it?
2. Think about the causes of this phenomenon.
3. Should we do something to change the situation?

Text A

The Joy Luck Club (Excerpt)

Amy Tan

1 I had taken my mother out to lunch at my favorite Chinese restaurant in hopes of putting her in a good mood, but it was a disaster.

2 When we met at the Four Directions Restaurant, she eyed me with immediate disapproval. "Ai-ya! What's the matter with your hair?" she said in Chinese.

3 "What do you mean, 'What's the matter,'" I said. "I had it cut." Mr. Rory had styled my hair differently this time, an asymmetrical blunt-line fringe that was shorter on the left side. It was fashionable, yet not radically so.

4 "Looks chopped off," she said. "You must ask for your money back."

5 I sighed. "Let's just have a nice lunch together, okay?"

6 She wore her tight-lipped, pinched-nose look as she scanned the menu, muttering, "Not too many good things, this menu." Then she tapped the waiter's arm, wiped the length of her chopsticks with her finger, and sniffed: "This greasy thing, do you expect me to eat with it?" She made a show of washing out her rice bowl with hot tea, and then warned other restaurant patrons seated near us to do the same. She told the waiter to make sure the soup was very hot, and of course, it was by her tongue's expert estimate "not even *lukewarm.*"

7 "You shouldn't get so upset," I said to my mother after she disputed a charge of two extra dollars because she had specified chrysanthemum tea, instead of the regular green tea. "Besides, unnecessary stress isn't good for your heart."

8 "Nothing is wrong with my heart," she huffed as she kept a disparaging eye on the waiter.

9 And she was right. Despite all the tension she places on herself — and others — the doctors have proclaimed that my mother, at age sixty-nine, had the blood pressure of a sixteen-year-old and the strength of a horse. And that's what she is. A horse, born in 1918, destined to be obstinate and frank to the point of tactlessness. She and I make a bad combination, because I'm a Rabbit, born in 1951, supposedly sensitive, with tendencies toward being thin-skinned and skittery at the first sign of criticism.

10 After our miserable lunch, I gave up the idea that there would ever be a good time to tell her the news: that Rich Schields and I were getting married.

11 "Why are you so nervous?" My friend Marlene Ferber had asked over the phone the other night. "It's not as if Rich is the scum of the earth. He's a tax attorney like you, for Chrissake. How can she criticize that?"

12　"You don't know my mother," I said. "She never thinks anybody is good enough for anything."

13　"So elope with the guy," said Marlene.

14　"That's what I did with Marvin." Marvin was my first husband, my high school sweetheart.

15　"So there you go," said Marlene.

16　"So when my mother found out, she threw her shoe at us," I said. "And that was just for openers."

17　My mother had never met Rich. In fact, every time I brought up his name — when I said, for instance, that Rich and I had gone to the symphony, that Rich had taken my four-year-old daughter, Shoshana, to the zoo — my mother found a way to change the subject.

18　"Did I tell you," I said as we waited for the lunch bill at Four Directions, "what a great time Shoshana had with Rich at the Exploratorium? He —"

19　"Oh," interrupted my mother, "I didn't tell you. Your father, doctors say maybe need exploratory surgery. But no, now they say everything normal, just too much constipated." I gave up. And then we did the usual routine.

20　I paid for the bill, with a ten and three ones. My mother pulled back the dollar bills and counted out exact change, thirteen cents, and put that on the tray instead, explaining firmly: "No tip!" She tossed her head back with a triumphant smile. And while my mother used the restroom, I slipped the waiter a five-dollar bill. He nodded to me with deep understanding. While she was gone, I devised another plan.

21　"Choszle!" -- Stinks to death in there! — muttered my mother when she returned. She nudged me with a little travel package of Kleenex. She did not trust other people's toilet paper. "Do you need to use?"

22　I shook my head. "But before I drop you off, let's stop at my place real quick. There's something I want to show you."

23　My mother had not been to my apartment in months. When I was first married, she used to drop by unannounced, until one day I suggested she should call ahead of time. Ever since then, she has refused to come unless I issue an official invitation.

24　And so I watched her, seeing her reaction to the changes in my apartment — from the pristine habitat I maintained after the divorce, when all of a sudden I had too much time to keep my life in order — to this present chaos, a home full of life and love. The hallway floor was littered with Shoshana's toys, all bright plastic things with scattered parts. There was a set of Rich's barbells in the living room, two dirty snifters on the coffee table, the disemboweled remains of a phone that Shoshana and Rich took part the other day to see where the voices came from.

25   "It's back here," I said. We kept walking, all the way to the back bedroom. The bed was unmade, dresser drawers were hanging out with socks and ties spilling over. My mother stepped over running shoes, more of Shoshana's toys, Rich's black loafers, my scarves, a stack of white shirts just back from the cleaner's.

26   Her look was one of painful denial, reminding me of a time long ago when she took my brothers and me down to a clinic to get out polio booster shots. As the needle went into my brother's arm and he screamed, my mother looked at me with agony written all over her face and assured me, "Next one doesn't hurt."

27   But now, how could my mother *not* notice that we were living together, that this was serious and would not go away even if she didn't talk about it? She had to say something.

28   I went to the closet and then came back with a mink jacket that Rich had given me for Christmas. It was the most extravagant gift I had ever received.

29   I put the jacket on. "It's sort of a silly present," I said nervously. "It's hardly ever cold enough in San Francisco to wear mink. But it seems to be a fad, what people are buying their wives and girlfriends these days."

30   My mother was quiet. She was looking toward my open closet, bulging with racks of shoes, ties, my dresses, and Rich's suits. She ran her fingers over the mink.

31   "This is not so good," she said at last. "It is just leftover strips. And the fur is too short, no long hairs."

32   "How can you criticize a gift!" I protested. I was deeply wounded. "He gave me this from his heart."

33   "That is why I worry," she said.

34   And looking at the coat in the mirror, I couldn't fend off the strength of her will anymore, her ability to make me see black where there was once white, white where there was once black. The coat looked shabby, an imitation of romance.

35   "Aren't you going to say anything else?" I asked softly.

36   "What I should say?"

37 "About the apartment? About *this*?" I gestured to all the signs of Rich lying about.

38   She looked around the room, toward the hall, and finally she said, "You have career. You are busy. You want to live like mess what I can say?"

39   My mother knows how to hit a nerve. And the pain I feel is worse than any other kind of misery. Because what she does always comes as a shock, exactly like an electric jolt, that grounds itself permanently in my memory. I still remember the first time I felt it.

40   "You know, I really don't understand you," said Marlene when I called her the night after I had shown my mother the mink jacket. "You can tell the IRS to piss up a rope, but you can't stand up to your own mother."

41　"I always intend to and then she says these little sneaky things, smoke bombs and little barbs, and..."

42　"Why don't you tell her to stop torturing you," said Marlene. "Tell her to stop ruining your life. Tell her to shut up."

43　"That's hilarious," I said with a half-laugh. "You want me to tell my mother to shut up?"

44　"Sure, why not?"

45　"Well, I don't know if it's explicitly stated in the law, but you can't *ever* tell a Chinese mother to shut up. You could be charged as an accessory to your own murder."

46　I wasn't so much afraid of my mother as I was afraid for Rich. I already knew what she would do, how she would attack him, how she would criticize him. She would be quiet at first. Then she would say a word about something small, something she had noticed, and then another word, and another, each one flung out like a little piece of sand, one from this direction, another from behind, more and more, until his looks, his character, his soul would have eroded away. And even if I recognized her strategy, her sneak attack, I was afraid that some unseen speck of truth would fly into my eye, blur what I was seeing and transform him from the divine man I thought he was into someone quite mundane, mortally wounded with tiresome habits and irritating imperfections.

Glossary

asymmetrical [eɪsɪ'metrɪkl] *a.*	irregular in shape or outline
attorney [ə'tɜːnɪ] *n.*	a professional person authorized to practice law; conducts lawsuits or gives legal advice
barb [bɑːb] *n.*	an aggressive remark directed at a person like a missile and intended to have a telling effect
barbell ['bɑːbel] *n.*	to which heavy discs are attached at each end; used in weightlifting
blunt [blʌnt] *a.*	not sharp
blur [blɜː] *v.*	(cause to) become unclear or indistinct
chrysanthemum [krɪ'sænθəməm] *n.*	type of garden flower which usually flowers in autumn 菊花
constipated ['kɒnstəpeɪtɪd] *a.*	have difficult or incomplete or infrequent evacuation of the bowel 患便秘症的
devise [dɪ'vaɪz] *v.*	come up with (an idea, plan, explanation, theory, or principle) after a mental effort
disembowel [dɪsɪm'baʊəl] *v.*	remove the entrails of

disparaging [dɪˈspærɪdʒɪŋ] a.	expressive of low opinion
divine [dɪˈvaɪn] a.	of, from or like god or a god
elope [ɪˈloʊp] v.	run away secretly with one's beloved
erode [ɪˈroʊd] v.	become ground down or deteriorate
explicit [ɪkˈsplɪsɪt] a.	clearly and fully expressed
fad [fæd] n.	an interest followed with exaggerated zeal
flung [flʌŋ] v.	the past tense of fling; throw violently or with force
fringe [frɪndʒ] n.	front hair cut so that it hangs over the forehead
greasy [ˈgriːzɪ] a.	containing an unusual amount of grease or oil
huff [hʌf] v.	blow hard and loudly
loafer [ˈloʊfə] n.	a low leather step-in shoe
lukewarm [luːkˈwɔːrm] a.	moderately warm
mink [mɪŋk] n.	fur coat made from the soft lustrous fur of minks
mundane [mʌnˈdeɪn] a.	belonging to this earth or world; not ideal or heavenly
mutter [ˈmʌtə] v.	a complaint uttered in a low and indistinct tone
nudge [nʌdʒ] v.	push into action by pestering or annoying gently
obstinate [ˈɒbstɪnət] a.	resistant to guidance or discipline
patron [ˈpeɪtrən] n.	regular customer at a shop
permanently [ˈpɜːmənəntlɪ] ad.	for a long time without essential change
pinch [pɪntʃ] v.	squeeze tightly between the fingers
pristine [ˈprɪstiːn] a.	immaculately clean and unused
radical [ˈrædɪkl] a.	having wide and important effects; thorough and complete
scum [skʌm] n.	worthless people
skitter [ˈskɪtərɪ] a.	moving quickly, restlessly, or irregularly
sneaky [ˈsniːkɪ] a.	marked by quiet and caution and secrecy; taking pains to avoid being observed
sniff [snɪf] v.	try the smell of; draw air in through the nose so that there is a sound
snifter [ˈsnɪftə] n.	a globular glass with a small top
speck [spek] n.	a tiny piece of anything
stink [stɪŋk] v.	smell badly and offensively
symphony [ˈsɪmfənɪ] n.	a long and complex sonata for symphony orchestra
tactless [ˈtæktləs] a.	lacking or showing a lack of what is fitting and considerate in dealing with others
triumphant [traɪˈʌmfənt] a.	joyful and proud especially because of triumph or success

Notes

1. About the author and the text.

Amy Ruth Tan was born in Oakland, California, on February 19, 1952. In 1989, Tan published her first novel *The Joy Luck Club* (《喜福会》), including stories of four immigrant mothers from China and their daughters raised in America, and the misunderstanding and conflicts between them. The novel became a surprise bestseller through word-of-mouth endorsements by independent booksellers. It was on the New York Times' bestseller list for more than 40 weeks, and was nominated for the National Book Award and the National Book Critics Award. It received the Commonwealth Gold Award and the Bay Area Book Reviewers Award. In 1994, *The Joy Luck Club* was adapted into a feature film, for which Tan was a co-screenwriter, with Ron Bass, and a co-producer, with Bass and Wayne Wang.

With great success in *The Joy Luck Club*, Tan continued to write four novels *The Kitchen God's Wife* (1991), *The Hundred Secret Senses* (1995), *The Bonesetter's Daughter* (2001) and *Saving Fish from Drowning* (2005). All of them enjoyed excellent sales and confirmed her reputation. Like most of American writers of recent Chinese immigrant ancestry, all Amy Tan's novels are closely related to themes concerning China, one way or another. Due to the fascinating artistic skills, cross-cultural themes, exotic content, etc., she had received more and more attention from both ordinary readers and academic circles.

2. He's a tax attorney like you, **for Chrissake**. (Para. 11)

It is an informal form of "for Christ's sake" (used as an exclamation of annoyance or exasperation).

3. ... what a great time Shoshana had with Rich at **the Exploratorium** (Para. 18)

It is the name of the zoo.

4. "**Choszle!**" — Stinks to death in there! (Para. 21)

"Stinks to death in there!" is the author's paraphrase of the mother's Chinese expression "Choszle!" (臭死了!).

5. She nudged me with a little travel package of **Kleenex**. (Para. 21)

Kleenex: 克里奈克斯牌面巾纸

6. ... when she took my brothers and me down to a clinic to get out **polio booster shot**. (Para. 26)

polio booster shot: 小儿麻痹症疫苗

7. Your father, doctors say maybe need exploratory surgery. But no, now they say everything normal, just too much constipated. (Para. 19)

What I should say? (Para. 36)

You have career. You are busy. You want to live like mess what I can say? (Para. 38)

The mother is an immigrant, so she speaks non-standard English sometimes.

8. You can tell **the IRS** to piss up a rope, but you can't stand up to your own mother. (Para. 40)

Internal Revenue Service 国税局

Comprehension Questions

Answer the following questions after reading the text.
1. What's the purpose of the author taking her mother out to lunch at her favorite Chinese restaurant?
2. Did the author convey the news of her getting married with Rich to her mother successfully? Why or why not?
3. Why did the author still take her mother to her apartment after the miserable lunch?
4. What's her mother's comments on the mink Rich gave her for Christmas?
5. Do you think the mother and the daughter understand each other? Why or why not?

Exercises

I Vocabulary

Section A   Paraphrase the sentences chosen from the text.
1. I'm a Rabbit, born in 1951, supposedly sensitive, with tendencies toward being thin-skinned and skittery at the first sign of criticism.
2. I couldn't fend off the strength of her will anymore, her ability to make me see black where there was once white, white where there was once black.
3. You can tell the IRS to piss up a rope, but you can't stand up to your own mother.
4. Then she says these little sneaky things, smoke bombs and little barbs, and...
5. You could be charged as an accessory to your own murder.

Section B   There are 10 sentences in this section. Beneath each sentence there are four words or phrases marked A, B, C and D. Choose one word or phrase that best completes the sentence.
1. The police said he had been hit with a _____ instrument, and so the wound had not been very serious.
   A. sharp   B. blunt   C. pointy   D. thick
2. The sign on the wall of the restaurant says this parking lot is for the use of _____ only.
   A. patronage   B. patronize   C. patrons   D. patronizing
3. It was coined by Cree Indians to _____ their northern cousins as eaters of raw flesh, and has long been regarded as somewhat derogatory.
   A. disperse   B. dispel   C. dispense   D. disparage

4. Mr. Quincy labored hard with the governor to obtain his assent, but he was _____.
   A. obstinate   B. flexible   C. intelligent   D. insightful
5. It was rather _____ of you to invite his ex-girlfriend to his wedding.
   A. tactless   B. sensible   C. wise   D. reasonable
6. If parents do not give their consent to their daughter's marriage, she can always _____ to Scotland.
   A. travel   B. elope   C. stroll   D. roam
7. The book celebrates the hostage' remarkable _____ over appalling adversity.
   A. failure   B. fall   C. triumph   D. retreat
8. The cartoon characters Snoopy and Charlie Brown were _____ by Charles M. Schultz.
   A. decided   B. dedicated   C. dealt   D. devised
9. Washing machine for sale — only 2 months old and in _____ condition.
   A. primary   B. raw   C. pristine   D. shabby
10. It's unbelievable that she got lost eventually — I had given her very _____ directions how to get here.
    A. implicit   B. implied   C. indirect   D. explicit

Section C Use the proper form of the following words given in the brackets to fill in the blanks.

1. Nothing was _____; everyone and everything was always on the move. (permanently)
2. I still can't figure how anything that big could have _____ up on me unawares. (sneaky)
3. A cottage upright, _____, its inner workings exposed on the floor. (disembowel)
4. My father complained that his suit _____ of mothballs. (stink)
5. Advancing culture is bound to _____ over declining culture. (triumphant)
6. We reposed great trust in his _____ and discretion. (tactlessness)
7. He was humble and meek, filled with self-_____ and abasement. (disparaging)
8. The fat captain was _____ through his cigar to the merry-eyed officer. (mutter)
9. It was a stunning act of _____ which has lasted. (radically)
10. I _____ myself to make sure I wasn't dreaming. (pinch)

Section D Use the proper form of the following phrases to fill in the blanks.

talk down to	resign oneself to	stand up to
be adamant about	be in limbo	squirrel away
hook up	have the presence of mind	loosen up

1. As a newcomer to China, I found out my own way to blend in and _____ with a couple of students for a few weeks.

2. Finally Being aware of your immediate environment and _____ at all times are key to ensure your safety.
3. For the sake of health, they _____ buying only organic food.
4. We had to _____ making a loss on the sale.
5. He seemed quite nervous at the beginning of the meeting, but he soon _____.
6. How dare you _____ me like this?
7. His life seemed stuck _____; he could not go forward and he could not go back.
8. Is this building going _____ the strongest gales?
9. She had money _____ in various bank accounts.

II Grammar
Choose the best answer to complete the following sentence from the respective four choices.
1. After _____ seemed an endless wait, it was her turn to enter the personnel manager's office.
   A. that   B. there   C. what   D. it
2. Professor Johnson is said _____ some significant advance in his research in the past year.
   A. having made   B. making   C. to have made   D. to make
3. He _____ unwisely, but he was at least trying to do something helpful.
   A. may have acted   B. must have acted
   C. should act   D. would act
4. He's _____ as a "bellyacher" — he's always complaining about something.
   A. who is known   B. whom is known   C. what is known   D. which is known
5. _____, he always tries his best to complete it on time.
   A. However the task is hard   B. However hard the task is
   C. Though hard the task is   D. Though hard is the task
6. Acute hearing helps most animals sense the approach of thunderstorm's long before people _____.
   A. do   B. hear   C. do them   D. hearing it
7. The central provinces have floods in some years, and _____.
   A. drought in others   B. droughts are others
   C. while other droughts   D. others in drought
8. I was very much put _____ by Mark's rude behavior; it really annoyed me.
   A. over   B. off   C. up   D. by
9. You _____ Jim anything about it. It was none of his business.
   A. needn't have told   B. needn't tell
   C. mustn't have told   D. mustn't tell
10. _____ at in this way, the present economic situation doesn't seem so gloomy.

A. Looking B. Looked C. Having looked D. To look
11. Time _____, the conference will be held as scheduled.
   A. permit B. permitting C. permitted D. permits
12. We've just installed two air-conditioners in the teaching building, _____ should make great differences in our life next summer.
   A. which B. what C. that D. they
13. Even as a girl, _____ to be her life, and theater audiences were to be her best teacher.
   A. performing by Catherine were
   B. it was known that Catherine's performances were
   C. knowing that Catherine's performances were
   D. Catherine knew that performing was
14. _____, Christina can now only watch it on TV at home.
   A. Obtaining not a ticket for the concert
   B. Not obtaining a ticket for the concert
   C. Not having obtained a ticket for the concert
   D. Not obtained a ticket for the concert
15. _____ enough time and money, the researcher would have been able to discover more in this field.
   A. Giving B. To give C. Given D. Being given

III Cloze

Decide which of the choices given below would best complete the passage if inserted in the corresponding blanks. Mark the best choice for each blank.

Marketers and cellphone makers are only too happy to (1) _____ the newest generation gap. Last fall, Firefly Mobile introduced the glowPhone for the preschool set; it has a small keypad with two speed-dial buttons (2) _____ an image of a mother and a father. AT&T promotes its wireless service with television commercials poking fun at a mom who doesn't understand her daughter's cellphone (3) _____. Indeed, IDC says (4) _____ from services and products sold to young consumers or their parents is expected to grow to $29 billion in 2010, up from $21 billion in 2005.

(5) _____, parents' ability to reach their children whenever they want affords families more pluses than minuses. Mr. Hampton, who is divorced, says it is easy to reach Katie even though they live in different time (6) _____. And college students who are (7) _____ for time, like Ben Blanton, a freshman who plays baseball at Vanderbilt University in Nashville, can text their parents when it suits them, asking them to (8) _____ errands or just saying hello.

"Texting is in between calling and sending and e-mail," he explained (9) _____ taking a break from study hall. Now he won't even consider writing a letter to his mother, Jan. "It's too time (10) _____," he said. "You have to go to the post office. Instead, I can sit and watch television and send a text, which is the same thing."

But as with any cultural shift (11) _____ parents and children — the birth of rock 'n' roll or the sexual revolution of the 1960s, for example — various gulfs emerge. Baby (12) _____ who warned decades ago that their out-of-touch parents couldn't be trusted now sometimes find themselves (13) _____ children who — (14) _____ the Internet and the cellphone — consider Mom and Dad to be clueless, too.

Cellphones, instant messaging, e-mail (15) _____ have encouraged younger users to create their own inventive, quirky and very private written language. That has given them the opportunity to essentially hide in plain sight. They are more connected than ever, but also far more independent.

In some cases, they may even become more (16) _____ from those closest to them, said Anita Gurian, a clinical psychologist and executive editor of AboutOurKids. org, a Web site of the Child Study Center at New York University.

"Cellphones demand parental (17) _____ of a different kind," she said. "Kids can do a lot of things in front of their parents without them (18) _____."

To be sure, parents have always (19) _____ about their children's well-being, independence and comportment — and the rise of the cellphone offers just the latest twist in that dynamic. However it all unfolds, it has helped (20) _____ communications companies to educate parents about how better to be in touch with their children.

1. A. fill   B. dig   C. enlarge   D. broaden
2. A. depicted   B. depicting   C. which depicting D. have depicted
3. A. word   B. saying   C. vernacular   D. behaviour
4. A. output   B. investment   C. input   D. revenue
5. A. So now   B. As now   C. So to speak D. So far
6. A. areas   B. regions   C. zones   D. places
7. A. pressing   B. pressed   C. stress   D. stressful
8. A. run   B. take   C. go   D. play
9. A. when   B. while   C. which   D. as
10. A. taking   B. using   C. consuming   D. assuming
11. A. involve   B. involved   C. involving   D. be involved
12. A. boom   B. booming   C. boomed   D. boomers
13. A. raise   B. raised   C. raising   D. being raised
14. A. owing   B. because   C. out of   D. thanks to
15. A. and the like B. and so   C. so the like D. and like
16. A. connected   B. associated   C. separated   D. alienated
17. A. development B. involvement C. evolvement   D. revolution

18. A. know	B. knew	C. knowing	D. known
19. A. concern	B. be concerned	C. been concerned	D. concerning
20. A. prompted	B. to prompt	C. prompting	D. prompt

IV Translation

Section A Translate the following Chinese sentences into English.

1. 我们常常光顾那家餐厅，他家的出品实在是太棒了。(patronize)
2. 最近媒体为了炒作而毁谤那位演员的慈善工作。(disparage)
3. 入侵部队遭遇了游击队的顽强抵抗。(obstinate)
4. 在同一时期，这项法案授权实行一套激进的方案来解决人口增长的问题。(radical)
5. 宪法的修改被称赞为民主的胜利。(triumph)
6. 他很擅长设计语言游戏，你可以将这些游戏放在课堂里跟学生一起玩。(devise)
7. 她很明显地提及了我的私人生活。(explicit)
8. 风雨的侵蚀使雕像变成了不成形的石块。(erode)
9. 像付账单和购买食品这种凡俗的事务无法引起她的兴趣。(mundane)
10. 英格兰夺冠的可能性变得非常靠后，以至于胜利的希望只能依靠神助了。(divine)

Section B Translate the following English paragraph into Chinese.

A conversation between a person of my age and one of hers is like a map of a maze: There are things that each of us knows, and that each of us knows the other knows, that can be talked about. But there are things that each of us knows that the other doesn't know we know, which must not be spoken of, no matter what. Because of our ages, and for reasons of decency, there are what Daffy would refer to as taboos: forbidden topics which we may stroll among like islands of horse dung in the road that, although perfectly evident to both of us, must not be mentioned or kicked at any cost.

V Topic for Discussion

From the excerpt of *Joy Luck Club*, we can clearly see the great divergence of manners of dealing with people and things in daily life between the mother and daughter. Discuss with your partner on what efforts both parties can make to narrow the distance between them so that smooth communication and understanding among family members can be maintained.

VI Written Work

Write a short essay of about 200 words on either of the topics.

Younger generations are becoming increasingly obsessed with technological devices like smart phones these days. On the contrary, their parents often are not so deft at using them and disapprove the overuse of these devices. Do you think technological devices are to be blamed for the widening of generation gap? Why or why not?

Text B
A Defining Gap: Seniors for Romney, Millennials for Obama

Susan Page

Age range
Millennials: 18 to 29
Seniors: 65 and older

Jack Ireton-Hewitt, 74, volunteers on behalf of Mitt Romney and likes his business background. "That's the kind of guy we need as president today," he says.

Alaysha Claiborne, 18, supports President Obama. "His personal story is very diverse, and my generation, we pride ourselves on our diversity."
By Doug Kapustin for *USA TODAY*

1   YORK, Penn. — At age 74, Jack Ireton-Hewitt is volunteering in his first campaign, walking door to door and manning an information booth at a county fair to help elect Republican Mitt Romney president. But the retired manufacturing executive has failed to persuade two targets close to home: His granddaughters, ages 19 and 21.
2   The first-time voters back President Obama.
3   That much-debated gender gap? The generation gap is wider. In a national *USA TODAY*/Gallup Poll, most 65-and-older seniors support Romney while young adults under 30 back Obama by almost 2-1. The 18-percentage-point difference in their presidential choices is one of the electorate's biggest demographic divides, and it helps define campaign strategies for both sides.
4   The enthusiasm of the Millennial Generation for Obama, who is now 50, fueled his election victory four years ago. Though still backing him, younger voters have lost some of their ardor while seniors have become significantly more engaged than in 2008 on behalf of the 65-year-old Romney — and they are much more likely to vote. At stake in this divide is not only the presidency but also the country's policy direction — shaping the debate on Social Security and Medicare spending, the need to invest in education and the priority placed on environment.

5   Ireton-Hewitt, for one, finds his granddaughters' point of view exasperating.

6   "Their big thing is Obama is going to lower the interest rates on their college loans," he says, noting that he worked his way through college and graduate school without borrowing a dime. The Chambersburg resident appreciates Romney's business background and his record in turning around the troubled Salt Lake City Winter Olympics in 2002. "That's the kind of guy we need as president today," he says.

7   At age 18, Alaysha Claiborne is working in her second campaign after volunteering for Obama before she was old enough to vote in 2008. She arrives at the campaign's storefront in downtown York in a bright yellow T-shirt and blue jeans to work a Saturday afternoon shift at the re-election phone bank.

8   There are political differences in her family, too. Her grandmother is "pretty conservative," says Claiborne, who will enter Temple University in Philadelphia this fall. Her generation has its own distinct perspective, she says. "Young people are more liberal and more accepting," and Obama's biracial background and international upbringing appeals to them. "His personal story is very diverse, and my generation, we pride ourselves on our diversity."

9   In some ways, the clashing generations reflect the changing face of America, especially when it comes to race and ethnicity. Among the seniors surveyed, 16% are Hispanic or racial minorities. Among those under 30, that proportion nearly triples, to 45%. Younger Americans overwhelmingly assess the nation's growing diversity as a good thing rather than a bad thing, by 56% −32%.

10   Seniors are inclined to see it as a bad thing for the country, by 44% −39%.

11   "I hate to use the word racially motivated; I don't think that's it," says William Frey, a demographer at the Brookings Institution who studies generational differences. "It's a fear of change and an unfamiliar change in a bad economy." That's one reason the new health care law is viewed with such suspicion by seniors, he says.

12   "Young people are interested in the future," he says. "They're not afraid of change."

13   Frey has created an index that measures what he dubs the "cultural generation gap," ranking states by the gulf between white seniors 65 and older and non-white children under 18, a mismatch that could spark conflicts over public policies and the allocation of resources. Three of the top six states on his index are among the dozen battlegrounds likely to decide the presidential election: Nevada, New Mexico and Florida. Swing states Colorado and North Carolina also are high on the list.

Do more or less?

14   Views of the role of government differ, too.

15   Two-thirds of seniors say the government is trying to do too much that would be better left to businesses and individuals; about one in four say the government is doing too little to solve the country's problems. Among those younger than 30, the

divide is much closer, 52% -47%, between those who say the government is doing too much or too little.

16 On no issue is the gap greater than on the question of same-sex marriage. Almost six in 10 Millennials say the next president should work to make gay marriages legal nationwide. Fewer than one in four seniors agree.

17 Asked to assess the importance of a dozen issues facing the next president, the youngest voters and the oldest ones reflect different priorities and self-interests:
- For those 18 to 29 years old, many of whom are preparing for or launching careers in a tough economic climate, the top-ranked issue is creating good jobs. Among those 65 and older, many of whom are retired or approaching retirement, that concern drops to sixth.
- For those 65 and older, ensuring the long-term stability of Social Security and Medicare — programs on which many of them rely — ranks second. Protecting those entitlement programs falls to seventh among those under 30.
- Seniors are more concerned about the way politics in Washington works, or doesn't work. By double digits, they put a higher priority on reducing corruption in the federal government (their top issue) and on overcoming political gridlock.
- Millennials, who may be starting families or still be in school themselves, put a higher priority on improving public schools and making college education affordable and available. As a group, they are more concerned about environmental issues such as global warming.

18 The findings are based on a *USA TODAY*/Gallup Poll taken July 19 - 22 of 1,030 adults, including 334 respondents who are 65 and older (margin of error +/-7 percentage points) and 128 respondents who are 18 to 29 (margin of error +/-11). The younger group largely mirrors the so-called Millennial Generation, of those born from 1981 to 1993. They are 18 to 31.

19 A major generation gap in presidential preference also was found in the daily Gallup poll, aggregated over three weeks, which has larger samples and lower margins of error. In the period from July 2 - 22, registered voters under 30 supported Obama by 14 points; those 65 and older backed Romney by 10 points.

20 The two group's differences in priorities are likely to sharpen the looming debate over how to reduce the federal deficit, including the possibility of raising taxes — an issue on which seniors express stronger and more negative views than young adults. This year's lame-duck session of Congress will consider the ax that is poised to slash spending if the legislators can't reach the budget deal that has eluded them.

21 The groups also shape this year's campaign appeals. Obama has tried to cut into Romney's lead among seniors by warning that his opponent wants to convert the popular Medicare program into a voucher system. (Romney supports giving seniors the

option of the current system or a new "premium support" plan to purchase private coverage.) The Romney camp is trying to win over voters, including young people, who backed Obama four years ago but are disappointed by the nation's continued economic travails. "It's OK to make a change," a new ad from the Republican National Committee says.

22 Still, the thrusts of both campaigns are aimed at drawing undecided voters and generating enthusiasm among core supporters. That's why the president talks so much about student loans and job-training programs while Romney spotlights concerns about the size of government and the deficit.

23 On a Saturday morning, several dozen GOP activists show up at Lancaster County Republican headquarters for the launch of Romney's local victory campaign. Asked why they're for the former Massachusetts governor, most cite taxes (too high), spending (out of control) and the health care law they deride as "ObamaCare."

24 "I don't want socialized medicine," says Beverly Rubin, 62, who was making calls in the phone bank set up in the basement. A paper sign taped to the door calls it the "GOP Victory Center." It's the first time Rubin has volunteered in a campaign since she was 14 and the candidate was Barry Goldwater.

25 "It's the fact that Barack Obama is president," she says. "I want to see a change. I think the country is going down completely the wrong path."

26 Upstairs, Immo Sulyok stands next to a life-size cardboard cutout of Romney in the back of the room. GOP county chairman Scott Boyd has offered volunteers who sign up on that day the chance to have their photo taken with the cutout and signed by the candidate — by auto-pen, he notes in the interest of full disclosure.

27 "To help the less fortunate, that's important, but this is not a sustainable model" for the U.S. government, says the white-haired Sulyok, who declines to give his age. "It feels good to go to a money tree, but that's not realistic. We don't have that far to go ... to be like Greece, Spain."

28 Mary Jo Sottek, 67, and her husband, Tom, 68, consider the question of why young people back Obama by such a wide margin.

29 "We believe in the Constitution," she says. "But younger people today. ..."

30 "With younger voters, it's the president's charisma," he says, shaking his head with apparent distaste.

"Everybody loves him".

31 At the Obama headquarters in York, 25 miles down Arsenal Road, the volunteers tend to be younger and are more casually dressed. Asked why they support the president, they cite his support of women's rights and gay rights, his global perspective, his relative youth.

32 "For me, it's the women's rights issue and issues like education which are

most important to me," says Hannah Miller, 21, a senior at Juniata College in Huntingdon, Pa. "I really want to have a say in what the future is going to be."

33   "The biggest thing for me — it's not so political, it's more of an interest in his leadership," says Hesham Abdelhamed, 23, a junior studying international relations at York College. He supports tighter government regulations on the banks and Obama's approach on foreign policy. "Everybody loves him" around the world, he says of the president.

34   Why is there a generational divide?

35   "The older generation may be more skeptical, more careful about their decisions," he suggests.

36   Irene Langley, 66, sports a small circular Obama campaign emblem on her cheek, courtesy of a fellow volunteer who specializes in face-painting. Langley has a theory for why many voters her age are inclined to back Romney. "The country is changing so fast, and I just think people may be afraid of change," the lifelong Democrat says. "The older people cling to their older ideas, and they won't let them go."

37   Dizzying developments in technology are part of that, she says. There's this: In the *USA TODAY* poll, three of four seniors were reached on land lines. Eight of 10 Millennials were called on cellphones.

38   The age divide gives the Romney camp one big advantage. Those 65 and older are the electorate's most reliable voters; young people are the least. In the survey, three of four seniors say they have given "a lot of thought" to the election, historically a sign they will show up at the polls. Four in 10 of the Millennials say the same.

39   "Our largest polling places in the county are our three senior homes," says Diane Moore, 43, the GOP's Election Day coordinator for Lancaster County. "In 2008, our college campuses came out very strong for Obama. We hadn't seen that before ... but I would think that support is not going to be as strong this time."

40   The Republican volunteers laugh when asked if they're certain to vote in November.

41   "100%," Mary Jo Sottek says.

42   "I'll be there, or I'll be dead," Sulyok says.

Notes

1. In a national *USA TODAY*/**Gallup Poll**, ... (Para. 3)

Gallup, Inc. is primarily a research-based performance-management consulting company. Some of Gallup's key practice areas are — employee engagement, customer engagement and well-being. Gallup has more than 40 offices in 27 countries. World headquarters are in Washington, D. C. Gallup currently has four divisions: Gallup

Poll, Gallup Consulting, Gallup University, and Gallup Press. The Gallup Poll is the division of Gallup that regularly conducts public opinion polls in more than 140 countries around the world. Gallup Polls are often referenced in the mass media as a reliable and objective audience measurement public opinion. 盖洛普民意调查

2. On a Saturday morning, several dozen **GOP** activists show up... (Para. 23)

GOP means Grand Old Party, which refers to The Republican Party, one of the two major contemporary political parties in the United States, along with the Democratic Party.

Questions for Discussion

1. According to the findings of the surveys in this article, what do you think are the reasons of the large divergence between older and younger generation?
2. Is the generation gap necessarily a bad thing? Could it benefit our society in any way?

Memorable Quotations

1. Young people are fitter to invent than to judge, fitter for execution than for counsel, and fitter for new projects than for settled business.

— Francis Bacon

2. When I was a boy of fourteen, my father was so ignorant I could hardly stand to have the old man around. But when I got to be twenty-one, I was astonished at how much the old man had learned in seven years.

— Mark Twain

3. Young men are apt to think themselves wise enough, as drunken men are apt to think themselves sober enough.

— Lord Chesterfield

4. It's all that the young can do for the old, to shock them and keep them up to date.

— George Bernard Shaw

Further Readings

1. Amy Tan, *The Joy Luck Club*
2. Margaret Mead, *Culture and Commitment: A Study of the Generation Gap*

Unit 4

Pre-reading Questions
1. Do you enjoy logging onto social media software?
2. How do you think of the authenticity of news on TV?
3. Will letter writing be killed by the modern communication tools?
4. Will the rise of social media undermine family traditions?

Text A

News in the Television Schedule

Jonathan Bignell

1 If we are to understand news in the television scheme, we have to first define what television news is. As we have seen in the discussion of newspaper discourse, news is a mediator of events, defining, shaping and representing the real by the use of linguistic and visual codes. The discourse of TV news is composed of language and visual images, organized by codes and conventions which the news viewer has to perceive and recognize in order for the viewer to construct sense. This competence in decoding news derives in part from the viewer's competence in the discourse which the news borrows from society at large. For instance, the presenters of TV news programmes adopt a formal dress code. Men wear suits, and women wear business clothes (blouse, jackets, unobtrusive jewellery). News presenters are thus coded as professional, serious, and authoritative. These connoted meaning are supported by the impersonal linguistic codes used in news presenters' speech (they hardly ever say "I"), and the lack of gestural signs which might connote emotion or involvement in the news stories they present. The mythic meaning that news presenters are neutral and authoritative is constructed from these connotations, which viewers recognize from other aspects of social life and not only from the codes of television.

2 Viewers of TV news will also make use of their knowledge of codes specific to the medium in which the news is broadcast. Like all other TV programmes, TV news is separated from other programmes and commercials by title sequences. Title sequences are syntagms of signs which signify boundaries between one part of the continual flow of TV material and the rest of it. News programmes contain interviewers which are visually coded in similar ways to current affairs programmes and some sports programmes. Camera shots alternate back and forth between speakers, signifying the to and fro of conversation, or unseen speakers put questions to people denoted in studio or outside locations. The news presenters' head-on address to the camera is also found in current affairs, sports, and quiz programmes, signifying the presenter's role in mediating between the viewer and the other components of the programme. News programmes feature actuality film with voice-over, which is also found in documentary programmes and signifies "observed reality". These examples show that TV news is not a unique television form, but rather genre of television whose codes draw on the viewer's knowledge of the codes of other genres of programme. The meanings of TV news derived from some codes which are borrowed from social life in general, and from codes used in

the TV medium.

3   As in the case of newspaper discourse, TV news does not consist of lists of fact, but of narrative reports of events. Like newspapers, TV news makes use of criteria of news value, where the set of priorities and assumptions shared by news broadcasters determines which news reports are given greatest significance within the news bulletin. In general, reports with high news value are those which appear near the beginning of the bulletin, just as the front pages of newspapers present stories with high perceived news value to readers. All four of the headline news stories announced at the beginning of *ITV News at Ten* and *BBC News* were the same stories on each programme (a White House gunman was arrested, a man imprisoned for murder was released after evidence was revealed as flawed, Prime Minister Tony Blair spoke about Britain's entry into the Euro currency zone, and Prince William attend a party). But these headline stories were present in a different order on each programme, and appeared in greater length at different points in each bulletin. Each news programme will contain a hierarchy of news items, with the first time in each segment having greater news value than the items which follow it. As in newspapers, the ranking of reports according to their perceived news value gives us an insight into the ideology of TV news, and the ideology of society in general.

4   The representation of reality offered by TV news is not reality itself, but reality mediated by the signs, codes, myths, and ideologies of news. News both shapes and reflects the dominant common sense notion of what is significant (because what is significant is what is in the news), and also therefore contributes to the ongoing process of constructing a dominant ideology through which we perceive our reality.

5   With that, one is now able to understand how news is schemed in television. News has a significant role in the broadcast output of television channels. Satellite cable offers all-day new channels, and all terrestrial television stations in Britain broadcast news several times each day. The longest news bulletins are in the early evening, the time when people return from work, and at the end of the "prime-time" mid-evening period when family entertainment programmes aim at a more adult audience. From the point of view of television stations, news not only serves to fulfill the requirement that they inform their audience about contemporary events, but is also used to manage the TV audience' pattern of viewing. A popular early-evening news programme may encourage viewers to remain watching that channel for subsequent entertainment programmes in the prime time which follows the news. Late-evening news bulletin occurs at times when adult-oriented programmes are shown, after the 9.00 p.m. "watershed", when children are presumed not to be watching, and watching the long late-evening news bulletin may encourage viewers to remain on that channel for subsequent programmes. BBC news at ten o'clock began in October 2000, replacing the former *Nine O'clock News*, and usually draws about five million viewers. On 7 February

2001, BBC1's evening news at 10.00 p.m. occurred after a popular factual programme, *Thief Catchers*: *A Car Wars Special* (about police units which target car crime) and the *National Lottery Update* revealing the winning numbers for that day's draw. About 80 per cent of news viewers have watched the preceding programme. On 6 February 2001 the start of the news was preceded by trailers for two programmes: the drama serial *The Best of Both Worlds* beginning on Sunday, and the *Omnibus* arts programme following the news. These trailers aim to retain viewers for other BBC1 programmes, since some viewers will have just tuned to watch *BBC News* and can be invited to remain on the channel afterwards, while other viewers may be tempted to switch channels away from the news and are reminded of other BBC1 programmes they might return to.

6 ITV's late-evening news bulletin was at 10.30 p.m. on 7 February 2001, but the news was broadcast even later in the evening for nearly two years under the name *ITN Nightly News*, after ITV executives had campaigned for more than five years to shift their news timeslot. The reason for placing the news later in the evening was to make room for the popular programmes, films and football matches in the mid-evening period. But in July 2000, the Independent Television Commission which regulates commercial television operation ordered ITV to return *News at Ten* to its 10.00 p.m. slot in early 2001. The current ITV *News at Ten* is 20 minutes long and is uninterrupted by commercial breaks. The programme can be moved to a later slot on Fridays and on one other day during the week, but is always named *News at Ten* because of the high recognition of this name among TV audiences. The newly repositioned news allows ITV to add 2.5 minutes of advertising to its peak time programming, and 20 seconds of extra trails for forthcoming programmes. This is significant because news is watched by comparatively high numbers of viewers in the ABC1 social categories (professional, managerial and skilled workers) who are the preferred audience for ads for such high-cost products as cars. So although ITV gained about £ 70 million a year from moving its news to 11.00 p.m., the inclusion of these additional ads around *News at Ten* will offset the loss incurred from shifting the news back to 10.00 p.m.

7 TV news is usually regarded as authoritative, with most people in Britain gaining their knowledge of news through TV rather than newspaper. The dominance of TV as a news medium come in part from the perceived impartiality of news broadcasting. There are rules of "balance" and "objectivity" in the regulations governing television broadcasting. Newspapers are not subject to these rules. The increasing dominance of TV as a news medium has been reinforced by a shift in newspaper coverage to other kinds of material, like lifestyle features or sensational stories, or to greater coverage of areas not extensively covered by TV news, like sport. The dominance of TV news derives also from its immediacy, since newspapers must be produced several hours before being distributed, while TV news can incorporate new

reports even during the programme broadcast. On Wednesday 7 February 2001, almost all national newspapers carried stories on the newly elected Prime Minister of Israel, Ariel Sharon, who featured in the main stories of his equivocal support for peace with Palestinians, but no newspaper had the opportunity to present a story about the arrest of a man who fired shots at the White House in Washington DC on 7 February 2001 because the event occurred after the newspaper publication deadlines.

8   So while there are evident parallels between the news values of newspaper journalists and television journalists, there are constraints imposed by the different timing of news production in the two media which determine the degree of immediacy which can be connoted in each. The different stories on the front pages of "quality" and "popular" newspapers also show that the news values of television news programmes are more similar to those of "quality" newspapers than to "popular" ones. This sharing of news values by "quality" newspaper and TV news is also paralleled by the authoritativeness, objectivity and balance which are connoted in TV news discourses and in "quality" newspapers' discourses. Like newspaper, television channels compete to attract audience and advertisers, but the differences in funding arrangements for British television channels make a direct comparison between them, and between television news and newspapers, much less straightforward.

9   In Britain, the BBC's two terrestrial channels are funded by a licence fee which must be paid by all owners of television sets. The regional TV companies broadcasting on the ITV channel, and other terrestrial channels Channel Four and Channel Five gain their income from advertisement. There are TV commercials before ITV's *News at Ten*. TV broadcasting companies funded by commercial advertising need to attract audiences for advertisers, and TV broadcasters funded by licence fee need to justify the compulsory payment of the licence fee by attracting large audiences. So broadcasters continually compete against each other to achieve large audiences for their programmes ("ratings"), and to encourage viewing of their own programmes rather than the competing programmes from their channels which are shown at the same time ("audience share"). On 7 February 2001 the ITV *News at Ten* was preceded by a trailer for the comedy drama serial *At Home with the Braithwaites* and *The Big Match* football coverage which followed the news, plus details of that evening's ITV programmes. These trailers can be regarded as an advertisement for the ITV channel (and the Carlton television company which broadcasts on this channel), attempting to attract audience share. Within *News at Ten* itself, results of football matches to be seen on *The Big Match* were broadcast without sound and viewers were reminded that *The Big Match* would follow (so that the results could remain a surprise for *Big Match* viewers), thus further advertising this ITV programme as well as informing viewers of sports news. News on TV is not only significant in itself, but also has an important role in the daily schedule and in the attraction and control of audiences.

Notes

1. About the author.

Jonathan Bignell is Professor of Television and Film in the University of Reading in the U. K. He is also the Head of the School of Arts and Communication Design. His main field of research is on television history and television and film analysis. *Beckett on Screen*: *The Television Plays* and *An Introduction to Television Studies* are two major books among his famous publications.

This essay is an excerpt taken and edited from his writing *Television News* from the book *Media Semiotics*.

2. All four of the headline news stories announced at the beginning of ***ITV*** *News at Ten*... (Para. 3)

ITV is the major commercial public service TV network in the United Kingdom. Launched in 1955 under the auspices of the Independent Television Authority (ITA) to provide competition to the BBC, it is also the oldest commercial network in the UK. Since the passing of the *Broadcasting Act* 1990, its legal name has been Channel 3, the number 3 having no real meaning other than to distinguish it from BBC One, BBC Two and Channel 4. In part, the number 3 was assigned as televisions would usually be tuned so that the regional ITV station would be on the third button, the other stations being allocated to the number within their name.

3. ... ***BBC*** *News* were the same stories on each programme... (Para. 3)

The British Broadcasting Company is an independent public media that is funded by the government. It is one of the biggest long-standing media around the world. The media serves it provides includes television, radio, publications, newspaper, English teaching and internet news serves.

4. On 7 February 2001, BBC1's evening news at 10.00 p.m. occurred after a popular **factual programme**... (Para. 5)

Factual programme is a genre of non-fiction television programming that documents actual events and people. These types of programs are also described as documentary, observational documentary, fly on the wall, docudrama, and reality television.

Glossary

authoritative [ɔːˈθɒrətətɪv] *a.*	an authoritative book, account etc. is respected because the person who wrote it knows a lot about the subject
bulletin [ˈbʊlətɪn] *n.*	a news report on radio or television
cable [ˈkeɪbl] *n.*	a plastic or rubber tube containing wires that carry

	telephone messages, electronic signals etc.
campaign [kæmˈpeɪn] v.	to lead or take part in a series of actions intended to achieve a particular result
contemporary [kənˈtemprərɪ] a.	belonging to the present time; modern
connote [kəˈnəʊt] v.	(*formal*) if a word connotes something, it makes you think of feelings and ideas that are not its actual meaning
constraint [kənˈstreɪnt] n.	restriction
draw [drɔː] n.	the act of choosing a winning number, ticket etc. in a lottery
equivocal [ɪˈkwɪvəkl] a.	ambiguous; mysterious or difficult to understand
forthcoming [fɔːθˈkʌmɪŋ] a.	a forthcoming event, meeting etc is one that had been planned to happen soon
incorporate [ɪnˈkɔːpəreɪt] v.	to include something as part of a group, system, plan etc
incur [ɪnˈkɜː] v.	to put yourself in an unpleasant situation by your own actions, so that you lose something, get punished etc
inform [ɪnˈfɔːm] v.	to formally or officially tell someone about something or give them information
impartiality [ɪmˌpɑːʃɪˈælətɪ] n.	the act of not giving special favour or support to any one person or group
immediacy [ɪˈmiːdɪəsɪ] n.	the quality of seeming to happen right now that makes something seem more important or urgent to you
offset [ˈɒfset] v.	if something such as a cost or sum of money offsets another cost, sum etc or is offset against it, it has an opposite effect so that the situation remains the same
preceding [prɪˈsiːdɪŋ] a.	[only before noun] (*formal*) happening or coming before the time, place, or part mentioned
retain [rɪˈteɪn] v.	to keep something or continue to have something
subsequent [ˈsʌbsɪkwənt] a.	(*formal*) coming after or following something else
straightforward [streɪtˈfɔːwəd] a.	simple and easy to understand
terrestrial [təˈrestrɪəl] a.	*technical* terrestrial TV / channels etc TV etc that is broadcast from the earth rather than from satellite
tempt [tempt] v.	to try to persuade someone to do something by making it seem attractive

timeslot ['taɪmslɒt] n.　　　　different periods of time in TV broadcasting
trailer ['treɪlə] n.　　　　　　an advertisement for a new film or television show, consisting of small scenes taken from it
tune [tjuːn] in phr v.　　　　to watch or listen to a broadcast on radio or television
watershed ['wɔːtəʃed] n.　　the (9 o'clock) watershed *BrE* the time in the evening after which television programmes that are not suitable for children may be shown

Comprehension Questions

Answer the following questions after reading the text.

1. In what way are the TV programs arranged to attract or maintain viewers?
2. Why did ITV change the timeslot of its late-evening news?
3. What makes TV a dominant news medium?
4. What is the biggest advantage that TV has over newspaper as a news medium?
5. What do TV and newspaper share in common in terms of new values?
6. How are BBC and ITV channels funded?

Exercises

I Vocabulary

Section A Paraphrase the following sentences chosen from the text.

1. Late-evening news bulletin occurs at times when adult-oriented programmes are shown, after the 9.00 p.m. "watershed", when children are presumed not to be watching, and watching the long late-evening news bulletin may encourage viewers to remain on that channel for subsequent programmes. (Para. 6)
2. So although ITV gained about £ 70 million a year from moving its news to 11.00 p.m., the inclusion of these additional ads around *News at Ten* will offset the loss incurred from shifting the news back to 10.00 p.m. (Para. 6)
3. This sharing of news values by "quality" newspaper and TV news is also paralleled by the authoritativeness, objectivity and balance which are connoted in TV news discourses and in "quality" newspapers' discourses. (Para. 8)

Section B There are ten sentences in this section. Beneath each sentence there are four words or phrases marked A, B, C and D. Choose one word or phrase that best completes the sentence.

1. The office will _____ you of any change of decision as soon as possible.
　　A. tell　　　　B. confirm　　　　C. inform　　　　D. provide
2. The palace is _____ to date back to the Han dynasty.

A. supposed   B. presumed   C. assured   D. told
3. Everyone should be _____ innocent until it is proved that he is guilty.
   A. presumed   B. assumed   C. resumed   D. consumed
4. When you get a minor burn, pour some cold water on it, which will help _____ the pain of the burn.
   A. relieve   B. relax   C. reveal   D. release
5. Fuel scarcities and price increases _____ automobile designers to scale down the largest models and to develop completely new lines of small cars and trunks.
   A. persuaded   B. prompted   C. imposed   D. enlightened
6. During the TV interview, the singer _____ that he was going to release his new album soon.
   A. revealed   B. rehearsed   C. relieved   D. renewed
7. As the manager was away on a business trip, I was asked to _____ the weekly staff meeting.
   A. preside   B. introduce   C. chair   D. dominate
8. His speech could not _____ the interest of his audience.
   A. remain   B. retain   C. relieve   D. renew
9. The factory is enlarged to make _____ for new machinery.
   A. space   B. place   C. room   D. out
10. Any expenses you may _____ will be chargeable to the company.
    A. occur   B. cost   C. have   D. incur

Section C   Use the proper form of the following words given in the brackets to fill in the blanks.

1. Saving the child's life took _____ over everything else. (precede)
2. We make more money this month than in the whole of the _____ quarter. (precede)
3. Is there any _____ for this? (precede)
4. Television brings a new _____ to world events. (immediate)
5. As soon as I got their email, I replied _____. (immediate)
6. This room is male _____. I am afraid it is not suitable for you ladies. (dominate)
7. The _____ role in this troop is the male gorilla. (dominate)
8. The subject for discussion today is Samsung's _____ of the market. (dominate)

Section D   Use the proper form of the following phrases to fill in the blanks.

| be presumed to | tempt to | tune in | campaign for |
| make room for | switch over | be preceded by | be paralleled by |

1. The commodity in the showcase is moved back to shelves to _____ the new promotion goods.

2. According to the law, an accused man _____ innocent until he is proved guilty.
3. E-business is very popular now — our company is _____ soon.
4. — Why is this programme so noisy?
   — Perhaps you are not properly _____.
5. The master's performance _____ a novice's debut.
6. Nothing can _____ me _____ join the army.
7. The president entered, _____ a group of professors.
8. She spent her life _____ children's welfare.

II Grammar

Choose the best answer to complete the following sentence from the respective four choices.

1. I know this is the correct train. The ticket agent said it would be on _____.
   A. Platform Four   B. the Platform Four
   C. Forth Platform   D. the Four Platform
2. Which of the following sentences is INCORRECT?
   A. They each have two tickets.
   B. They cost twenty Yuan each.
   C. Each they have bought the same book.
   D. They were given two magazines each.
3. If there were no subjunctive mood, English _____ much easier to learn.
   A. could have been   B. would be
   C. will be   D. would have been
4. Land belongs to the state; there is _____ thing as private ownership of land.
   A. no such a   B. not such   C. not such any   D. no such
5. Which of the following sentences has an object complement?
   A. The directors appointed John manager.
   B. I gave Marry a Christmas present.
   C. You have done Peter a favor.
   D. She is teaching children English.
6. In "How much do you think he earns?" how much is _____ of the sentence.
   A. the subject   B. the adverbial   C. the object   D. the complement
7. "It seems that she was there at the conference." The sentence means that _____.
   A. she seems to be there at the conference
   B. she seemed to be there at the conference
   C. she seems to have been there at the conference
   D. she seemed to being there at the conference
8. "The man preparing the document is the firm's lawyer" has all the following possible meanings EXCEPT _____.

A. the man who has prepared the documents
B. the man who has been preparing the document
C. the man who is preparing the documents
D. the man who will prepare the documents

9. Which of the following adverbs can NOT be used to complete "_____ everybody came"?
   A. Nearly   B. Quite   C. Practically   D. Almost

10. Which of the following words can NOT be used to complete "We've seen the film _____"?
    A. before   B. recently   C. lately   D. yet

11. It _____ to see so many children in that rural area cannot even afford elementary education.
    A. pains her   B. makes her pain   C. is paining   D. is pained

12. Our boss, Mr. Thompson, _____ a raise in salary for ages, but nothing has happened yet.
    A. was promising   B. has been promising
    C. promised   D. has promised

13. A dream is to a person is _____ wings are to a bird.
    A. that   B. which   C. what   D. as

14. The man sitting opposite me smiled dreamily, as if _____ something wonderful in the past.
    A. to remember   B. remembered
    C. having been remembered   D. remembering

15. I _____ him the Christmas gift by mail because he came home during the Christmas holidays.
    A. ought to have sent   B. couldn't have sent
    C. must have sent   D. needn't have sent

III Cloze

The mass media is a essential part of our culture, yet it can also be a helper, adviser and teacher to our young generation. The mass media affects the lives of our young by acting as a (an) (1) _____ for a number of institutions and social contacts. In this way, it (2) _____ a variety of functions in human life. The time spent in front of the TV box is usually at the (3) _____ of leisure: there is less time for games, amusement and rest. (4) _____ by what is happening on the screen, children not only imitate what they see but also directly (5) _____ themselves with different characters. Americans have been concerned about the (6) _____ of violence in the media and its (7) _____ harm to children and adolescents for at least forty years. During this period, new media (8) _____, such as video games, cable television, music videos, and the Internet. As they continue to gain popularity, these media, (9) _____ television, (10) _____ public concern and research attention. Another large societal concern on our young generation (11) _____ by the media, is body image. (12) _____ forces can influence body image positively or negatively. (13) _____ one, societal and cultural norms and mass media marketing (14) _____ our concepts of beauty. In the mass media, the images of (15) _____ beauty fill magazines and newspapers, (16) _____ from our televisions and entertain us (17) _____ the movies. Even in advertising, the mass media (18) _____ on accepted cultural values of thinness and fitness for commercial gain. Young adults are presented with a (19) _____ defined standard of attractiveness, a(n) (20) _____ that carries unrealistic physical expectations.

1. A. alternative   B. preference   C. substitute   D. Representative
2. A. accomplishes   B. fulfills   C. provides   D. suffices
3. A. risk   B. mercy   C. height   D. expense
4. A. Absorbed   B. Attracted   C. Aroused   D. Addicted
5. A. identify   B. recognize   C. unify   D. equate
6. A. abundance   B. incidence   C. prevalence   D. recurrence
7. A. disposed   B. hidden   C. implicit   D. potential
8. A. merged   B. emerged   C. immerged   D. submerged
9. A. apart from   B. much as   C. but for   D. along with
10. A. promote   B. propel   C. prompt   D. prosper
11. A. inspired   B. imposed   C. delivered   D. contributed
12. A. External   B. Exterior   C. Explicit   D. Exposed
13. A. As   B. At   C. For   D. In
14. A. mark   B. effect   C. impact   D. shock
15. A. generalized   B. regularized   C. standardized D categorized
16. A. boom   B. bottom   C. brim   D. beam
17. A. over   B. with   C. on   D. at
18. A. play   B. take   C. profit   D. resort
19. A. barely   B. carefully   C. narrowly   D. subjectively
20. A. ideal   B. image   C. stereotype   D. Criterion

IV Translation
Section A Translate the following Chinese sentences into English.
1. 他厨艺精湛，无人能与之匹敌。(parallel)
2. 俗话说，大祸来临之前总是格外地平静。(precede)
3. 商家通常以提高售价来抵消增加的成本。(offset)
4. 我们翻新房间时保留了原有的阳台。(retain)
5. 来自权威方面的消息证实了这一新政将会实行。(authoritative)

6. 并非所有他的朋友都去参加宴会。(all)
7. 帮忙救人的不全是志愿者。(all)
8. 他的研究只是出于好奇，并不是为了钱。(for)
9. 很多难民死于饥饿。(from)
10. 代表们一致选她为学生会主席。(object complement)

Section B Translate the following English paragraphs into Chinese.

While it is easy for parents to worry that iPads, iPhones and Instagram are undermining the family, it is not always that simple. As Danah Boyd, a digital anthropologist, points out, our cyber behaviour needs to be viewed in a much bigger social context. Take the oft-cited concern that electronic media are separating children from their parents (or grandparents). To a casual observer, this might seem self-evident, given how much time children tend to spend online, roaming cyber space or chatting with friends.

Similarly, while the rise of social media might undermine the type of family traditions that grandparents say they love, it is also creating new links. Parents today can monitor what teenagers are saying to each other far more closely than before. Kids can talk — or Skype or FaceTime — with their relatives all over the world on Christmas Day. Family news or holiday snaps can be shared on social media platforms.

V Topics for Discussion

1. We watch TV very often, but we seldom look at it from an analytical point of view. Interview your classmates to find out how they comment on our TV programmes and the arrangement of them. And then report to the class.
2. What are the makings of a good comparison? Can you find answers by analyzing this text?

VI Written Work

Media are playing an increasingly important role in our life, through which we obtain information, communicate with others, and establish our values and judge from that. Some politicians even speak directly to the press rather than to the government officer. How do you think of that? Write a comment of about 200 words on the role of media today.

Text B
How to Establish Your Professional Network Through Social Media

1 After getting his M. B. A. from the College of William and Mary, Chris Perry knew he'd have to venture beyond Williamsburg, Va., to find a good job in marketing and branding.

2 The best jobs in his field are in big cities like New York, and industry recruiters weren't coming to his university. So, through the career website LinkedIn he started reaching out to people who worked at companies that he had an interest in. His first few introductions didn't get much response. Mr. Perry acknowledges that his notes were cordial but may have sounded too self-serving. So he softened his approach.

3 "I'd put in the title that I was a recent M. B. A. graduate looking for advice," says Mr. Perry. "I'd focus on talking about them during informational interviews and I'd mention any accomplishments of theirs that I may have read about."

4 He also participated in LinkedIn industry groups that allowed him to communicate directly with contacts he couldn't have reached without a chain of introductions.

5 One fellow group member worked for Reckitt Benckiser, a British consumer-goods company with a major office in Parsippany, N. J. The contact agreed to speak with Mr. Perry on condition that he not ask for a reference. After a pleasant conversation, the contact ended up forwarding Mr. Perry's résumé to the HR department, which helped him get an interview and a job. He's now a senior leader on Reckitt's e-commerce team.

6 Social-media websites like LinkedIn have made job hunting easier by automating many tasks. But one-click networking invitations fall short when trying to reach people, say experts. Instead, job hunters need to engage other professionals on a more personal level. This includes getting introductions to people outside of your network who can help you with your career. The trick is knowing how to ask.

7 Focus on your first- and second-degree connections. The former are contacts that have already accepted your invitation to join your network, or vice versa, and the latter are contacts known to your first-degree connection. Third-degree connections require more than one introduction and can be difficult to reach, as you may not have a mutual acquaintance.

8 Consider whom you want to get an introduction from. Do research on LinkedIn, Google and even Glassdoor to find out what kind of employee your chosen first-degree contact is, says Dan Schawbel, a workplace expert from Boston and author of *Promote*

Yourself: The New Rules of Career Success.

9   "You really don't want an endorsement from somebody that's not liked at work or who has a poor workplace reputation," says Mr. Schawbel. "How much do you really know about that person that you connected with at that trade show?"

10   When asking for an introduction, make it easy for your first-degree contact by mentioning how you'd like to be introduced and the reasons you need help, writing out the introduction to be forwarded and providing something in return for the effort. Networking works best when both parties can offer the other something useful.

11   You should also give your contact an easy way out in case he or she isn't comfortable making the introduction, says New York career coach Melissa Llarena. "Always be gracious, since at the very least they might offer useful advice or a referral to somebody else that can help you with an introduction," she says.

12   Groups are one way to contact second- and third-degree LinkedIn members directly. But don't join a group and start contacting individual members without making an earnest attempt to participate in community dialogue. You could get ejected from the group by the moderators.

13   Answer some questions and start new topics. Go beyond "liking" updates by making thoughtful comments on new posts or by sharing relevant links. You want to show regular engagement, says Mr. Schawbel. That includes answering any network requests promptly.

14   Preface any requests with regular status updates to show that you're active. It will also give you and your contact something to reference. Just don't share the same personal updates about your cats across all of your social-media accounts. Try to keep your LinkedIn updates on a more professional level.

15   You'll get a much better response if your profile is up-to-date and includes a photo. That includes making your profile relevant to the job that you want to get, says Ms. Llarena.

16   Once you've established a regular dialogue, take the relationship offline as soon as you can. Ask for 30 minutes and treat your contact to coffee or lunch.

Notes

1. After getting his M. B. A. from the **College of William and Mary**, ... (Para. 1)

It is the second oldest university in the USA, a top university from which four US presidents are its graduates.

2. So, through the career website **LinkedIn**... (Para. 2)

LinkedIn is a global platform open for all professionals for communication.

3. Do research on LinkedIn, Google and even **Glassdoor** to ... (Para. 8)

It is a free jobs and career community that offers the world an inside look at jobs and companies.

4. ... says New York **career coach** Melissa Llarena. (Para. 11)

Career coaches are professionals that help staffs to see their problems in jobs and find their own solutions, often can be found in companies and education.

Questions for Discussion

1. Do you have an account in Linkedin?
2. Have you any experience with talking to professionals through such social media?
3. How do you think of the social media?

Memorable Quotations

1. If people in the media cannot decide whether they are in the business of reporting news or manufacturing propaganda, it is all the more important that the public understand that difference, and choose their news sources accordingly.

   — Thomas Sowell

2. I believe in equality for everyone, except reporters and photographers.

   — Gandhi

3. Trying to determine what is going on in the world by reading newspapers is like trying to tell the time by watching the second hand of a clock.

   — Ben Hecht

4. The public have an insatiable curiosity to know everything. Except what is worth knowing. Journalism, conscious of this and having tradesman-like habits, supplies their demands.

   — Oscar Wilde

Further Readings

1. Bignell, J., *An Introduction to Television Studies*. 3rd edition
2. Bignell, J. and Weissmann, E., *Cultural Difference? Not So Different after All*.

Unit 5

Pre-reading Questions:
1. How do you think global aging will challenge the world economy?
2. What recommendations would you make to tackle the problem of population aging?

Text A
The World Turns Gray

Phillip J. Longman

1 Worldwide, as recently as 1972, a woman gave birth to an average of 5.6 children over her lifetime. Global population, as a result, was doubling every generation. Citing the trend, a hoary group of intellectuals known as the Club of Rome issued an influential study, titled "The Limits to Growth," that told what it all meant. The 21st century, said the club, would inevitably be marked by declining standards of living as human population exceeded the "carrying capacity" of the Earth, leading to mass famine and energy shortages.

2 But in the years since this Malthusian prophecy, a change has occurred in human behavior that is as revolutionary as it is unheralded: Around the world, fertility rates are plummeting. Today, women on average have just half the number of children they did in 1972. In 61 countries, accounting for 44 percent of the Earth's population, fertility rates are now at or below replacement levels.

3 That doesn't mean the Earth's population will fall anytime soon. Thanks to the high fertility rates of the past, a large percentage of the world's population is still of childbearing age. Life expectancy is also up. Globally, the average life span has jumped from 49.5 years in 1972 to more than 63 years. Consequently, according to projections by the United Nations, the world's population will slowly increase at an average rate of 1.3 percent a year during the next 50 years, and it could decline by midcentury if fertility continues to fall.

Birth Dearth

4 So there is a new problem for mankind. Global aging. Next year, for the first time in history, people over 60 will outnumber kids 14 or younger in industrial countries. Even more startling, the population of the Third World, while still comparatively youthful, is aging faster than that of the rest of the world. In France, for example, it took 140 years for the proportion of the population age 65 or older to double from 9 percent to 18 percent. In China, the same feat will take just 34 years. In Venezuela, 22. "The developed world at least got rich before it got old," notes Neil Howe, an expert on aging. "In the Third World the trend is reversed."

5 And that means trouble. For one thing, the cost of supporting a burgeoning elderly population will place enormous strains on the world's economy. Instead of there being more workers to support each retiree — as was the case while birthrates were still

rising — there will be fewer. Instead of markets growing, they will shrink, at least in large parts of the globe.

6   Economists define a recession as two or more consecutive quarters of declining gross domestic product. Yet as Peterson points out in his new book, *Gray Dawn*, in the world's richest and most productive countries, the number of working-age people will be dropping well over 1 percent a year within 20 years. Even assuming healthy increases in productivity, such a continuing contraction in the work force could mean decades of declining economic output.

Productivity Problem

7   Yet economics alone are not enough to explain people's reproductive behavior. After all, in general the world's highest birthrates are in the poorest countries. Teresa Castro, a fertility expert at the Spanish government's Superior Council for Scientific Research, points to diffuse cultural factors at work. In Spain, she says, the Roman Catholic prohibition against birth control is now widely ignored. The church, she says, "lost all influence in family matters years ago and now serves only as a setting for rites of passage," such as weddings, baptisms, and funerals. Another key factor is the incorporation of a majority of women into the work force. This change, says Castro, "has come about so rapidly that there are not enough day-care facilities for working women who would like to have children."

8   Spain may lead the world in its diminishing fertility, but there are plenty of runners-up. Italy is in the midst of a bambini bust that will cause it to lose more than half its native younger workers with each new generation. The Czech Republic, Romania, and Bulgaria all are producing children at a rate of just 1.2 per woman. Germany, Japan, Greece, Russia, Portugal, Hungary, and Ukraine have similar fertility rates. American women, though still not producing enough babies to replace the population, are fertility goddesses by comparison, with a lifetime average of two children each.

9   For the developed world, fiscal consequences of these trends are dire. Over the next 25 years, the number of persons of pensionable age (65 and over) in industrial countries will rise by 70 million, predicts the Organization for Economic Cooperation and Development (OECD), while the working-age population will rise by only 5 million. Today, working taxpayers outnumber nonworking pensioners in the developed world by 3 to 1. By 2030, absent increases in retirement ages, this ratio will fall to 1.5 to 1. In Italy and other places, it will drop to 1 to 1 or lower.

10   Of course, there will be fewer children to feed and educate. But most experts agree that while aging societies may be able to divert some resources that now go to the young, the increasing cost of supporting the elderly is almost certain to consume these savings many times over.

11　Throughout the developed world, total public spending per old person is two to three times as great as public spending per child. And in the future, that gap will probably widen. The elderly consume far more health care resources than do children, and new technologies to extend life are bound to escalate health care costs.

12　Who will pay the bills? One option is to raise taxes on the diminishing number of workers. But according to official projections, doing so would require increasing the total tax burden on workers by the equivalent of 25 to 40 percent of their taxable wages, an unthinkable prospect in industrial countries, where payroll tax rates already sometimes exceed 40 percent. Another option would be to cut benefits, but given the political and ethical obstacles, this approach is likely to be put off for as long as possible.

13　That leaves borrowing. As aging nations attempt to avoid hard choices, they are likely to rack up mountains of debt. And, at some point, that could destabilize the world economy. For example, with neither tax increases nor benefit cuts, Japan will have to increase its public-debt levels from a little more than 20 percent of gross domestic product today to over 100 percent by 2050, according to OECD. In Europe, public indebtedness would have to rise from under 60 percent of GDP to nearly 110 percent.

14　Like all Latin American countries, Brazil has seen a dramatic decline in its fertility rate over the last generation. In 1960, a Brazilian woman on average had more than six children over her lifetime; today, her counterpart has just 2.3 children. As a result, in a land once known for its celebration of dental-floss bikinis and youthful carnival exuberance, pension debt has become the public's central preoccupation.

15　China also is struggling with pension and health care bills it can't afford. The large generation born in the first half of the 1950s will become elderly within the next two decades. Yet because of China's one-family/one-child policy, begun in the late 1970s, the number of workers is shrinking dramatically. Increasingly, the typical family pattern in China today is the "one-two-four household," with one child supporting two parents and four grandparents.

16　Other parts of Asia are aging even faster than China. Over the next decade, Japan, for example, will suffer a 25 percent drop in the number of workers under age 30. In 1985, only 28 percent of the world's elderly lived in Asia; by 2025, Asia's share will increase to 58 percent.

17　Aside from the Muslim countries of North Africa and the Middle East, it's hard to find any part of the world that isn't aging. For many Third World countries, the challenge of supporting a growing elderly population is compounded by huge out-migrations of younger people. The nations of the Caribbean, for example, have lost 5.6 million mostly working-age citizens to emigration since 1950. This trend, combined with falling fertility rates and increasing life expectancy among the elderly, has given countries like Martinique, Barbados, and Aruba populations that are nearly as old as that of the United States.

18   Even Africa, the world's youngest continent, is more and more burdened by aging issues. Indeed, because of migration and the ravages of the AIDS epidemic, the number of working-age persons in sub-Saharan Africa available to support each elder is shrinking, causing enormous societal strains.

19   The plight of Grace Ngondo provides a good case study. Sitting in her thatch-roofed, rondavel hut along a dusty road in Epworth, Zimbabwe, Ngondo reflected recently on the good life she had expected in old age. When her late husband, a farm worker, first retired, Ngondo counted on her children for the same reverence and support she had once given her own aging parents, and for a while she received it. Her eldest son provided clothing and food. There was chicken stewing in the pot and meat hanging from a long wire. "I lived like a white person in those days," she recalls.

20   But now the wire is rusty and bare, and like millions of aging Africans these days, Ngondo must work to eat. Two of her sons have died of diseases which Ngondo says had AIDS-like symptoms. A third son has moved away. Following the death of her husband and a brother-in-law, Ngondo now finds herself responsible for supporting more than a dozen grandchildren, nieces, and nephews. To make ends meet, she toils in the fields until the heat of the day overcomes her. Then she walks to the local school to sell ice cream to the departing children.

21   But like their African counterparts, the elderly in even the richest countries will most likely be called upon to work much later in life and to take more of a role in rearing the next generation. That may dash some people's dreams of an early retirement to the golf course or fishing hole, but in exchange for longer lives in a less crowded world, it may be a fair price to pay.

Notes

1. ... as human population exceeded the "**carrying capacity**" of the Earth... (Para. 1)

The carrying capacity of a biological species in an environment is the maximum population size of the species that the environment can sustain indefinitely, given the food, habitat, water and other necessities available in the environment. In population biology, carrying capacity is defined as the environment's maximal load.

2. But in the years since this **Malthusian prophecy**, ... (Para. 2)

Malthusian prophecy refers to the prediction made by an English economist, Thomas Malthus (1766—1834). He predicted that food production would increase arithmetically (1, 2, 3, 4, 5...), but population would increase geometrically (1, 2, 4, 8, 16...). Eventually the demand for food by the increasing population would exceed the world's capacity to produce. The results would be war, famine, pestilence and strife.

3. **Life expectancy** is also up. (Para. 3)

Life expectancy is the expected (in the statistical sense) number of years of life remaining at a given age.

4. ... elderly population will **place** enormous **strains on** the world's economy. (Para. 5)

To place or put a strain on means to cause problems for someone or to make a situation difficult. e.g., Children put tremendous strains on a marriage.

5. ... two or more consecutive quarters of declining **gross domestic product**. (Para. 6)

GDP is the market value of all officially recognized final goods and services produced within a country in a given period.

6. ... as a setting for **rites of passage**, ... (Para. 7)

A rite of passage is a ritual event that marks a person's progress from one status to another. Rites of passage are often ceremonies surrounding events such as other milestones within puberty, coming of age, marriage and death.

7. ... predicts **the Organization for Economic Cooperation and Development (OECD)**. (Para. 9)

The Organization for Economic Co-operation and Development is an international economic organization of 34 countries founded in 1961 to stimulate economic progress and world trade. It is a forum of countries committed to democracy and the market economy, providing a platform to compare policy experiences, seek answers to common problems, identify good practices, and co-ordinate domestic and international policies of its members.

8. Italy is in the midst of a **bambini bust** that will... (Para. 8)

Bambini bust refers to the fact that Italians' baby boom goes bust. Long known for its large families, the nation now has a very low birthrate.

Glossary

birthrate ['bɜːθreɪt] n.	a measure of how many children are born during a period of time in a particular place
burgeon ['bɜːdʒən] v.	begin to grow or increase rapidly; flourish
carnival ['kɑːnɪvəl] n.	a public celebration where people wear special clothes and dance and play music in the roads
childbearing ['tʃaɪldbeərɪŋ] n.	the process of giving birth to children
comparatively [kəm'pærətɪvlɪ] ad.	when compared to something else or to what is usual
counterpart ['kaʊntəpɑːt] n.	a person or thing holding a position or performing a

	function that corresponds to that of another person or thing in another place
day-care [ˈdeɪkɛə] a.	daytime care for the needs of people who cannot be fully independent, such as children or elderly people
dearth [dɜːθ] n.	a scarcity or lack of something:
decline [dɪˈklaɪn] v.	become smaller, fewer, or less; decrease
diffuse [dɪˈfjuːz] v.	spread or cause to spread over a wide area or among a large number of people
diminish [dɪˈmɪnɪʃ] v.	to become less, or to make something becomeless
dire [ˈdaɪə] a.	(of a situation or event) extremely serious or urgent
economics [ekəˈnɒmɪks] n.	the branch of knowledge concerned with the production, consumption, and transfer of wealth
economist [ɪˈkɒnəmɪst] n.	an expert in economics
exuberance [ɪɡˈzjuːbərəns] n.	the quality of being full of energy, excitement, and cheerfulness
famine [ˈfæmɪn] n.	extreme scarcity of food
fertility [fəˈtɪlɪtɪ] n.	the ability to conceive children or young
fiscal [ˈfɪskəl] a.	of or relating to government revenue, especially taxes: monetary and fiscal policy
hoary [ˈhɔːrɪ] a.	ancient or venerable
intellectual [ɪntəˈlektjʊəl] n.	a person possessing a highly developed intellect
outnumber [aʊtˈnʌmbə] v.	to be larger in number than another group
output [ˈaʊtpʊt] n.	the amount of something produced by a person, machine, or industry
pensionable [ˈpɛnʃənəbl] a.	entitling to or qualifying for a pension
pensioner [ˈpɛnʃənə] n.	a person who receives a pension
plight [plaɪt] n.	a dangerous, difficult, or otherwise unfortunate situation
plummet [ˈplʌmɪt] v.	fall or drop straight down at high speed
productivity [prɒdʌkˈtɪvətɪ] n.	rate at which goods are produced
prophecy [ˈprɒfəsɪ] n.	a statement that something will happen in the future, especially one made by someone with religious or magic powers
recession [rɪˈseʃən] n.	a period of temporary economic decline during which trade and industrial activity are reduced, generally identified by a fall in GDP in two successive quarters.
resource [rɪˈsɔːs] n.	(usually resources) a stock or supply of money, materials, staff, and other assets that can be drawn

	on by a person or organization in order to function effectively
reverence ['revərəns] n.	deep respect for someone or something
reverse [rɪ'vɜːs] v.	to change a situation or change the order of things so that it becomes the opposite
span [spæn] n.	the full extent of something from end to end
startling ['stɑːtlɪŋ] a.	very surprising, astonishing, or remark
symptom ['sɪmptəm] n.	a physical or mental feature that is regarded as indicating a condition of disease, particularly such a feature that is apparent to the patient
taxpayer ['tækspeɪə] n.	a person who pays taxes
unheralded [ʌn'herəldɪd] a.	not previously announced, expected, or recognized
Venezuela [venə'zweɪlə] n.	委内瑞拉
youthful ['juːθfəl] a.	young or seeming young

Comprehension Questions

Answer the questions after reading the text.

1. What's the main problem discussed in this article? What do you think are the negative effects of global aging?
2. The Club of Rome said that the 21st Century would inevitably be marked by declining standards of living as human population exceeded the "carrying capacity" of the Earth, leading to mass famine and energy shortages. Do you agree with their viewpoints or not?
3. Are the fertility rates still rising around the world? Worldwide, how many children on average did a woman give birth to over her lifetime in 1972? Today, how many children on average does a woman have?
4. Neil Howe, an expert on aging, is quoted as saying, "The developed world at least got rich before it got old. In the Third World the trend is reversed." What does he mean?
5. Will the number of working-age people in the world's richest and most productive countries be dropping within 20 years according to Peterson? What effect will it have on the economic output of these countries?
6. Does the Roman Catholic Church have a big influence in family matters in Spain? What functions the church serves today?
7. What will be the fiscal consequences of the diminishing fertility for the developed world? Who will pay the bills for taking care of the increasing number of the elderly? What are the author's suggestions for how a country can get more money to care for the elderly?

8. What is China's typical family pattern today? Do you think China will give up its one family/one child policy in the years to come? Why or why not?

Exercises

I Vocabulary

Section A Paraphrase the sentences chosen from the text.
1. Thanks to the high fertility rates of the past, a large percentage of the world's population is still of childbearing age.
2. For many Third World countries, the challenge of supporting a growing elderly population is compounded by huge out-migrations of younger people.
3. Consequently, according to projections by the United Nations, the world's population will slowly increase at an average rate of 1.3 percent a year during the next 50 years, and it could decline by midcentury if fertility continues to fall.
4. Indeed, because of migration and the ravages of the AIDS epidemic, the number of working-age persons in sub-Saharan Africa available to support each elder is shrinking, causing enormous societal strains.
5. As a result, in a land once known for its celebration of dental-floss bikinis and youthful carnival exuberance, pension debt has become the public's central preoccupation.

Section B There are ten sentences in this section. Beneath each sentence there are four words or phrases marked A, B, C and D. Choose one word or phrase that best completes the sentence.

1. That country has serious social and _____ problems.
   A. economical   B. economy   C. economic   D. economics
2. The exploitation of natural _____ was hampered by the lack of technicians
   A. resources   B. sources   C. materials   D. elements
3. The soldier was _____ of running away when the enemy attacked.
   A. scolded   B. charged   C. accused   D. punished
4. Now, don't tell anyone else what I've just told you. Remember, it's _____.
   A. controversial   B. secretive   C. confidential   D. sacred
5. The oil price rise reactivated the boom in commodity prices and _____ inflation, which reached an annual rate of 15% in the spring of 1974.
   A. boosted   B. harnessed   C. staggered   D. embarked
6. I would like to get another table like this one, but the company that made it is out of _____.
   A. order   B. business   C. practice   D. style
7. Another round of war in the region obviously would _____ international relations.
   A. put strains on   B. push forward   C. promote   D. enhance
8. Soil _____ refers to quality of a soil that enables it to provide essential chemical

elements in quantities and proportions for the growth of specified plants.
   A. prosperity   B. fertility   C. efficiency   D. effectiveness
9. We won the battle even though we were _____ by the enemy.
   A. outnumbered   B. excelled   C. surpassed   D. defeated
10. The _____ on this apartment expires in a year's time.
    A. treaty   B. lease   C. engagement   D. subsidy

Section C Use the proper form of the following words given in the brackets to fill in the blanks.
1. Dental problems may be a _____ of other illness. (symptomatic)
2. With 20 girls and 10 boys in the class, the boys _____ by the girls. (outnumber)
3. Let's _____ the order — I'll give the first talk and you the second. (reversal)
4. We must direct our efforts toward relieving the _____ of children living in poverty. (plight)
5. Stock prices _____ 40 percent during the scandal. (plummet)
6. The problem is how to _____ power without creating anarchy. (diffusion)
7. The government has taken various measures to pull the economy out of _____. (recess)
8. The trout population in the stream is _____ now that the water is clean. (burgeon)

Section D Use the proper form of the following phrases to fill in the blanks.

| put a strain on | reflect on | in the midst of | count on |
| in exchange for | serve as | rack up | bound to |

1. He left his flat _____ a rainstorm.
2. The accusations _____ relations between the two countries.
3. He carried bags of groceries _____ a nickel.
4. Whatever you're doing, you can _____ me.
5. His misleading and irresponsible comments were _____ attract criticism.
6. The square now _____ the town's chief car park.
7. He _____ with sadness _____ the unhappiness of his marriage.
8. Japan is _____ record trade surpluses with the United States.

II Grammar

Choose the best answer to complete the following sentence from the respective four choices.
1. Which of the following italicized phrases indicates a subject-predicate relation?
   A. *Mr. Smith's passport* has been issued.
   B. *John's travel details* have not been finalized.

C. *The visitor's arrival* was reported in the news.
   D. The new bookstore sells *children's stories*.
2. Which of the following italicized parts is used as an object?
   A. *What* do you think has happened to her?
   B. *Who* do you think the visiting professor is?
   C. *How much* do you think he earns every month?
   D. *How quickly* would you say he would come?
3. Which of the following italicized parts is a subject clause?
   A. It is sheer luck *that the miners are still alive after ten days*.
   B. He has to face the fact *that there will be no pay rise this year*.
   C. She said *that she had seen the man earlier that morning*.
   D. We are quite certain *that we will get there in time*.
4. _____ it may be, there is no place like home.
   A. As humble   B. Though humble   C. Humble as   D. If humble
5. He wrapped her up with great care, the night _____ dark and frosty.
   A. is   B. was   C. been   D. being
6. Almost all metals are good conductors, and silver _____ the best of all.
   A. is   B. was   C. been   D. being
7. Not far from the school there was a garden, _____ owner seated in it playing chess with his little grandson every afternoon.
   A. its   B. whose   C. which   D. that
8. He wrote a lot of novels, many of _____ were translated into foreign languages.
   A. it   B. them   C. which   D. that
9. There _____ no further business, I declare the meeting closed.
   A. is   B. was   C. been   D. being
10. Having been attacked by terrorists, _____ .
    A. doctors came to their rescue   B. the tall building collapsed
    C. an emergency measure was taken   D. warning were given to tourists
11. _____ under a microscope, a fresh snowflake has a delicate six pointed shape.
    A. Seen   B. Sees   C. Seeing   D. To see
12. Written in great haste, _____ .
    A. Jim made a lot of mistakes in the report
    B. there are plenty of errors in the report
    C. we found several mistakes in his report
    D. the report is full of errors.
13. Paper produced every year is four times _____ the weight of the world's production of vehicles.
    A. /   B. that of   C. which   D. of
14. I should like to rent a house, modern, comfortable and _____ in a quiet

neighborhood.

A. all in all B. above all C. after all D. over all

15. Einstein won the Nobel Prize in 1921 and enjoyed great fame in Germany until the rise of Nazism _____ he was expelled from Germany because he was a Jew.

A. when B. who C. then D. which

III Cloze

Decide which of the choices given below would best complete the passage if inserted in the corresponding blanks. Mark the best choice for each blank.

Most people would be (1) _____ by the high quality of medicine (2) _____ to most Americans. There is a lot of specialization, a great deal of (3) _____ to the individual, a (4) _____ amount of advanced technical equipment, and (5) _____ effort not to make mistakes because of the financial risk which doctors and hospitals must (6) _____ in the courts if they (7) _____ things badly.

But the Americans are in a mess. The problem is the way in (8) _____ health care is organized and (9) _____. (10) _____ to public belief it is not just a free competition system. To the private system has been joined a large public system, because private care was simply not (11) _____ the less fortunate and the elderly.

But even with this huge public part of the system, (12) _____ this year will eat up 84.5 billion dollars — more than 10 per cent of the U.S. Budget — large numbers of Americans are left (13) _____. These include about half the 11 million unemployed and those who fail to meet the strict limits (14) _____ income fixed by a government trying to make savings where it can.

The basic problem, however, is that there is no central control (15) _____ the health system. There is no (16) _____ to what doctors and hospitals charge for their services, other than what the public is able to pay. The number of doctors has shot up and prices have climbed. When faced with toothache, a sick child, or a heart attack, all the unfortunate person concerned can do is (17) _____ up.

Two thirds of the population (18) _____ covered by medical insurance. Doctors charge as much as they want (19) _____ that the insurance company will pay the bill.

The rising cost of medicine in the U.S.A. is among the most worrying problems facing the country. In 1981 the country's health bill climbed 15.9 percent — about twice as fast as prices (20) _____ general.

1. A. compressed B. impressed C. obsessed D. repressed
2. A. available B. attainable C. achievable D. amenable
3. A. extension B. retention C. attention D. exertion
4. A. countless B. titanic C. broad D. vast

5. A. intensive	B. absorbed	C. intense	D. concentrated
6. A. run into	B. come into	C. face	D. defy
7. A. treat	B. deal	C. maneuver	D. handle
8. A. which	B. that	C. what	D. when
9. A. to finance	B. financed	C. the finance	D. to be financed
10. A. Contrary	B. Opposed	C. Averse	D. Objected
11. A. looking for	B. looking into	C. looking after	D. looking over
12. A. which	B. what	C. that	D. it
13. A. over	B. out	C. off	D. away
14. A. for	B. in	C. with	D. on
15. A. over	B. on	C. under	D. behind
16. A. boundary	B. restriction	C. confinement	D. limit
17. A. paid	B. paying	C. pay	D. to have paid
18. A. is being	B. are	C. have been	D. is
19. A. knowing	B. to know	C. they know	D. known
20. A. in	B. with	C. on	D. for

IV Translation

Section A Translate the following Chinese sentences into English.

1. 如果旱季还持续下去，池塘中的水量将减少。(diminish)
2. 由于生态环境受到破坏，这个自然保护区的鸟类数量急剧下降。(decline)
3. 对在华跨国公司的本土化战略进行案例分析给他们带来了一些新思路。(case study)
4. 国家和地方政府都十分关注该机构对人口增长的预测。(projection)
5. 政府出于政治目的蓄意使战争逐步升级。(escalate)
6. 厨房的水池生锈了，他花了两个小时才把它卸下来，换成了一个新的。(replace)
7. 专家称，这些年中国的离婚人数在逐年增加。(on the rise)
8. 人口老龄化会给一个国家的政治、经济、社会、文化等带来多方面的影响。(aging)

Section B Translate the following English paragraph into Chinese.

Rapid aging in China has been driven by three distinctive developments. First, robust economic growth over the past decades has been associated with increased average life expectancy in China — from 68 in 1981 to 74 today. Second, the generation of baby boomers (those Chinese born in the 1950s and 1960s) has started to join the older population. Third, the draconian population control policy, introduced in the early 1980s, resulted in an extremely low fertility rate, further increasing the proportion of the older population.

V Topics for Discussion

According to "The World Turns Gray", increasingly, the typical family pattern in China today is the "one-two-four household," with one child supporting two parents and four grandparents. Please discuss with your classmates: who should be responsible for taking care of the elderly? Should it be the central government, the local government, the family members, or the charity organizations? And in what way can they take care of the elderly?

VI Written Work

Nowadays, a great number of Chinese have already emigrated abroad or are currently in the process. Please write a paper on the impact of emigration on China's economy, culture and society.

Text B
Oil's New World Order

Daniel Yergin

1 For more than five decades, the world's oil map has centered on the Middle East. No matter what new energy resources were discovered and developed elsewhere, virtually all forecasts indicated that U.S. reliance on Mideast oil supplies was destined to grow. This seemingly irreversible reality has shaped not only U.S. energy policy and economic policy, but also geopolitics and the entire global economy.

2 But today, what appeared irreversible is being reversed. The outline of a new world oil map is emerging, and it is centered not on the Middle East but on the Western Hemisphere. The new energy axis runs from Alberta, Canada, down through North Dakota and South Texas, past a major new discovery off the coast of French Guyana to huge offshore oil deposits found near Brazil.

3 This shift carries great significance for the supply and the politics of world oil. And, for all the debates and speeches about energy independence throughout the years, the transformation is happening not as part of some grand design or major policy effort, but almost accidentally. This shift was not planned — it is a product of a series of unrelated initiatives and technological breakthroughs that, together, are taking on a decidedly hemispheric cast.

4 The search for a "hemispheric energy policy" for the United States has been a subject of discussion ever since the oil crises and supply disruptions of the 1970s. Yet it was never easy to pin down exactly what such a policy would mean. Some years ago, an

economic adviser to a presidential candidate dropped in to see me, explaining the directive that his boss had given him: "You know that Western hemispheric energy policy that I have been giving speeches about? Could you talk to some people around the country and find out what I actually mean by a Western hemispheric energy policy?"

5 The notion of "hemispheric energy" in the 1970s and 1980s rested on two pillars. One was Venezuela, which had been a reliable petroleum exporter since World War II. The other was Mexico, caught up in a great oil boom that had transformed the United States' southern neighbor from an oil importer into a major exporter.

6 But since Hugo Chavez took power in Venezuela, its petroleum output has fallen — about 25 percent since 2000. Moreover, Venezuela does not seem quite the pillar to rely on when its leader denounces "the U. S. empire" as "the biggest menace on our planet" and aligns his country with Iran. And Mexico, which depends on oil for 35 percent of its government revenue, is struggling with declining output. Without reform to its oil sector and international investment, it could become an importer of oil later this decade.

7 The new hemispheric outlook is based on resources that were not seriously in play until recent years — all of them made possible by technological breakthroughs and advances. They are "oil sands" in Canada, "pre-salt" deposits in Brazil and "tight oil" in the United States.

8 In little more than a decade, Canada's oil sands have gone from being a fringe resource to a major one. Oil sands (sometimes known as "tar sands") are composed of very heavy oil mixed with clay and sand. The oil is so heavy and molasses-like that, for the most part, it does not flow until it is separated from the sand and clay and treated. To do that on a large scale and on a commercial basis has required substantial advances in engineering over the past 15 years.

9 Oil sands production in Canada today is 1.5 million barrels per day — more oil than Libya exported before its civil war. Canadian oil sands output could double to 3 million barrels per day by the beginning of the next decade. This increase, along with its other oil output, would make Canada a larger oil producer than Iran — becoming the world's fifth largest, behind Russia, Saudi Arabia, the United States and China.

10 The oil sands have become particularly controversial because of environmental groups' vigorous opposition to the proposed 1,700-mile Keystone XL pipeline, which would carry oil from Alberta to the Texas coast. The pipeline is waiting for the Obama administration to say "yea" or "nay." Though large, it would increase the length of the oil pipeline network in the United States by just 1 percent.

11 The main reason given for the opposition is the carbon dioxide associated with oil sands production, but the impact of this should be considered in the context of the overall release of CO_2. When measured all the way from "well to wheels" — that is, from production to what comes out of an auto tailpipe — oil sands average 5 to 15

percent more carbon dioxide than the average barrel of oil used in the United States. And this country uses other streams of oil that generate CO_2 in the same range.

12　Even while the environmental argument rages, oil sands are proving to be a major contributor to energy security. Although it is easy to assume that most U.S. oil imports come from the Middle East, the largest individual share by far — nearly a quarter of the total — comes from Canada, part of a dense network of economic ties that makes Canada the United States' largest trading partner. More than half of Canada's oil exports to the United States come from oil sands, and that share will rise steeply in the years ahead.

13　At the other end of that hemispheric oil axis is Brazil. When Brazil began to develop ethanol from sugar in the 1970s, it did so based on the conviction that the country had no oil. As it turns out, Brazil has lots of oil. Just the increase in Brazilian oil production since 2000 is more than one and a half times greater than the country's entire ethanol output.

14　In the middle of the last decade, new breakthroughs in technology made possible the identification and development of huge oil resources off the southern coast of Brazil that until then had been hidden below a belt of salt a mile thick. The salt had rendered unreadable the seismic signals necessary to determine whether oil was there. "The breakthrough was pure mathematics," said Jose Sergio Gabrielli de Azevedo, the president of Petrobras, Brazil's national oil company. "We developed the algorithms that enabled us to take out the disturbances and look right through the salt layer." Once discovered, further technical advances were required to cope with the peculiarities of the salt layer, which, sludge-like, keeps shifting.

15　Developing these "pre-salt" resources, as they've become known, is a big technical, political and logistical challenge for Brazil, and will require huge investments. But, if development proceeds at a reasonable pace, Brazil could be producing 5 million barrels of oil per day by around 2020, about twice Venezuela's current output — and more than half the current output of Saudi Arabia. That would make Brazil, not Venezuela, the powerhouse of Latin American oil, and could make it a major exporter to the United States.

16　The third major supply development has emerged right here in the United States: the application of shale-gas technology — horizontal drilling and hydraulic fracturing, a process popularly known as "fracking" — to the extraction of oil from dense rock. The rock is so hard that, without those technologies, the oil would not flow. That is why it is called "tight oil."

17　Case study No. 1 is in North Dakota, where, just eight years ago, a rock formation known as the Bakken, a couple of miles underground, was producing a measly 10,000 barrels of oil per day. Today, it yields almost half a million barrels per day, turning North Dakota into the fourth-largest oil-producing state in the country, as well as the state with the lowest unemployment rate.

18 Similar development is taking place in other parts of the country, including South Texas and West Texas. Altogether, tight oil production is growing very fast. The total output in the United States was just 200,000 barrels per day in 2000. Around 2020, it could reach 3 million barrels per day — a third of the total U.S. oil production. (And that is a conservative estimate; others are much higher.)

19 Together, these three developments will radically alter the global flow of oil. The Western Hemisphere will still require supplies from the rest of the world, but not to the same degree — and certainly nowhere near the growing amounts forecast just a few years ago. The need could fall by as much as half by 2020, which will mean declining imports from the Middle East and West Africa.

20 Oil that would have gone west from those regions will instead flow in increasing volumes to the east — to the booming emerging markets of Asia. And those markets will be in urgent need of additional supplies. China, which today consumes half as much oil as the United States, could by the beginning of the next decade overtake America as the world's largest oil consumer. All of this points to a major geopolitical shift, with Asian economies having an increasing stake in the stability of Mideast oil supplies. It also raises a very significant question over the next several years: How will responsibility be shared among the great powers for the stability of the Persian Gulf?

21 For the United States, these new sources of supply add to energy security in ways that were not anticipated. There is only one world oil market, so the United States — like other countries — will still be vulnerable to disruptions, and the sheer size of the oil resources in the Persian Gulf will continue to make the region strategically important for the world economy. But the new sources closer to home will make our supply system more resilient. For the Western Hemisphere, the shift means that more oil will flow north to south and south to north, rather than east to west. All this demonstrates how innovation is redrawing the map of world oil — and remaking our energy future.

Notes:

1. Daniel Yergin

Daniel Yergin is chairman of IHS Cambridge Energy Research Associates and the author of *The Quest: Energy, Security, and the Remaking of the Modern World*.

2. ... but also **geopolitics** and the entire global economy. (Para. 1)

Geopolitics is the study of the effects of geography (human and physical) on international politics and international relations. 地缘政治学

Quotations

1. At twenty years of age the will reigns; at thirty the wit; at forty the judgment.

   — Benjamin Franklin

2. Wisdom doesn't automatically come with old age. Nothing does — except wrinkles. It's true, some wines improve with age. But only if the grapes were good in the first place.

   — Abigail Van Buren

Further Readings

1. Betty Friedan, *The Fountain of Age*
2. Thomas Wolfe, *Look Homeward, Angel*
3. Maya Angelou, *I Know Why the Caged Bird Sings*

Unit 6

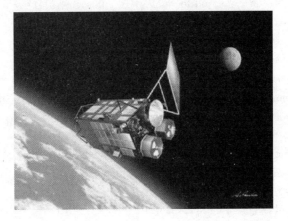

Pre-reading Questions
1. Do you know any invention in your life?
2. Are there some things that never should have been invented? What are they and why?

Text A
Is Technology a Threat to Liberal Society?

Irving Kristol

1 What I want to talk about today is the question of the place of science and technology in a liberal democracy in the decades ahead. I think that is not a matter about which one can be smug. I think we must anticipate some very serious problems involving the place of science and technology in our society. These are problems we are going to have to face up to, although they may not be problems we like to face.

Progress and Perfection

2 There is a very interesting historical controversy concerning why the Greeks and the Chinese did not develop the technology that their theoretical science evidently made possible. One theory, which has been elaborated by Marxist historians primarily but not exclusively, makes the reason for this failure to convert pure science into an "institutional" one — namely, that there was slavery, or that labor was depreciated, not held in high esteem; and therefore, though pure science developed to a considerable degree in the ancient world, applied science and technology did not. There is another theory for why pure science developed while applied technology did not — namely, that the ancient Greeks and the Chinese were very wise people. They knew that although science is beautiful when contemplated in its theoretical aspects, when it is transformed into technology it becomes a form of power. And power is the power for good and for evil. The theory goes on to say that the ancients decided that this was not a power they cared to entrust men with, and therefore deliberately, systematically discouraged the application of pure theory to the development of technology.

3 This notion is preserved for us in our literature, in the myth of *Doctor Faustus*, for instance. The idea that there is something diabolical about science, the idea that the power that science gives you over the world is a power that comes not from God but from the devil — this idea was certainly very strong until around the sixteenth and seventeenth centuries. At that point, we saw the emergence of the modern idea of science and technology, that not only is pure science good but the development of all the inherent potentialities of science and technology is also good.

4 For this change of perception and this change of perspective to take place, certain basic assumptions had to be changed as well. Two new grand intellectual ideas emerged to legitimate the modern scientific enterprise. One was that man could be trusted with this power, that man was not a creature of original sin, that man was not a creature of innate perversity — and that he was, if not perfectible in the literal sense, then perfectible enough to permit one to entrust to humanity the power that science,

when converted into technology, gives us. The second basic idea that the Greeks did not have was that history was progressive, consisting of a series of stages whereby humanity perfected itself. Therefore, since the future would be better than the past and human beings in the future would be better than they had been in the past, there really was no great cause for concern in giving humanity this new and great power.

5   These two ideas, when conformed, give us the essence of what we call in our textbooks the Enlightenment — meaning that it's a good thing to get as much knowledge as possible and to make it as widely available as possible. Enlighten everyone, make knowledge freely available to all who seek it. This set of beliefs is the basis of our liberal democratic society.

Brave New Worlds

6   During the past few decades, however, these assumptions have become less firmly held. It seems clear to me, at any rate, that these assumptions have become problematic, and will probably become more problematic in the years ahead.

7   I think the first great blow to the Enlightenment's view of the world, the modern view of the world, was the explosion of the atom bomb. It suddenly became very clear to us indeed that the power of science is a power for evil as well as for good. And not only for evil but for unlimited evil. Suddenly, humanity had within its grasp the power to destroy itself and the entire world quickly, without much effort. And the question was bound to occur to us: Is it unthinkable that humanity should do such a thing? Once we really looked at the world and thought about the matter, we came to the conclusion that no, it wasn't unthinkable. As a matter of fact, though we may have been slow in coming to that conclusion, our children were not. It's clear that the generation that came to maturity in the 1950s, after the explosions at Hiroshima and Nagasaki, saw the world rather differently from those of us who had the good luck, as it were, to be born and raised during the Depression.

8   The skepticism that then began to emerge about the necessary benefits of science and technology was reinforced by the upsurge of concern for ecology, the environmentalist movement. One must understand the environmentalist and the ecological movements in their full seriousness. These are not just movements for improving the world. These are movements that, in their full thrust, challenge the basic assumptions upon which modern civilization — modern, liberal, democratic civilization — was created. They question whether the furthest development of science and the richest, most ample application of technology necessarily are going to lead to a good society and a good world. And it is quite clear that, among young people today, there is a great deal of doubt and skepticism about this.

9   Oddly enough, throughout the twentieth century, even when the basic assumptions of our worldview and our society were not being explicitly challenged, there

was one area of our culture where one could find it under very critical scrutiny. I trust that many of you read science fiction. One of the fascinating facts of our cultural history of the past 50 years is the way in which science fiction, having begun on an optimistic note very early on — long before the hydrogen bomb — became extremely pessimistic. If you look at the worlds that are described in science-fiction stories of the 1920s, 1930s, and 1940s, you will find they are not usually the kinds of worlds that most of us would want to live in. They are not, to begin with, liberal; practically all of them are despotisms. Some are benevolent despotisms, some malevolent despotism. But none of them is a self-governing community, and always for the same reason: Someone has to keep control of the knowledge that can destroy the entire civilization. And there is usually one group that has control of that knowledge: a good group, or a bad group. But what you do not have is anything like a liberal society, a self-governing political community of the kind that we have grown up in, where knowledge is free, where knowledge can be published freely, where knowledge can be circulated widely, and where it is assumed that all this will somehow lead to a good end result.

10 Now the premonitions of science fiction over the past 40 years have come home to roost in actuality in our lifetime. It really is a fact that in 30 or 40 or 50 years, these premonitions will be coping with a reality. It will happen that almost anyone with a smattering of college chemistry and physics will be able to create some form of atomic weapon. It's quite clear that, at the rate things are going, in 40 or 50 years almost anybody will be able to create explosives of a kind that can destroy an entire city. And if anyone can, it is possible to surmise that someone will, the world being what it is and human beings what they are. It is also quite clear that, given the tremendous developments in chemistry, some high school student puttering around in his basement is going to come up with a nerve gas that could decimate an entire country. Something like that will happen as science gets more and more sophisticated, as young people become masters of technologies that only a genius could dream of 50 years ago.

Educating the Scientist

11 All of these things are on the horizon. I don't say this to scare you; I say this as a matter of fact. It is clear that this is going to happen. The real question is: How are we going to cope with it? Humanity has not perfected itself in any great degree as a result of the progress of science and technology in these past four centuries. It certainly has not perfected itself in its basic feelings of benevolence toward other human beings. And it is clear to me, therefore, that the basic premises of our liberal society are going to be under challenge and scrutiny. We're going to have to think about what we can do with the results of scientific enlightenment, with the results of the spread of scientific and technological knowledge as this knowledge becomes ever more powerful.

12 I hope we will approach this problem with the intention of preserving our

liberal democratic society. But that is going to be extremely difficult. It will involve not the training of better technologists, but rather the moral education of scientists and technologists. And this may well turn out to be the biggest single challenge facing the scientific community — its own moral education, its own assumption of moral responsibility for the use and abuse of scientific knowledge. For this, you need an education not in science but in the humanities, because you don't get moral education by studying science. You may acquire good moral habits by studying science, but you don't get a moral education. You don't learn to think about problems of good and evil by studying science. That's what the humanities are for. And scientists, I believe, in the decades ahead, are going to have to become much more attentive than they have been to the humanities, in their own self-defense.

Glossary

actuality [æktjʊˈælɪtɪ] n.	the state of actually existing objectively
ample [ˈæmpl] a.	more than enough in size or scope or capacity
anticipate [ænˈtɪsɪpeɪt] v.	regard something as probable or likely
assumption [əˈsʌmpʃn] n.	a statement that is assumed to be true and from which a conclusion can be drawn
atomic [əˈtɒmɪk] a.	of or relating to or comprising atoms
benevolent [bəˈnevələnt] a.	intending or showing kindness
circulate [ˈsɜːkjəleɪt] v.	become widely known and passed on
contemplate [ˈkɒntempleɪt] v.	look at thoughtfully; observe deep in thought
decimate [ˈdesɪmeɪt] v.	kill in large numbers
depreciate [dɪˈpriːʃɪeɪt] v.	lower the value of something
despotism [ˈdespətɪzəm] n.	a form of government in which the ruler is an absolute dictator (not restricted by a constitution or laws or opposition etc.)
diabolical [daɪəˈbɒlɪkl] a.	showing the cunning or ingenuity or wickedness typical of a devil
environmentalist [ɪnvaɪrənˈmentəlɪst] n.	someone who works to protect the environment from destruction or pollution
humanity [hjuːˈmænətɪ] n.	all of the living human inhabitants of the earth
hydrogen [ˈhaɪdrədʒən] n.	colorless and smell-less gas which burns very easily
hypotheses [haɪˈpɒθəsiːz] n.	臆断, 假设 (singular form: hypothesis)
institutional [ɪnstɪˈtjuːʃənl] a.	relating to or constituting or involving an institution
legitimate [lɪˈdʒɪtɪmət] v.	make legal
malevolent [məˈlevələnt] a.	wishing or appearing to wish evil to others; arising from intense ill will or hatred

perfectible	[pəˈfektəbl] adj.	capable of becoming or being made perfect
perversity	[pəˈvɜːsɪtɪ] n.	deliberate and stubborn unruliness and resistance to guidance or discipline
premise	[ˈpremɪs] n.	a statement that is assumed to be true and from which a conclusion can be drawn
premonition	[priːməˈnɪʃn] n.	a feeling of evil to come; an early warning about a future event
problematic	[prɒbləˈmætɪk] a.	open to doubt or debate
putter	[ˈpʌtə] v.	do random, unplanned work or activities or spend time idly
scrutiny	[ˈskruːtənɪ] n.	the act of examining something closely (as for mistakes)
skepticism	[ˈskeptɪsɪzəm] n.	doubt about the truth of something
smattering	[ˈsmætərɪŋ] v.	a small number or amount
smug	[smʌg] a.	marked by excessive complacency or self-satisfaction
surmise	[səˈmaɪz] v.	imagine to be the case or true or probable
thrust	[θrʌst] n.	the force used in pushing
upsurge	[ˈʌpsɜːdʒ] v.	a sudden or abrupt strong increase

Notes

1. About the author and the text.

Irving Kristol (1920—2009) is widely considered to be the founder of American neo-conservatism. He was the managing editor of *Commentary* magazine from 1947 to 1952 and the cofounder of the U. K. -based *Encounter*. After eight years as the executive vice president of Basic Books, Mr. Kristol became a professor of social thought at the New York University Graduate School of Business. In July 2002, President George W. Bush awarded him the Presidential Medal of Freedom.

The article is an excerpt from the talk given by Irving Kristol at the Polytechnic Institute of New York in 1975.

2. … namely, that there was slavery, or that labor was depreciated, not **held in high esteem**; … (Para. 2)

  hold… in high esteem: 对……十分看重

3. This notion is preserved for us in our literature, in the myth of **Doctor Faustus**, for instance. (Para. 3)

  The Tragical History of the Life and Death of Doctor Faustus, commonly referred to simply as *Doctor Faustus*, is a play by Christopher Marlowe, based on the Faust story, in which a man sells his soul to the devil for power and knowledge. *Doctor Faustus* was first published in 1604, eleven years after Marlowe's death and at least twelve years after the first performance of the play.

4. One was that man could be trusted with this power, that man was not a creature of **original sin**, that man was not a creature of innate perversity... (Para. 4)

According to a Christian theological doctrine, original sin, also called ancestral sin, is humanity's state of sin resulting from the fall of man, stemming from Adam's rebellion in Eden. It deals with Adam's sin of disobedience in eating from the Tree of Knowledge of Good and Evil and its effects upon the rest of the human race. This condition has been characterized in many ways, ranging from something as insignificant as a slight deficiency, or a tendency toward sin yet without collective guilt, referred to as a "sin nature", to something as drastic as total depravity or automatic guilt of all humans through collective guilt.

5. It seems clear to me, **at any rate**, that these assumptions have become problematic ... (Para. 6)

at any rate: 无论如何，至少

e. g. At any rate, there will be no wedding presents in heaven.

Comprehension Questions

1. What was the historical controversy concerning why the Greeks and the Chinese did not develop the technology?
2. What are the two new grand intellectual ideas that emerged to legitimate the modern scientific enterprise?
3. What is the attitude of young people towards the development of science and application of technology?
4. What kinds of worlds are described in science-fiction stories of the 1920s, 1930s, and 1940s?
5. What is the biggest single challenge facing the scientific community?

Exercises

I Vocabulary
Section A Paraphrase the sentences chosen from the text.

1. ... there really was no great cause for concern in giving humanity this new and great power. (Para. 4)
2. These two ideas, when conformed, give us the essence of what we call in our textbooks the Enlightenment. (Para. 5)
3. And not only for evil but for unlimited evil. (Para. 7)
4. One of the fascinating facts of our cultural history of the past 50 years is the way in which science fiction, having begun on an optimistic note very early on — long before

the hydrogen bomb — became extremely pessimistic. (Para. 9)
5. Now the premonitions of science fiction over the past 40 years have come home to roost in actuality in our lifetime. (Para. 10)
6. All of these things are on the horizon. (Para. 11)
7. That's what the humanities are for. (Para. 12)

Sections B There are ten sentences in this section. Beneath each sentence there are four words or phrases marked A, B, C and D. Choose one word or phrase that best completes the sentence.

1. The city suffered _____ damage as a result of the earthquake.
   A. considered   B. considerate   C. considerable   D. considering
2. When I walked to the street, I found there was a large crowd of demonstrators _____ against the war.
   A. protesting   B. preserving   C. prosecuting   D. protecting
3. Experts say walking is one of the best ways for a person to _____ healthy.
   A. preserve   B. stay   C. maintain   D. reserve
4. Our newly-built teaching building seems _____ enough to last a hundred years.
   A. steady   B. substantial   C. sophisticated   D. spacious
5. The chairman in the room didn't have enough time so far to go into it _____, but she gave as an idea about her plan.
   A. in conclusion   B. in turn   C. at length   D. instead of
6. Chinese people are often puzzled by ways of expression that the native speaker of English does not even have to _____.
   A. think over   B. think about   C. think out   D. think for
7. The policeman in the city come under close _____ after the miserable incident happened.
   A. specification   B. appreciation   C. apprehension   D. scrutiny
8. All citizens are requested to _____ with the regulations in this country.
   A. agree   B. comply   C. consent   D. conform
9. He was thinking of something bewildered him for a long time, and he found it difficult to _____ with calmness.
   A. consider   B. contemplate   C. contact   D. contrive
10. Because of its feature of intimacy with human, mobile phone is usually considered more than just a medium; it is _____.
    A. corporation   B. company   C. enterprise   C. firm

Section C Use the proper form of the following words given in the brackets to fill in the blanks.

1. If only one had an _____ supply of money! (limit)
2. It is reported that the old coins have been withdrawn from _____. (circulate)
3. The project was based on the _____ that the economy was expanding. (assume)

4. The amount of grant the institution received from the local government was _____ reduced. (progress)
5. The new movie has been criticized a lot for apparently _____ violence (legitimate)
6. The animals in the farm grew restless as if in _____ of an earthquake. (anticipate)
7. This election demonstrates _____ in action. (democratic)
8. We _____ a new system so that it could keep me informed of the danger. (perfect)
9. In the modern times, many young girls quit school for marrying a rich old man, which is _____ in my generation. (think)
10. Sally has often been criticized by her colleagues in the company for an excessively _____ view of life. (pessimism)

Section D Use the proper form of the following phrases to fill in the blanks.

| face up to | hold... in high esteem | entrust ... with | at any rate |
| within one's grasp | to begin with | come up with | on the horizon |

1. _____ this most sacred responsibility, how could she betray that trust by saying nothing?
2. Victory is _____, so we must keep playing the game to win.
3. We have several choices what to do. _____, we could do nothing!
4. There is some excitement _____, but I can't tell you about it.
5. She's finding it difficult to _____ the possibility of an early death.
6. Edwards's always chasing after rainbows and never _____ a really practical idea.
7. He doesn't understand me, or _____ not fully.
8. My grandfather is _____ by his friends for his wise judgment on important matters.

II Grammar

Choose the best answer to complete the following sentence from the respective four choices.
1. You _____ Jim anything about it. It was none of his business.
   A. needn't have told   B. needn't tell
   C. mustn't have told   D. mustn't tell
2. As it turned out to be a small house party, we _____ so formally.
   A. need not have dressed up   B. must not have dressed up
   C. did not need to dress up   D. must not dress up
3. We could _____ our friend with a detached house when she came, but she had specifically asked for a small flat.

A. provide   B. have provided
   C. not provide   D. not have provided
4. Jack _____ the 8:20 bus because he didn't leave home till 8:25.
   A. couldn't have caught   B. ought to have caught
   C. shouldn't have caught   D. must not have caught
5. "Stephanie must be in the dormitory now."
   "No, she _____ be there. I saw her in the classroom a minute ago."
   A. mustn't   B. can't   C. couldn't   D. wouldn't
6. Nancy's gone to work but her car's still there. She _____ by bus.
   A. must have gone   B. should have gone
   C. ought have gone   D. Could have gone
7. She _____ fifty or so when I first met her at a conference.
   A. had been   B. must be   C. has been   D. must have been
8. Which of the following sentences expresses "probability?"
   A. You must leave immediately.
   B. You must be feeling rather tired.
   C. You must be here by eight o'clock.
   D. You must complete the reading assignment on time.
9. Since it is already midnight, we _____.
   A. had better leaving   B. ought to have leave
   C. should take our leave   D. might as well leave
10. Loudspeakers were fixed in the hall so that everyone _____ an opportunity to hear the speech.
    A. ought have   B. must have   C. may have   D. should have

III Reading Comprehension

Go over the passage quickly and choose the best answer from the four choices marked A, B, C and D.

Ultralight（超轻型的）airplanes are a recent development in aviation that provide what aviation enthusiasts have long been seeking: an inexpensive airplane that is easy to fly. The ultralight plane was born of the marriage of the hang glider and the go-kart（微型单座竞赛车）engine around 1974, when John Moody mounted a 12-horsepower go-kart engine on his Icarus H hang glider.

Today's ultralights are not just hang gliders with engines; they are "air recreation vehicles". Modern ultralight planes use snowmobile（雪地机动车）engines that let them cruise at about 50 miles per hour, climb at about 500 feet per minute, and carry combined payloads of pilot and fuel up to about 200 pounds, which is about equal to an ultralight plane's weight when empty. More than ten thousand ultralight planes were sold last year at prices ranging from $2,800 to $7,000. But the main reason for the increasing popularity of these aircraft is not that they are inexpensive, but that they are fun to fly.

The modern ultralight plane would look very familiar to the earliest pioneers of aviation. Otto Lilienthal made more than 2,000 flights in Germany in the 1890's in what were actually hang gliders. Octave Chanute designed and built many early hang gliders. Augustus Herring, Chanute's assistant, used these gliders as models for a glider that he built for himself. On this glider, Herring installed a compressed-air motor and flew 267 feet in 1898. The Wright brothers' Flyer was the grandfather of today's ultralight planes. The pilot sat right out in the open, just as in modern ultralights, and used controls that were much the same as those used in today's machines.

Though most ultralight planes are used for pleasure flying, some are also used for crop dusting, aerial photography, and even military observation service. The likelihood is that further uses will be found for ultralight planes, but their greatest use will continue to be as air recreational vehicles.

1. The author seems to feel that ultralight airplanes are _____.
   A. a toy for the rich
   B. nothing but hang gliders
   C. a new development that meets the needs of aviation enthusiasts
   D. the most important development in aviation since the Wright brothers' Flyer

2. According to the passage, today's ultralight airplanes _____.
   A. are inexpensive but difficult to fly
   B. are more like go-karts than like hang gliders
   C. cannot climb as last or as high as hang gliders
   D. are not too different from the earlier aircraft

3. The author compares John Moody's use of a go-kart engine on a hang glider to _____.
   A. a marriage
   B. the flight of Icarus
   C. cruising in a snowmobile
   D. soaring and gliding from a high altitude

4. Which of the following statements is an opinion?
   A. Ultralight planes use snowmobile engines that let them cruise at about 50 miles per hour.
   B. John Moody used a 12-horse-power engine to power his Icarus II hang glider.
   C. The use of ultralight planes will increase in such areas as crop dusting and aerial photography.
   D. Otto Lilienthal made more than 2,000 flights in Germany in the 1890's in what were actually hang gliders.

5. The author finds great similarity between _____.
   A. the weight of the hang glider and that of the ultralight airplane

B. ultralight airplanes and military aircraft
C. the inventiveness of John Moody and that of Octave Chanute
D. the controls used in the Wright brothers' Flyer and those used in today's ultralight airplanes

6. The best title for this passage is _____.
   A. The Flying Snowmobile
   B. The History of Recent Aviation
   C. How the Ultralight Plane Flies
   D. The Ultralight Plane, a Recent Development

IV Translation

Section A Translate the following Chinese sentences into English.

1. 你不应该该把那辆不安全的车卖给我，你的不端行为迟早会得到报应。(come home to roost)
2. 那个在车里的婴儿不知为什么就大哭起来。(somehow)
3. 30年后他们最终成为永久的城市居民。(transform into)
4. 从许多方面讲，小孩子可以说是生活在一个跟成人不同的世界里。(as it were)
5. 我们的祖先必须应付寒冷、饥饿以及野兽的袭击。(cope with)
6. 医生说你还身体太弱不能工作，但是你可以起床在房前屋后走动走动几天。(putter around)
7. 做坏事的人到头来总会遭到惩罚的。(be bound to)
8. 我没有想到我最好的朋友会拒绝我的邀请。(occur to)
9. 我父亲病情不但没好转，反而恶化了。(but rather)
10. 安全驾驶之规则适用于每个人。(apply to)

Section B Translate the following English paragraphs into Chinese.

What is the nature of the scientific attitude, the attitude of the man or woman who studies and applies physics, biology, chemistry, geology, engineering, medicine or any other science?

We all know that science plays an important role in our societies. However, many people believe that our progress depends on two different aspects of science. The first aspect is the application of the machines, products and systems of knowledge that scientists and technologists develop. The second is the application of the special methods of thought and action that scientists use in their work.

V Topics for Discussion

Nowadays, science and technology are developing very fast, which have great influence on our daily life and society. Work with your classmates to discuss what the world will be like in 2050, raising as many imaginative questions as you can.

VI Written Work

With the development of science and technology, man's life has been more comfortable and colorful. However, science and technology may also bring certain harm and disaster. Write a short essay of about 200 words on the topic — Science and Technology: Good or Evil?

Text B
Modern Science and Technology and the Challenges of Third World Countries

John Ndubueze

1 We live in a highly sophisticated world where everything is almost achievable. There would probably have been no changes between the world of today and that of three centuries ago if necessity and serendipitous discoveries had not driven men to achieve great things. Science and technology have had huge positive effects on every society. The world today has gone digital, even human thought. Our world has been reduced to a global village and is better for it.

2 The benefits of science and technology far outweigh every perceived shortcoming. Some of the biggest effects of technology are in the area of communication; through the internet and mobile phones. There is advancement of communication and expansions of economic commerce. Today we hear of information and communication technology (ICT). Any institution worth its name must have it in place to be really outstanding. Information technology has become boosted in today's generation; from the field of communication, business, education, and down to the entertainment industry. Through information technology, work performances are boosted with less effort and greater productivity by using various operations. Without computers or the internet, it will be difficult for people all over the world to get their questions answered. One may use the internet to locate a wealth of information with which to answer an essay question that may have been assigned at school, communicate with people, conduct transactions, access news, buy and advertise goods. The list is endless.

3 The advancement of science and technology allow mass communication today so that we not only have the television, radio and newspaper, but even mobile phones which renders a multipurpose service; from long distance calls, listening to radio and music, playing games, taking pictures, recording voice and video, and browsing the

internet. The benefits we obtain as a result of services from ICT have become widespread in our generation today. It improves the productive level of individuals and workers because people's knowledge of life beyond the area they lived in is now unlimited. This idea of mass communication also profoundly affects politics as leaders now have many ways they talk directly to the people. Apart from going on air to use radio or television, politicians resort to the social media for some of their political comments and campaign. Information about protests and revolutions are being circulated online, especially through social media. This has caused political upheavals and resulted in change of government in most countries today.

4 Furthermore, current global issues are much more accessible to the public. Communication has been brought also to the next level because one can find new ways to be able to communicate with loved ones at home.

5 Science and technology expand society's knowledge. Science helps humans gain increased understanding of how the world works, while technology helps scientists make these discoveries. Learning has maximized because of different media that are being developed which are all interactive and which bring learning experiences to the next level. Businesses have grown and expanded because of breakthroughs in advertising.

6 Modern technology has changed the way many companies produce their goods and handle their business. The idea and use of video and web conferencing, for instance, has helped companies remove geographical barriers and given them the opportunity to reach out to employees and clients throughout the world. In today's economy, it has helped companies reduce the cost and inconveniences of travelling, allowing them to meet as often as they could like without having to worry about finding the budget to settle it. Modern technology helps companies reduce their carbon footprint and become green due to the fact that almost anything can be done from a computer.

7 There have been advances in medical care through the development of science and technology. Advances in medical technology have contributed immensely in extending the life span of people. People with disabilities or health problems are now more and more able to live closer to normal lives. This is because science contributes to developing medications to enhance health as well as technology such as mobile chairs and even electronics that monitor current body levels. Most devices used by the physically challenged people are customized and user friendly.

8 Science and technology increase road safety. Nowadays, law enforcement officers use Laser technology to detect when automobiles are exceeding speed limits. Technology has led to the development of modern machines such as cars and motorcycles which allow us to be mobile and travel freely and airplanes which travel at a supersonic speed.

9 Another machine, the air-conditioner, provides cool comfort, especially during

hot weather. In offices where dress codes exist, people can afford to wear suits without being worried about the weather. It guarantees convenience even when the climate says otherwise.

10 Moreover, present day factories have modern facilities like machines and soft ware that facilitate production. These machines work with greater speed and perfection incomparable with human skills. These machines have enabled markets to have surplus products all over the world. For the soft ware, they make it possible for machines to be programmed, for production to be regulated, to monitor the progress being recorded and so on.

11 Modern technology indeed has been great. For third world countries, however, it has been challenging, especially the area of production. Only consuming and not being able to manufacture does not favor any country when it comes to balance of trade. The most sensitive parts of technology are the theoretical or conceptual parts and technical parts. These are the backbone of technological development anywhere in the world. Without the ideas, there will not be technology. Third world countries need to go back to the basics, that is, to the primitive. There must be meeting ground for tradition and modern technological invention. Third world countries engage in import substitution strategy where they import half finished goods and complete the tail end of the production process domestically. Third world countries started wrongly. They started with climbing the ladder from the top which is very wrong and difficult. They thought that being able to purchase and operate modern technological products qualifies for advancement in science and technological development. This makes third world countries to be a dependent system because working in the factories are routine work and this inevitably links to the issue of the idea of technology transfer. They should seek for technological transfer, but the problem is that no nation is ready to transfer her hard earned technological knowledge to any other nation for some certain reasons which drive nations into competition; world politics and economic prowess. That is the struggle to lead or dominate other nations technologically, economically and politically. Be the first to invent new gadgets and latest electronics including those used in modern warfare, use other nations as market for finished goods, and to have a strong voice and be able to influence other countries. They should consider embarking on technological espionage so as to acquire the rudiments for technological development if they must liberate themselves from the shackles of technological domination.

12 In conclusion, it's not until third world countries begin to put embargo on the importation of certain electronics and mechanical goods that the necessity to be creative would replace the habit of consuming foreign products. Countries like Thailand, Burma, Brazil, and South Africa and so on, should be emulated. These countries experienced colonialism yet they did not allow it to overwhelm their creative prowess. Industry and determination saw them emerge as economic giants in the world today.

Third world countries should emulate them by carrying out proper feasibility studies to ascertain which technology will suit their country; giving more financial boost to this area, training people to become experts; motivating and encouraging individuals who are naturally endowed and technologically inclined to display their bests of talents. These measures if strictly adhered to will go a long way to help the advancement of these countries in the area of science and technology. If these countries must achieve greatness before the next decade, they have to make conscious and unrelenting efforts. The time starts now! The more they delay, the more backward they become.

Notes

1. Our world has been reduced to a **global village** and is better for it. (Para. 1)

Global village is a term closely associated with Marshall McLuhan, popularized in his books *The Gutenberg Galaxy: The Making of Typographic Man* (1962) and *Understanding Media* (1964). McLuhan described how the globe has been contracted into a village by electric technology and the instantaneous movement of information from every quarter to every point at the same time.

2. Today we hear of **information and communication technology** (ICT). (Para. 2)

Information and Communications Technology or ICT, is often used as an extended synonym for information technology (IT), but is a more specific term that stresses the role of unified communications and the integration of telecommunications (telephone lines and wireless signals), computers as well as necessary enterprise software, middleware, storage, and audio-visual systems, which enable users to access, store, transmit, and manipulate information.

3. The advancement of science and technology allow **mass communication** today so that we not only have the television, radio and newspaper, but even mobile phones which renders a multipurpose service; ... (Para. 3)

Mass communication technically refers to the process of transferring or transmitting a message to a large group of people — typically, this requires the use of some form of media such as newspapers, television, or the Internet. Another definition of the term, and perhaps the most common one, refers to an academic study of how messages are relayed to large groups of people instantaneously. This area of study, most often referred to as mass comm, is offered at many colleges and universities worldwide as an area of study, and some colleges teach nothing but mass comm. Due to its pertinence to all people around the world, mass comm is becoming more popular and may offer graduates careers in various countries worldwide.

4. Modern technology helps companies reduce their **carbon footprint** and become green due to the fact that almost anything can be done from a computer. (Para. 6)

A carbon footprint is the amount of greenhouse gas emissions produced, either directly or indirectly, through daily activities. These greenhouse gases are usually measured in metric tons of carbon dioxide. A carbon footprint can be measured for an individual person, a household, a company or other group of people, or a state or nation. It is a small yet vital part of our larger, all-encompassing ecological footprint.

5. Technology has led to the development of modern machines such as cars and motorcycles which allow us to be mobile and travel freely and airplanes which travel at a **supersonic speed**. (Para. 8)

Supersonic is any speed above the speed of sound. The speed of sound depends on many different variables. One is the atmospheric pressure at a given altitude. The higher you are the less the pressure and the faster the speed of sound. Anything traveling faster than 761.2 miles per hour at sea level would be traveling at supersonic speeds.

6. Only consuming and not been able to manufacture does not favor any country when it comes to **balance of trade**. (Para. 11)

Balance of trade: the difference between the value of goods and services exported out of a country and the value of goods and services imported into the country. The balance of trade is the official term for net exports that makes up the balance of payments. The balance of trade can be a "favorable" surplus (exports exceed imports) or an "unfavorable" deficit (imports exceed exports).

7. This makes third world countries to be a dependent system because working in the factories are routine work and this inevitably links to the issue of the idea of **technology transfer**. (Para. 11)

Technology transfer, also called transfer of technology (TOT) and technology commercialization, is the process of transferring skills, knowledge, technologies, methods of manufacturing, samples of manufacturing and facilities among governments or universities and other institutions to ensure that scientific and technological developments are accessible to a wider range of users who can then further develop and exploit the technology into new products, processes, applications, materials or services.

Questions for Discussion

1. How did technological advances affect our daily life?
2. Should young people adapt with the changes of technology now?

Memorable Quotes

1. The whole of science is nothing more than a refinement of everyday thinking.

— Albert Einstein

2. Our scientific power has outrun our spiritual power. We have guided missiles and misguided men.

— Martin Luther King Jr.

3. Software is a great combination between artistry and engineering. When you finally get done and get to appreciate what you have done it is like a part of yourself that you've put together. I think a lot of the people here feel that way.

— Bill Gates

4. Design is not just what it looks like and feels like. Design is how it works.

— Steve Jobs

Further Readings

1. Stephen Hawking, *A Brief History of Time*
2. Bill Bryson, *Life Ascending: The Ten Great Inventions of Evolution*
3. Carl Sagan, *The Demon-haunted World*

Unit 7

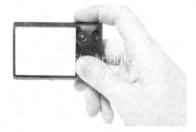

Pre-reading Questions
1. Do you prefer the traditional photos or digital photos? Why or why not?
2. Will digital photos replace traditional photos?

Text A
Digital Photography Does Not Exist?

Lev Manovich

1 It is easiest to see how digital (r) evolution solidifies rather than destroys certain aspects of modern visual culture — the culture synonymous with the photographic image — by considering not photography itself but a related film-based medium — cinema. New digital technologies promise to radically reconfigure the basic material components (lens, camera, lighting, film) and the basic techniques (the separation of production and post-production, special effects, the use of human actors and non-human props) of the cinematic apparatus as it has existed for decades. The film camera is increasingly supplemented by the virtual camera of computer graphics which is used to simulate sets and even actors (as in *Terminator 2* and *Jurassic Park*). Traditional film editing and optical printing are being replaced by digital editing and image processing which blur the lines between production and post-production, between shooting and editing.

2 At the same time, while the basic technology of film-making is about to disappear, being replaced by new digital technologies, cinematic codes find new roles in the digital visual culture. New forms of entertainment based on digital media and even the basic interface between a human and a computer are being increasingly modeled on the metaphors of movie making and movie viewing. With Quicktime technology built into every Macintosh sold today, the user makes and edits digital "movies" using software packages whose very names (such as Director and Premiere) make a direct reference to cinema. Computer games are also increasingly constructed on the metaphor of a movie, featuring realistic sets, arid characters, complex camera angles, dissolves, and other codes of traditional filmmaking. Many new CD-ROM games go even further, incorporating actual movie-like scenes with live actors directed by well known Hollywood directors. Finally, SIGGRAPH, the largest international conference on computer graphics technology, offers a course entitled "Film Craft in User Interface Design" based on the premise that "The rich store of knowledge created in 90 years of filmmaking and animation can contribute to the design of user interfaces of multimedia, graphics applications, and even character displays."

3 Thus, film may soon disappear — but not cinema. On the contrary, with the disappearance of film due to digital technology, cinema acquires a truly fetishistic status. Classical cinema has turned into the priceless data bank, the stock which is guaranteed never to lose its value as classic films become the content of each new round

of electronic and digital distribution media — first video cassette, then laser disk, and, now, CD-ROM (major movie companies are planning to release dozens of classic Hollywood films on CD-ROM by the end of 1994). Even more fetishized is "film look" itself — the soft, grainy, and somewhat blurry appearance of photographic image which is so different from the harsh and flat image of a video camera or the too clean, too perfect image of computer graphics. The traditional photographic image once represented the inhuman, devilish objectivity of technological vision. Today, however, it looks so human, so familiar, so domesticated — in contrast to the alienating, still unfamiliar appearance of a computer display with its 1,280 by 1,024 resolution, 32 bits per pixel, 16 million colors, and so on. Regardless of what it signifies, any photographic image also connotes memory and nostalgia, nostalgia for modernity and the twentieth century, the era of the pre-digital, pre-post-modern. Regardless of what it represents, any photographic image today first of all represents photography.

 4 So while digital imaging promises to completely replace the techniques of film-making, it at the same time finds new roles and brings new value to the cinematic apparatus, the classic films, and the photographic look. This is the first paradox of digital imaging.

 5 But surely, what digital imaging preserves and propagates are only the cultural codes of film or photography. Underneath, isn't there a fundamental physical difference between film-based image and a digitally encoded image?

 6 The most systematic answer to this question can be found in William Mitchell's recent book *The Reconfigure Eye: Visual Truth in the Post-Photographic Era*. Mitchell's entire analysis of the digital imaging revolution revolves around his claim that the difference between a digital image and a photograph is grounded in fundamental physical characteristics that have logical and cultural consequences. In other words, the physical difference between photographic and digital technology leads to the difference in the logical status of film-based and digital images and also to the difference in their cultural perception.

 7 How fundamental is this difference? If we limit ourselves by focusing solely, as Mitchell does, on the abstract principles of digital imaging, then the difference between a digital and a photographic image appears enormous. But if we consider concrete digital technologies and their uses, the difference disappears. Digital photography simply does not exist.

 8 The biggest alleged difference concerns the relationship between the original and the copy in analog and in digital cultures. Mitchell writes: "The continuous spatial and tonal variation of analog pictures is not exactly replicable, so such images cannot be transmitted or copied without degradation ... But discrete states can be replicated precisely, so a digital image that is a thousand generations away from the original is indistinguishable in quality from any one of its progenitors. Therefore, in digital visual

culture, an image file can be copied endlessly, and the copy is distinguishable from the original by its date since there is no loss of quality." This is all true — in principle. However, in reality, there is actually much more degradation and loss of information between copies of digital images than between copies of traditional photographs. A single digital image consists of millions of pixels. All of this data requires considerable storage space in a computer; it also takes a long time (in contrast to a text file) to transmit over a network. Because of this, the current software and hardware used to acquire, store, manipulate, and transmit digital images uniformly rely on lossy compression — the technique of making image files smaller by deleting some information. The technique involves a compromise between image quality and file size — the smaller the size of a compressed file, the more visible are the visual artifacts introduced in deleting information. Depending on the level of compression, these artifacts range from barely noticeable to quite pronounced. At any rate, each time a compressed file is saved, more information is lost, leading to more degradation.

9   One may argue that this situation is temporary, and once cheaper computer storage and faster networks become commonplace, lossy compression will disappear. However, at the moment, the trend is quite the reverse with lossy compression becoming more and more the norm for representing visual information. If a single digital image already contains a lot of data, then this amount increases dramatically if we want to produce and distribute moving images in a digital form (one second of video, for instance, consists of 30 still images). Digital television with its hundreds of channels and video on-demand services, the distribution of full-length films on CD-ROM or over Internet, fully digital post-production of feature films — all of these developments will be made possible by newer compression techniques. So rather than being an aberration, a flaw in the otherwise pure and perfect world of the digital, where even a single bit of information is never lost, lossy compression is increasingly becoming the very foundation of digital visual culture. This is another paradox of digital imaging — while in theory digital technology entails the flawless replication of data, its actual use in contemporary society is characterized by the loss of data, degradation, and noise; the noise which is even stronger than that of traditional photography.

10   Even the pixel-based representation, which appears to be the very essence of digital imaging, can no longer be taken for granted. Recent computer graphics software have bypassed the limitations of the traditional pixel grid which limits the amount of information in an image because it has a fixed resolution. Live Picture, an image editing program for the Macintosh, converts a pixel-based image into a set of equations. This allows the user to work with an image of virtually unlimited size. Another paint program Matador makes possible painting on a tiny image which may consist of just a few pixel as though it were a high-resolution image (it achieves this by breaking each pixel into a number of smaller sub-pixels). In both programs, the pixel is no longer a "final

frontier"; as far as the user is concerned, it simply does not exist.

11　Mitchell's third distinction concerns the inherent mutability of a digital image. While he admits that there has always been a tradition of impure, re-worked photography, Mitchell identifies straight, unmanipulated photography as the essential, "normal" photographic practice: "There is no doubt that extensive reworking of photographic images to produce seamless transformations and combinations is technically difficult, time-consuming, and outside the mainstream of photographic practice. When we look at photographs we presume, unless we have some clear indications to the contrary, that they have not been reworked." This equation of "normal" photography with straight photography allows Mitchell to claim that a digital image is radically different because it is inherently mutable: "the essential characteristic of digital information is that it can be manipulated easily and very rapidly by computer." It is simply a matter of substituting new digits for old... Computational tools for transforming, combining, altering, and analyzing images are as essential to the digital artist as brushes and pigments to a painter.

12　Yet Mitchell's idea that digital imaging destroys the innocence of straight photography by making all photographs inherently mutable is questionable. Straight photography has always represented just one tradition of photography; it always coexisted with equally popular traditions where a photographic image was openly manipulated and was read as such. Equally, there never existed a single dominant way of reading photography; depending on the context the viewer could and continue to read photography as representations of concrete event, or as illustrations which do not claim to correspond to events which have occurred. Digital technology does not subvert "normal" photography because "normal" photography never existed.

Notes

1. About the author.

Lev Manovich is an author of books on new media theory, professor in Computer Science program at City University of New York, Graduate Center, U. S. and visiting professor of European Graduate School in Saas-Fee, Switzerland. Manovich's research and teaching focuses on digital humanities, new media art and theory, and software studies. His best known book is *The Language of New Media*, which has been widely reviewed and translated into eight languages. According to two reviewers, this book offers "the first rigorous and far-reaching theorization of the subject", and "it places new media within the most suggestive and broad ranging media history since MarshallMcLuhan". Manovich's new book *Software Takes Command* was published in 2013 by Continuum. This text is taken and edited from his writing "The Paradoxes of Digital Photography" from *The Photography Reader*.

2. ... certain aspects of modern **visual culture**... (Para. 1)

Visual culture as an academic subject is a field of study that generally includes some combination of cultural studies, art history, critical theory, philosophy, and anthropology, by focusing on aspects of culture that rely on visual images.

3. ... of the **cinematic apparatus** as it has existed for decades. (Para. 1)

Baudry (1970) was among the first film theorists to suggest that the cinematic apparatus or technology has an ideological effect upon the spectator. In the simplest instance the cinematic apparatus purports to set before the eye and ear realistic images and sounds.

4. The film camera is increasingly supplemented by the virtual camera of **computer graphics** which... (Para. 1)

Computer graphics are graphics created using computers and, more generally, the representation and manipulation of image data by a computer with help from specialized software and hardware.

5. *Terminator 2*, *Judgment Day* (《终结者2》) (Para. 1)

It is a 1991 American science fictionaction film, the second installment of the Terminator franchise and the sequel to The Terminator (1984). Directed by James Cameron and written by Cameron and William Wisher, Jr., it stars Arnold Schwarzenegger, Linda Hamilton, Robert Patrick, and Edward Furlong.

6. *Jurassic Park* (《侏罗纪公园》) (Para. 1)

It is a 1993 American science fiction adventure film directed by Steven Spielberg and the first of the Jurassic Parkfranchise. It is based on the 1990 novel of the same name by Michael Crichton, with a screenplay by Crichton and David Koepp. It stars Sam Neill, Laura Dern, Jeff Goldblum, Richard Attenborough, Ariana Richards, Joseph Mazzello, Martin Ferrero, Samuel L. Jackson and Bob Peck.

7. With **Quicktime** technology, ... (Para. 2)

It is an extensible multimedia framework developed by Apple Inc., capable of handling various formats of digital video, picture, sound, panoramic images, and interactivity. The classic version of QuickTime is available for Windows XP and later, as well as Mac OS X Leopard and later operating systems. A more recent version, QuickTime X, is currently available on Mac OS X Snow Leopard, Lion, and Mountain Lion.

8. ... built into every **Macintosh** sold today, ... (Para. 2)

The Macintosh marketed as Mac, is a line of personal computers (PCs) designed, developed, and marketed by Apple Inc. It is targeted mainly at the home, education, and creative professional markets, and includes the descendants of the original iMac, the entry-level Mac mini desktop model, the Mac Pro tower graphics workstation, and the MacBook Air and MacBook Pro laptops. Its Xserve server was discontinued on January 31, 2011.

9. ..., nostalgia for **modernity** and... (Para. 3)

It typically refers to a post-traditional, post-medieval historical period, one marked by the move from feudalism (or agrarianism) toward capitalism, industrialization, secularization, rationalization, the nation-state and its constituent institutions and forms of surveillance

10. **William Mitchell** (Para. 6)

William J. Mitchell, Professor of Architecture and Media Arts and Sciences at MIT, holds the Alexander W. Dreyfoos, Jr. (1954) Professorship and directs the Media Lab's Smart Cities research group. He was formerly Dean of the School of Architecture and Planning and Head of the Program in Media Arts and Sciences, both at MIT.

His book, *The Reconfigure Eye: Visual Truth in the Post-Photographic Era*, provides the first systematic, critical analysis of the digital imaging revolution. It describes the technology of the digital image in detail and looks closely at how it is changing the way we explore ideas, at its aesthetic potential, and at the ethical questions it raises.

Glossary

aberration	[æbəˈreɪʃn] n.	the act of departing from the right, normal, or usual course
alienate	[ˈeɪliəneɪt] v.	(used with object), alienated, alienating; to make indifferent or hostile
analog	[ˈænəlɔːg] n.	thing that is similar to another thing
artifact	[ˈɑːtəfækt] n.	thing made by man, esp. a tool or weapon of archaeological interest
blur	[blɜː] v.	(cause sth. to) become unclear or indistinct
commonplace	[ˈkɒmənpleɪs] n.	event, topic etc. that is ordinary or usual computer graphics 电脑图形图像
convert	[kənˈvɜːt] v.	change from one form to another; change one's belief
devilish	[ˈdevəlɪʃ] a.	wicked; cruel
dissolve	[dɪˈzɒlv] v.	disappear; fade away
encode	[ɪnˈkəʊd] v.	put (a message, etc.) into code
entail	[ɪnˈteɪl] v.	make (sth.) necessary; involve
equation	[ɪˈkweɪʒn] n.	等式，方程式
fetishism	[feˈtʃɪsəm] n. adj.	belief in or use of fetishes. Fetishistic, the form of fetishism
inherent	[ɪnˈhɪərənt] a.	existing as a natural or permanent feature of sth.
interface	[ˈɪntəfeɪs] n.	surface common to two areas

lossy ['lɒsɪ] a. (of a material or transmission line) causing appreciable loss or dissipation of energy
manipulate [mə'nɪpjuleɪt] v. control or handle (sth) with skill
metaphor ['metəfə] n. use of a word or phrase to indicate sth different from the literal meaning
mutable ['mju:təbl] a. can be changed or subjective to change
pixel ['pɪksl] n. the smallest element of an image that can be individually processed in a video display system 像素
progenitor [prəʊ'dʒenɪtə] n. ancestor (of a person, an animal or a plant)
pronounced [prə'naʊnst] a. very noticeable
prop [prɒp] n. moveable object, e.g., a piece of furniture or a costume, used in a performance
reconfigure [ri:kən'fɪgə] v. to change the shape or formation of; remodel; restructure
replicable ['replɪkəbl] a. capable of replication
resolution [rezə'lu:ʃn] n. process of separating something or being separated into constituent parts. 分解，分辨率
simulate ['sɪmjuleɪt] v. reproduce by means of a model, etc., e.g. for study or training purposes
solidify [sə'lɪdɪfaɪ] v. (cause sth. to) become solid, hard or firm
spatial ['speɪʃl] a. of, concerning or existing in space
subvert [səb'vɜ:t] v. destroy the authority of sth.
synonymous [sɪ'nɒnɪməs] a. have the same meaning
tonal ['təʊnl] a. of (a) tone or tones

Comprehension Questions

Answer the following questions after reading the text.
1. How do cinematic codes influence the digital visual culture?
2. How is the conception of photographic image changing?
3. What is the first paradox of digital imaging? Can you explain it?
4. How does William Mitchell explain the differences between a digital image and a photograph?
5. Why lossy compression is becoming popular?
6. What is the second paradox of digital imaging?

Exercises

I Vocabulary

Section A Paraphrase the following sentences chosen from the text.

1. However, in reality, there is actually much more degradation and loss of information between copies of digital images than between copies of traditional photographs.
2. This is another paradox of digital imaging — while in theory digital technology entails the flawless replication of data, its culture use in contemporary society is characterized by the loss of data, degradation, and noise; the noise which is even stronger than that of traditional photography.
3. There is no doubt that extensive reworking of photographic images to produce seamless transformations and combinations is technically difficult, time-consuming, and outside the mainstream of photographic practice.
4. Computational tools for transforming, combining, altering, and analyzing images are as essential to the digital artist as brushes and pigments to a painter.
5. Straight photography has always represented just one tradition of photography; it always coexisted with equally popular traditions where a photographic image was openly manipulated and was read as such.

Section B There are ten sentences in this section. Beneath each sentence there are four words or phrases marked A, B, C and D. Choose one word or phrase that best completes the sentence.

1. This project would _____ a huge increase in defense spending.
   A. result   B. assure   C. entail   D. accomplish
2. If you keep on taking on more work than you can do, your health will _____.
   A. decline   B. degrade   C. degenerate D. deteriorate
3. There are two main requirements before the fifth generation computer can become a reality and it is these that scientists are _____.
   A. anticipating B. tackling   C. manipulating D. speculating
4. If you don't _____ the children properly, Mr. Chiver, they'll just run riot.
   A. mobilize   B. warrant   C. manipulate D. supervise
5. The human race has already paid a heavy price for its slow _____ to environmental threats.
   A. response   B. responsibility C. resolution D. resistance
6. I can't drive fast, for the heavy mist _____ my view.
   A. blur   B. daze   C. dazzle   D. cloud
7. The playwright's recent work _____ many of his followers.
   A. disassociate B. detach   C. alienate   D. disunite
8. Her disapproval of racism is _____. That is why she has chosen to work with this NGO to protect the victim.

A. bold   B. pronounced   C. assured   D. decided
9. The message is _____ in a unique form so that others cannot read it.
   A. organized   B. decoded   C. structured   D. encoded
10. The computer can _____ conditions in the outer space.
    A. monitor   B. imitate   C. simulate   D. change

Section C Use the proper form of the following words given in the brackets to fill in the blanks.

1. What _____ distinguish the English from the Scottish? (character)
2. The protagonist is _____ as brave and passionate in the novel. (character)
3. The town is just a _____ place. I cannot understand why so many people come to visit here. (character)
4. The twins are so alike that no one can _____ one from the other. (distinguish)
5. This kind of flower is _____ from others by its scent. (distinguish)
6. Jane Austen is a _____ novelist whose works have been loved by many people. (distinguish)
7. Poverty is not necessarily _____ with miser. Some of them often give the most. (synonym)
8. You have been cheated. It is just a _____ jewel, which doesn't cost that much. (simulate)
9. The pilot to be has been trained in the _____ of fight condition. (simulate)
10. We cannot _____ this machine, for it is too old. (configure)

Section D Use the proper form of the following phrases to fill in the blanks.

in the status of	at any rate	revolve around	as such
be characterized by	for decades	be replaced by	model on
on the premises that	coexist with		

1. For some teachers, the preparation of a lesson nowadays _____ the use of internet.
2. It is quite possible that traditional photos will _____ digital photos.
3. The suspect is _____ being questioned.
4. _____, the photographer will come to shoot tomorrow.
5. The research has been carried out _____.
6. The painting of this famous artist is _____ the unconventional use of colors.
7. The plan is based _____ interest rates would continue to fall.
8. The design of the music hall is _____ on Roman forms.
9. Legend has it that dogs can never _____ cats.
10. I can't call this film a big success _____ but it's very popular.

II Grammar

Choose the best answer to complete the following sentence from the respective four choices.

1. Which of the following italicized phrases indicates CAUSE?
   A. Why don't you do it *for the sake of your friends*?
   B. I wish I could write *as well as you*.
   C. *For all his efforts*, he didn't get an A.
   D. Her eyes were red *from excessive reading*.
2. Do you know Tim's brother? He is _____ than Tim.
   A. much more sportsman
   B. more of a sportsman
   C. more of sportsman
   D. more a sportsman
3. The experiment requires more money than _____ .
   A. have been put in
   B. being put in
   C. has been put in
   D. to be put in
4. There ought to be less anxiety over the perceived risk of mountain climbing than _____ in the public mind today.
   A. exists
   B. exist
   C. existing
   D. to exist
5. It was _____ we had hoped.
   A. more a success than
   B. a success more than
   C. as much of a success as
   D. a success as much as
6. That trumpet player was certainly loud. But I wasn't bothered by his loudness _____ by his lack of talent.
   A. so much as
   B. rather than
   C. as
   D. than
7. In the sentence "It's no use *waiting for her*", the italicized phrase is _____ .
   A. the object
   B. an adverbial
   C. a complement
   D. the subject
8. Fat cannot change into muscle _____ muscle changes into fat.
   A. any more than
   B. no more than
   C. no less than
   D. much more than
9. John is _____ hardworking than his sister, but he failed in the exam.
   A. no less
   B. no more
   C. not less
   D. no so
10. Intellect is to the mind _____ sight is to the body.
    A. what
    B. as
    C. that
    D. like
11. If negotiations for the trade agreements take _____ , food industries in both countries will be seriously affected.
    A. much too long
    B. too much longer
    C. too much long
    D. much long
12. We both could hardly listen to each other, _____ ?
    A. could I
    B. couldn't you
    C. could we
    D. couldn't we
13. We _____ the new-comer with an apartment, but he specifically asked for a

single room.
A. could provide B. could have provided
C. Couldn't provide D. couldn't have provided
14. The torpedo is designed in such a way that once _____ nothing can be done to retrieve it.
A. fired B. being fired C. they fired D. having fired
15. _____, he would not have recovered so fast.
A. Hadn't he been taken good care of
B. Had he not been taken good care of
C. Had not he been taken good care of
D. Had he been not taken good care of

III Cloze

Fill in the blanks with worlds from the following list. Use the words in their proper form. Pay attention each word is used only once.

combine	computer	change	by	dozen
depend	different	display	enable	eye
exist	follow	function	processing	possible
since	time	technologies		

Computerized design systems that flawlessly (1) _____ real photographed objects and objects synthesized (2) _____ the computer. Satellites that can photograph the license plate of your car and read the (3) _____ on your watch. "Smart" weapons that recognize and (4) _____ their targets in effortless pursuit — the kind of new, post-modern, post-industrial dance to which we were all exposed during the televised Gulf War. New medical imaging (5) _____ that map every organ and function of the body. On-line electronic libraries that (6) _____ any designer to acquire not only millions of photographs digitally stored but also (7) _____ of styles which can be automatically applied by a computer to any image.

All of these and many other recently emerged technologies of image-making, image manipulation, and vision (8) _____ on digital computers. All of them, as a whole, allow photographs to perform new, unprecedented, and still poorly understood (9) _____. All of them radically (10) _____ what a photograph is.

Indeed, digital photographs function in an entirely (11) _____ way from traditional — lens and film based — photographs. For instance, images are obtained and displayed by sequential scanning; they (12) _____ as mathematical data which can be (13) _____ in a variety of modes — sacrificing color, spatial or temporal resolution. Image (14) _____ techniques make us realize that any photograph contains more information than can be seen with the human (15) _____. Techniques of 3-D (16) _____ graphics make (17) _____ the synthesis of photo images — yet, this realism is always partial, (18) _____ these techniques do not permit the synthesis of any arbitrary scene.

IV Translation
Section A Translate the following Chinese sentences into English.
1. 长大并不一定意味着成熟。(synonymous)
2. 大气层千变万化，难以模拟。(simulate)
3. 众叛亲离的下场是他应得的，正所谓"自食其果"。(alienate)
4. 在数字化的时代，照片的副本和正本之间已经没有区别了。(distinguish / distinguishable)
5. 控制媒体，就能操作民众的思想。(manipulate)
6. 我知道得太多了，于我无益。(more than)
7. 获取知识不容易，传授知识也不容易。(not... more than)
8. 这个囚徒获得了假释，前提是他必须每天到社区报到。(on the premises that)

Section B Translate the following English paragraph into Chinese.
Why is it that the more connected we get, the more disconnected I feel? Every advance in communications technology is a setback to the intimacy of human interaction. With e-mail and instant messaging over the Internet, we can now communicate without seeing or talking to one another. With voice mail, you can conduct entire conversations without ever reaching anyone. If my mother has a question, I just leave the answer on her machine.

V Topics for Discussion
1. Do you agree that traditional way of photography will be replaced by digital photos? Discuss with your classmate.
2. The information technology has become an essential part of our life and greatly influences our life. We do benefit from it. But there are critics doubt the danger of its essentiality. What is your opinion? Organize a debate on the relevant topic.

VI Written Work
Write a short essay of about 200 words on the following topic.

People say that the very advancement in communications technology is a setback to the intimacy of human interaction. What is the major advantages and disadvantages of the prevalence of modern communications technology in our daily life?

Text B
THE iPHONE: Three Revolutionary Products in One
— An iPod That Makes Calls

1   By 2005 iPod sales were skyrocketing. An astonishing twenty million were sold that year, quadruple the number of the year before. The product was becoming more important to the company's bottom line, accounting for 45% of the revenue that year, and it was also burnishing the hipness of the company's image in a way that drove sales of Macs.

2   That is why Jobs was worried. "He was always obsessing about what could mess us up," board member Art Levinson recalled. The conclusion he had come to: "The device that can eat our lunch is the cell phone." As he explained to the board, the digital camera market was being decimated now that phones were equipped with cameras. The same could happen to the iPod, if phone manufacturers started to build music players into them. "Everyone carries a phone, so that could render the iPod unnecessary."

3   His first strategy was to do something that he had admitted in front of Bill Gates was not in his DNA: to partner with another company. He began talking to Ed Zander, the new CEO of Motorola, about making a companion to Motorola's popular RAZR, which was a cell phone and digital camera that would have an iPod built in. Thus was born the ROKR. It ended up having neither the enticing minimalism of an iPod nor the convenient slimness of a RAZR. Ugly, difficult to load, and with an arbitrary hundred-song limit, it had all the hallmarks of a product that had been negotiated by a committee, which was counter to the way Jobs liked to work. Instead of hardware, software, and content all being controlled by one company, they were cobbled together by Motorola, Apple, and the wireless carrier Cingular. "You call this the phone of the future?"

4   Jobs was furious. "I'm sick of dealing with these stupid companies like Motorola," he told Tony Fadell and others at one of the iPod product review meetings. "Let's do it ourselves." He had noticed something odd about the cell phones on the market: They all stank, just like portable music players used to. "We would sit around talking about how much we hated our phones," he recalled. "They were way too complicated. They had features nobody could figure out, including the address book. It was just Byzantine." George Riley, an outside lawyer for Apple, remembers sitting at meetings to go over legal issues, and Jobs would get bored, grab Riley's mobile phone, and start pointing out all the ways it was "brain-dead." So Jobs and his team became excited about the prospect of building a phone that they would want to use. "That's the best motivator of all," Jobs later said.

5   Another motivator was the potential market. More than 825 million mobile phones were sold in 2005, to everyone from grammar schoolers to grandmothers. Since most were junky, there was room for a premium and hip product, just as there had been in the portable music-player market. At first he gave the project to the Apple group that was making the AirPort wireless base station, on the theory that it was a wireless product. But he soon realized that it was basically a consumer device, like the iPod, so he reassigned it to Fadell and his teammates.

6   Their initial approach was to modify the iPod. They tried to use the trackwheel as a way for a user to scroll through phone options and, without a keyboard, try to enter numbers. It was not a natural fit. "We were having a lot of problems using the wheel, especially in getting it to dial phone numbers," Fadell recalled. "It was cumbersome." It was fine for scrolling through an address book, but horrible at inputting anything. The team kept trying to convince themselves that users would mainly be calling people who were already in their address book, but they knew that it wouldn't really work.

7   At that time there was a second project under way at Apple: a secret effort to build a tablet computer. In 2005 these narratives intersected, and the ideas for the tablet flowed into the planning for the phone. In other words, the idea for the iPad actually came before, and helped to shape, the birth of the iPhone.

8   One of the engineers developing a tablet PC at Microsoft was married to a friend of Laurene and Steve Jobs, and for his fiftieth birthday he wanted to have a dinner party that included them along with Bill and Melinda Gates. Jobs went, a bit reluctantly. "Steve was actually quite friendly to me at the dinner," Gates recalled, but he "wasn't particularly friendly" to the birthday guy.

9   Gates was annoyed that the guy kept revealing information about the tablet PC he had developed for Microsoft. "He's our employee and he's revealing our intellectual property," Gates recounted. Jobs was also annoyed, and it had just the consequence that Gates feared. As Jobs recalled:

This guy badgered me about how Microsoft was going to completely change the world with this tablet PC software and eliminate all notebook computers, and Apple ought to license his Microsoft software. But he was doing the device all wrong. It had a stylus. As soon as you have a stylus, you're dead. This dinner was like the tenth time he talked to me about it, and I was so sick of it that I came home and said, "Fuck this, let's show him what a tablet can really be."

10   Jobs went into the office the next day, gathered his team, and said, "I want to make a tablet, and it can't have a keyboard or a stylus." Users would be able to type by touching the screen with their fingers. That meant the screen needed to have a feature that became known as multi-touch, the ability to process multiple inputs at the same time. "So could you guys come up with a multi-touch, touch-sensitive display for me?" he asked. It took them about six months, but they came up with a crude but

workable prototype.

11   Jony Ive had a different memory of how multi-touch was developed. He said his design team had already been working on a multi-touch input that was developed for the trackpads of Apple's MacBook Pro, and they were experimenting with ways to transfer that capability to a computer screen. They used a projector to show on a wall what it would look like. "This is going to change everything," Ive told his team. But he was careful not to show it to Jobs right away, especially since his people were working on it in their spare time and he didn't want to quash their enthusiasm. "Because Steve is so quick to give an opinion, I don't show him stuff in front of other people," Ive recalled. "He might say, 'This is shit,' and snuff the idea. I feel that ideas are very fragile, so you have to be tender when they are in development. I realized that if he pissed on this, it would be so sad, because I knew it was so important."

12   Ive set up the demonstration in his conference room and showed it to Jobs privately, knowing that he was less likely to make a snap judgment if there was no audience. Fortunately he loved it. "This is the future," he exulted.

13   It was in fact such a good idea that Jobs realized that it could solve the problem they were having creating an interface for the proposed cell phone. That project was far more important, so he put the tablet development on hold while the multi-touch interface was adopted for a phone-size screen. "If it worked on a phone," he recalled, "I knew we could go back and use it on a tablet."

14   Jobs called Fadell, Rubinstein, and Schiller to a secret meeting in the design studio conference room, where Ive gave a demonstration of multi-touch. "Wow!" said Fadell. Everyone liked it, but they were not sure that they would be able to make it work on a mobile phone. They decided to proceed on two paths: P1 was the code name for the phone being developed using an iPod trackwheel, and P2 was the new alternative using a multi-touch screen.

15   A small company in Delaware called FingerWorks was already making a line of multi-touch trackpads. Founded by two academics at the University of Delaware, John Elias and Wayne Westerman, FingerWorks had developed some tablets with multi-touch sensing capabilities and taken out patents on ways to translate various finger gestures, such as pinches and swipes, into useful functions. In early 2005 Apple quietly acquired the company, all of its patents, and the services of its two founders. FingerWorks quit selling its products to others, and it began filing its new patents in Apple's name.

16   After six months of work on the trackwheel P1 and the multi-touch P2 phone options, Jobs called his inner circle into his conference room to make a decision. Fadell had been trying hard to develop the trackwheel model, but he admitted they had not cracked the problem of figuring out a simple way to dial calls. The multi-touch approach

was riskier, because they were unsure whether they could execute the engineering, but it was also more exciting and promising. "We all know this is the one we want to do," said Jobs, pointing to the touchscreen. "So let's make it work." It was what he liked to call a bet-the-company moment, high risk and high reward if it succeeded.

17   A couple of members of the team argued for having a keyboard as well, given the popularity of the BlackBerry, but Jobs vetoed the idea. A physical keyboard would take away space from the screen, and it would not be as flexible and adaptable as a touchscreen keyboard. "A hardware keyboard seems like an easy solution, but it's constraining," he said. "Think of all the innovations we'd be able to adapt if we did the keyboard onscreen with software. Let's bet on it, and then we'll find a way to make it work." The result was a device that displays a numerical pad when you want to dial a phone number, a typewriter keyboard when you want to write, and whatever buttons you might need for each particular activity. And then they all disappear when you're watching a video. By having software replace hardware, the interface became fluid and flexible.

18   Jobs spent part of every day for six months helping to refine the display. "It was the most complex fun I've ever had," he recalled. "It was like being the one evolving the variations on 'Sgt. Pepper.'" A lot of features that seem simple now were the result of creative brainstorms. For example, the team worried about how to prevent the device from playing music or making a call accidentally when it was jangling in your pocket. Jobs was congenitally averse to having on-off switches, which he deemed "inelegant." The solution was "Swipe to Open," the simple and fun on-screen slider that activated the device when it had gone dormant. Another breakthrough was the sensor that figured out when you put the phone to your ear, so that your lobes didn't accidentally activate some function. And of course the icons came in his favorite shape, the primitive he made Bill Atkinson design into the software of the first Macintosh: rounded rectangles. In session after session, with Jobs immersed in every detail, the team members figured out ways to simplify what other phones made complicated. They added a big bar to guide you in putting calls on hold or making conference calls, found easy ways to navigate through email, and created icons you could scroll through horizontally to get to different apps — all of which were easier because they could be used visually on the screen rather than by using a keyboard built into the hardware.

Notes

1. **iPod** is a line of portable media players designed and marketed by Apple Inc.
2. **Macs** include Macbook Air, Macbook Pro, Mac mini, iMac, and Mac Pro.
3. **Motorola Razr** (styled **RAZR**, pronounced "razer") is a series of mobile phones by Motorola, part of the 4LTR line.

4. **The Motorola Rokr** (**styled ROKR**) is a series of mobile phones from Motorola, part of a 4LTR line developed before the spin out of Motorola Mobility.

5. **Cingular** was the second largest wireless provider of USA.

6. **Byzantine**, complex and intricate.

7. **Trackwheel** is BlackBerry devices that precede the BlackBerry ® Pearl 8100 Series, as the primary control for user navigation.

8. **A tablet computer**, or simply tablet, is a mobile computer with display, circuitry and battery in a single unit.

9. In computing, **multi-touch** refers to a touch sensing surface's (trackpad or touchscreen) ability to recognize the presence of two or more points of contact with the surface.

10. In computer science, an **interface** is the point of interaction with software, or computer hardware, or with peripheral devices such as a computer monitor or a keyboard.

11. **Trackpad** is a pointing device featuring a tactile sensor, a specialized surface that can translate the motion and position of a user's fingers to a relative position on screen.

12. The **BlackBerry** is a line of wireless handheld devices and services designed and marketed by BlackBerry. The first BlackBerry device, an email pager, was released in 1999. The most recent BlackBerry devices are the Z10, Q10 and Q5. The Z10 and Q10 were announced on January 30, 2013, and the Q5 was announced on May 14, 2013.

Memorable Quotation

Telephone, an invention of the devil which abrogates some of the advantages of making a disagreeable person keep his distance.

— Ambrose Bierce

Further Readings

1. Connor, S. *Postmodernist Culture*
2. V. Amelunxen, Florian Rotzer. (eds). *Photography after Photography*

Unit 8

Pre-reading Questions

1. Can you name some well-known charity organizations or people in China or all over the world? If so what are they?

2. What is the responsibility of charity organizations? Have you ever done or will you do anything for charity?

3. Why do people do charity work?

Text A
ChildFund International

Anonymous

Helping children in poverty has always been at our heart, although how we do it has changed over time. What's been consistent is our desire to ever improve how we make an impact — we've fostered a spirit of innovation from the beginning.

History

1 Our founder, Dr. J. Calvitt Clarke, was an early innovator in gathering support for his cause: He started the "child sponsorship" concept we know today, asking a sponsor to donate to help one child. Acting on its growing understanding of what works for children, ChildFund moved from running orphanages to helping families and communities fight poverty at its roots. Because helping an individual child only goes so far, we added community-level interventions. We determined the best way forward for lasting change was to have local people lead those local programs, because they understand cultural nuances and their local needs best. We added a focus on the whole child — not just physical needs, but emotional and social ones, as well. As we grew, we knew our sponsors would want to know their dollars were being well spent, so we created a Code of Fundraising Ethics: our continuing promise that we will conduct ourselves with accountability, integrity, stewardship and honesty. We created the Emergency Action Fund, which allows our emergency response teams to provide immediate relief and long-term assistance to children in wars, droughts, hurricanes and more. We established the first of our Child-Centered Spaces to help children affected by war recover, learn, play and heal. These spaces, which we now offer in any kind of emergency, help children return to a sense of normalcy, hope and calm. We conducted an in-depth study on child poverty, which revealed that children acutely feel not only the physical but also the emotional and social impacts of poverty. As a result, we found that listening to children's voices when it comes to how poverty affects them makes a profound difference in how we help them improve their futures. We listen before we act. And when we help, it's as a partner.

Accountability

2 Today, worldwide, 400 million children live in extreme poverty. All children — including those 400 million — have rights to the support, protection and care they need to grow up healthy and strong. As a child-focused international development

organization, ChildFund exists to change underlying factors that prevent children from fully experiencing these rights. We work with families and communities to support children at each stage of their development, promoting children's well-being, knowledge and skills so that they may participate in society to their fullest potential.

3   Since our beginnings, our approach has evolved into one of community development, focused on strengthening families and community structures that make up a child's environment. The individual sponsor-to-child relationship supports this work, with sponsor funds pooled to improve life in the communities where sponsored children live.

4   Today, support from sponsors is what allows us to remain in communities long term, building relationships with local partner organizations and focusing on children's changing needs as they grow up. Support from diverse donors and institutions allows ChildFund to expand and deepen its work with children and families even more. Sponsors' friendship and encouragement further elevate ChildFund's impact for children, families and communities, increasing their well-being.

5   This sustained, diverse support, in effect, makes ChildFund's work sustainable. It has allowed us to build and refine programming to address children's rights and needs across multiple areas, from education to health to nutrition and more. Our work is grounded in a theory of change that identifies the age-appropriate resources children at any age need to fully experience their rights.

6   After 75 years, here are some things we know: We know that poverty is more than just lack of material assets — that it is a complex experience involving not only deprivation, but also social exclusion and vulnerability. All of these threaten children's development. We know that children's experience of poverty differs from that of adults and changes as they grow from infancy through childhood and adolescence to young adulthood. We know that children need support throughout their transitions from one stage to the next. We know that at every age, children have unique gifts to offer their communities. We know that harmful policies and practices entrenched at local, national and international levels often cause or perpetuate poverty. Alongside parents, communities and government partners, ChildFund advocates for policies and funding to change conditions and systems that harm children. We know that children are most severely affected by disasters, and that such disruptions occur more often in the developing world. ChildFund approaches emergency response through the means of child protection and supports communities to become more resilient. We know that a child's earliest years are the most important — that during this sensitive time, the foundations for a child's future development are laid, and disruptions have lifelong consequences. We know that a child needs loving caregivers, health care, nutrition, clean water and sanitation, education, opportunity and safety. If any one of these is missing in a child's life, his or her potential may remain out of reach. ChildFund

achieves its greatest impact by working to ensure all these elements are in place, using evidence-based practices tailored to local needs and culture. We know that a child's well-being and protection require the support of family and community. ChildFund works with community members — of all ages — to create the protective environments children need. We know that locally owned change is the most sustainable — that when community members join hands to create an environment where children can thrive, children do.

7   ChildFund mobilizes global relationships linking children, sponsors, parents, teachers, community members, community leaders, local organizations, schools, local and national governments, foundations, corporations and more. Together, we make it possible for children to dream, achieve and contribute — at every age. ChildFund exists to help deprived, excluded and vulnerable children have the capacity to improve their lives and the opportunity to become young adults, parents and leaders who bring lasting and positive change in their communities. We promote societies whose individuals and institutions participate in valuing, protecting and advancing the worth and rights of children.

Issues We Work On

Example 1: Belarus Youth with Disabilities Overcomes Misperceptions to Enter College

8   Eighteen-year-old Vlad was born with cerebral palsy. His speech is unclear, and he cannot handle a pen or use a computer keyboard. And, yet, Vlad is a brilliant student. Teachers educated Vlad at his Belarus home. Though the boy couldn't write, he easily solved math problems in his head. By the age of 15, he had read many literature classics and could easily cite quotes by Dumas or analyze Dostoyevsky's and Tolstoy's works.

9   Vlad dreamed about becoming a lawyer who advocates for the rights of people with disabilities. But he faced a serious roadblock: Belarus' system of entrance exams to its universities does not consider the special needs of a person with disabilities. The examination must be written, and parents are not allowed to be in a classroom during the exam. Personal assistants to help with writing or reading are typically unavailable.

10   In a quest to get their son admitted to college, Vlad's parents petitioned several universities to allow him special assistance to take entrance exams, but they were turned down by most. In 2012, Vera, a vice rector at Baranovichi University, received training in inclusive education, a program conducted by ChildFund through the USAID-funded project Community Services to Vulnerable Groups.

11   Before the training program, Vera, like many other Belorussian educators, believed that children with communication problems also suffered from cognitive disability, often a misconception. But at the training, Vera was deeply impressed by the

examples of academic achievements and talents that American children with disabilities have developed through proper support and teaching.

12   As a result, Vera decided to change the rigid entrance procedure at her university. She shared her new knowledge with her colleagues and obtained their full support. A special team was arranged to provide Vlad with adequate assistance during the testing process. At the exams, Vlad gave his answers verbally, and a faculty member wrote it down. This minor adjustment allowed Vlad to pass the tests.

13   "The results inspired all of my colleagues," Vera says. "The rector of our university and the members of the state educational board that inspected the exams applauded. Vlad showed brilliant results! He got the highest scores among all the applicants. We are very proud that the boy will become our student. Vlad is very persistent, and there is no doubt he will became a successful advocate for the rights of people with disabilities." Because of widespread media coverage, Vlad's story became known all over Belarus and was praised by the minister of education, who said that 2013 will bring reforms to the entrance examination process at all Belarussian universities.

14   At Vera's university, she has continued advocacy efforts by designing a course on inclusive education for students in preschool education. The course was recently approved by the Ministry of Education for university curriculum all over the country.

Example 2: Philippines Children Make Progress after Typhoon

15   As you approach Tambulilid school, the singing and laughter of children gets louder and louder. It's great to hear children having fun and being children again. Nearly one month after Typhoon Haiyan struck islands in the Philippines, ravaged communities are slowly getting back on their feet. In the devastated city of Ormoc, ChildFund is addressing the immediate needs of impacted families by distributing food packs and essential items including hygiene kits, roofing materials and cooking utensils.

16   ChildFund is also focusing on providing psychosocial support to children. In disaster situations, children are particularly vulnerable. While parents are out looking for shelter, food, water and emergency assistance, children are often left unsupervised, increasing their susceptibility to abuse, exploitation and harassment. Children are often separated from loved ones and exposed to levels of destruction that have long-term effects on their psychological and physical development.

17   ChildFund was quick to establish Child-Centered Spaces immediately following Typhoon Haiyan to provide a safe haven for children to play, socialize, learn and express themselves in a caring and supportive environment. At Tambulilid school, where ChildFund established its first CCS after the typhoon, a young mother, Rein, says: "I leave my daughter here while I stand in the long distribution line for food. She is only 5 years old. It is important she has a safe place to play under supervision." At a CCS, children take part in activities that help them overcome the traumatic experience

they went through. It is also a place where children can be children again.

18 "For a few hours every day, I can forget what happened and play with friends," says a smiling Angel, age 7. Marcela, a local ChildFund staff member, explains: "Children take part in drawing, singing, dancing, playing and storytelling, which allow emotional expression." Today, children are drawing. They are enjoying themselves. Marcela adds: "At first, most children drew pictures of the typhoon and the destruction, but in more recent days, they are drawing their family and friends. This is an important sign in post-trauma healing. Child-centered spaces help in this respect."

19 More than 300 children participate daily at Tambulilid, one of three CCSs run by ChildFund in Ormoc. "We conduct separate sessions for different age groups, where we provide age-appropriate structured activities," Marcela says. "Many youths are trained facilitators and have volunteered to conduct sessions for younger children, because they want to be active in the community's recovery. We have also mobilized many volunteers. ChildFund has worked in Ormoc through a local partner organization for many years, and we have a strong relationship with the local community. We train our volunteers to provide basic support to children dealing with distress and shock from their situations, and to recognize children who need to be referred for more specialized services."

20 Although food aid has arrived in Ormoc, malnutrition is still an issue as a number of children appear to be underweight. ChildFund provides food to children at the CCS. Marcela says: "The first day we opened the CCS, we served pancit (a type of Filipino noodles). It was the first time children ate a cooked meal since the typhoon struck. They were extremely hungry. They ate everything up quickly and they had a smile back on their faces. The second day we served pandesal (a popular bread roll in the Philippines made of flour, eggs, yeast, sugar, and salt)." Today, it is spaghetti with tomato sauce. It makes a nice change from the rice and canned sardines they eat every day in the evacuation centers.

21 While the situation in Ormoc is improving, basic survival resources — food, drinking water, shelter and access to medical treatment — are still needed. Schools were expected to reopen sometime this month, but with school buildings extensively damaged, this is unlikely. Schools are in need of major repair to be safely occupied, and learning and teaching materials need to be replaced if classes are to resume as intended. There is still no date for the restart of pre-school and day care activities at this time — highlighting the critical importance of ChildFund's Child-Centered Spaces.

23 ChildFund has opened 13 CCSs impacted areas in the Philippines, but thousands of children still require psychosocial support to overcome trauma from the typhoon. With your support, ChildFund will be able to open more spaces for affected children.

Glossary

accountability	[əkaʊntəˈbɪlɪtɪ] n.	responsibility to someone or for some activity
address	[əˈdres] v.	speak to; give a speech to; deal with verbally
advocacy	[ˈædvəkəsɪ] n.	active support of an idea or cause etc.; especially the act of pleading or arguing for sth.
Belarus	[ˈbelərəs] n.	白俄罗斯，白俄罗斯共和国
Belorussian	[beləˈrʌʃn] a.	白俄罗斯人的；白俄罗斯人
cerebral palsy	[ˈserɪbrəl] [ˈpɔːlzɪ]	[医] 大脑性麻痹
coverage	[ˈkʌvərɪdʒ] n.	The extent to which sth. is covered cognitive disability 认知障碍；智能障碍
curriculum	[kəˈrɪkjuləm] n.	an integrated course of academic studies
donate	[dəʊˈneɪt] v.	give to a charity or good cause
deprivation	[deprɪˈveɪʃən] n.	a state of extreme poverty; the disadvantage that results from losing sth.
deprived	[dɪˈpraɪvd] a.	marked by deprivation especially of the necessities of life or healthful environmental influences
devastated	[ˈdevəsteɪt] a.	ravaged
disruption	[dɪsˈrʌpʃən] n.	an act of delaying or interrupting the continuity
evolve	[ɪˈvɒlv] v.	work out; undergo development or evolution
elevate	[ˈelɪveɪt] v.	give a promotion to or assign to a higher position; raise from a lower to a higher position
entrench	[ɪnˈtrentʃ] v.	fix firmly or securely
exploitation	[eksplɔɪˈteɪʃən] n.	the act of making some area of land or water more profitable or productive or useful; development
evacuation	[ɪvækjuˈeɪʃən] n.	the act of removing the contents of sth.
facilitator	[fəˈsɪlɪteɪtə] n.	someone who makes progress easier
hygiene kits	[ˈhaɪdʒiːn] n.	卫生用品
harassment	[ˈhærəsmənt] n.	a feeling of intense annoyance caused by being tormented
intervention	[ɪntəˈvenʃən] n.	the act of intervening in a situation
integrity	[ɪnˈtegrɪtɪ] n.	an undivided or unbroken completeness or totality with nothing wanting
mobilize	[ˈməʊbəlaɪz] v.	make ready for action; call to arms
misperception	[mɪspəˈsepʃən] n.	an idea or impression that is not correct 错误知觉；错误想法
misconception	[mɪskənˈsepʃən] n.	an idea that is not correct

malnutrition [mælnjʊˈtrɪʃən] n.	a state of poor nutrition
nuance [njuːˈɑːns] n.	a small difference in sound, feeling, appearance, or meaning
normalcy [ˈnɔrmlsɪ] a.	situation in which everything is normal
orphanage [ˈɔːfənɪdʒ] n.	a public institution for the care of orphans; the condition of being a child without living parents
petition [pɪˈtɪʃən] v.	request formally and in writing
pool [puːl] v.	combine into a common fund; join or form a pool of people 联营、合伙经营
perpetuate [pəˈpetʃʊeɪt] v.	cause to continue or prevail
psychosocial [saɪkəʊˈsəʊʃəl] a.	of or relating to processes or factors that are both social and psychological in origin
resilient [rɪˈzɪlɪənt] a.	elastic; rebounds readily
rector [ˈrektə] n.	dean; principle; headmaster
ravaged [ˈrævɪdʒ] a.	having been robbed and destroyed by force and violence
resume [rɪˈzjuːm] v.	restart
stewardship [ˈstjuːədʃɪp] n.	the position of steward 管理工作
sustained [səˈsteɪnd] a.	maintained at length without interruption or weakening; continuous
sanitation [senɪˈteɪʃən] n.	the state of being clean and conducive to health
susceptibility [səseptəˈbɪlətɪ] n.	the state of being susceptible; easily affected
session [ˈseʃən] n.	a meeting devoted to a particular activity; the time during which a school holds classes
thrive [θraɪv] v.	grow stronger; gain in wealth
traumatic [trɔːˈmætɪk] a.	of or relating to a physical injury or wound to the body; psychologically painful
utensil [juːˈtensəl] n.	tools or objects that you use in order to help you to cook, serve food, or eat.
unsupervised [ʌnˈsuːpəvaɪzd] a.	without supervision
vulnerability [vʌlnərəˈbɪlətɪ] n.	the state of being vulnerable or exposed; susceptibility to injury or attack

Notes

1. About the text (the origin of **ChildFund International**).

ChildFund International, formerly known as Christian Children's Fund, is a child development organization based in Richmond, Virginia, United States. It provides assistance to deprived, excluded and vulnerable children in 30 countries, including the

United States. ChildFund was founded on October 6, 1938 as China's Children Fund by Presbyterian minister Dr. J. Calvitt Clarke to aid Chinese children displaced by the War of Resistance Against Japanese Aggression. As the mission expanded to other countries, the name was changed on February 6, 1951 to Christian Children's Fund. In June 2002, Christian Children's Fund and 11 other international child sponsorship organizations founded a worldwide network, ChildFund Alliance. The ChildFund Alliance comprises twelve organizations that partner to improve the lives of children and their families in 55 countries. Alliance members meet organizational standards of governance, fundraising and fiscal responsibility. The partnership fosters opportunities for pooled resources and collaborative activities to reach more children in need. On July 1, 2009, Christian Children's Fund changed its name to ChildFund International.

2. **Baranovichi University** 巴拉诺维奇州大学 (Para. 10)

Baranovichi state University is an institution of higher education established in accordance with the order of the president of the republic of Belarus dated on June 23, 2004. It is not only a high professional school focused on training highly-qualified specialists with deep theoretical and practical knowledge, but also a center of scientific research and a powerful ideological support. It is a diversified structure combining education, research and innovation activities.

3. In 2012, Vera, a vice rector at Baranovichi University, received training in **inclusive education**, a program conducted by ChildFund through the **USAID**-funded project Community Services to Vulnerable Groups. (Para. 10)

"inclusive education" 是个多义词，它可以指全纳教育，融合教育。

The United States Agency for International Development (**USAID**) is the United States Government agency primarily responsible for administering civilian foreign aid. Responding to President Barack Obama's pledge in his 2013 State of the Union Address to "join with our allies to eradicate extreme poverty in the next two decades," USAID has adopted as its mission statement "to partner to end extreme poverty and to promote resilient, democratic societies while advancing the security and prosperity of the United States." USAID operates in Africa, Asia, Latin America and Eastern Europe. President John F. Kennedy created USAID from its predecessor agencies in 1961 by executive order. USAID's programs are authorized by the Congress in the Foreign Assistance Act, which the Congress supplements through directions in annual funding appropriation acts and other legislation. Although technically an independent federal agency, USAID operates subject to the foreign policy guidance of the President, Secretary of State, and the National Security Council.

4. The course was recently approved by **the Ministry of Education**... (Para. 14)

The Ministry of Education is a governmental agency in charge of regulating the education system. 教育部

5. ... following **Typhoon Haiyan** to provide a safe haven for children to ...

(Para. 17)

Typhoon Haiyan (海燕台风), known in the Philippines as Typhoon Yolanda, was one of the strongest tropical cyclones ever recorded; devastating portions of Southeast Asia, particularly the Philippines, in early-November 2013. It is the deadliest Philippine typhoon recorded in modern history, killing at least 6,300 people in that country alone. Haiyan is also the strongest storm recorded at landfall, and the strongest typhoon ever recorded in terms of one-minute sustained wind speed. As of January 2014, bodies were still being found.

6. ChildFund has worked in **Ormoc** through... (Para. 19)

Ormoc is a city in the province of Leyte, Philippines. According to the 2010 census, it has a population of 191,200 people. Ormoc is the economic, cultural, commercial and transportation hub of western Leyte. Ormoc City is an independent component city, not subject to regulation from the Provincial Government of Leyte. However, the city is part of the VI Congressional District of Leyte together with Albuera, Kanaga, Merida, Palompon and Isabel. On 8 November 2013, the city was largely destroyed by Super Typhoon Yolanda (Haiyan), having previously suffered severe destruction and loss of life in 1991 from torrential flooding during Tropical Storm Thelma. The city's name is derived from ogmok, an old Visayan term for "lowland" or "depressed plain".

Comprehension Questions

Answer the following questions after reading the text.

1. How many innovations does ChildFund International have? What are they?
2. What are child rights according to ChildFund International and how does it help children?
3. What is the mission of ChildFund International?
4. How did Vlad's story change Belarussian universities?
5. What did ChildFund International do for Philippines children?

Exercises

I Vocabulary

Section A Paraphrase the sentences chosen from the text below.

1. Because helping an individual child only goes so far, we added community-level interventions. We determined the best way forward for lasting change was to have local people lead those local programs, because they understand cultural nuances and their local needs best. (Para. 1)
2. The individual sponsor-to-child relationship supports this work, with sponsor funds

pooled to improve life in the communities where sponsored children live. (Para. 3)
3. Our work is grounded in a theory of change that identifies the age-appropriate resources children at any age need to fully experience their rights. (Para. 5)
4. In a quest to get their son admitted to college, Vlad's parents petitioned several universities to allow him special assistance to take entrance exams, but they were turned down by most. (Para. 10)
5. While the situation in Ormoc is improving, basic survival resources — food, drinking water, shelter and access to medical treatment — are still needed. Schools were expected to reopen sometime this month, but with school buildings extensively damaged, this is unlikely. (Para. 21)

Section B There are ten sentences in this section. Beneath each sentence there are four words or phrases marked A, B, C and D. Choose one word or phrase that best completes the sentence.

1. New leaders need to assess these dimensions and quickly figure out how to converge and _____ the organization.
   A. evolve into   B. evolve from   C. evolve to   D evolve around
2. When my kids go a weekend without pizza and TV while camping, they think they are suffering great _____.
   A. deficiency   B. deprivation   C. depression   D. starvation
3. President Obama's _____ in Libya, achieving a similar result, cost just over a billion.
   A. insult   B. innovation   C. indifference   D. intervention
4. A special team was arranged to provide Vlad with adequate _____ during the testing process.
   A. help   B. aid   C. assistance   D. favor
5. Therefore, the _____, legitimacy, survival and effectiveness of this Organization depend on you all.
   A. integrity   B. goodness   C. purity   D. virtue
6. Johnston, who works in the bone-marrow transplant unit at McMaster, has a background in sports _____.
   A. nutrition   B. nullity   C. nuisance   D. nuance
7. The orphanage is supported by the _____ of townspeople.
   A. allowance   B. compensations   C. subsidies   D. charity
8. I have the honor of introducing to you, Mr. Alan, who _____ will you on his recent tour abroad.
   A. address   B. speak   C. talk   D. converse
9. The old custom of St. Monday — when no work was done — was gradually phased out and to compensate, work stopped around midday on Saturday and did not _____ until Monday morning.

A. last   B. begin   C. start   D. resume
10. The old lady has developed a _____ cough which cannot be cured completely in a short time.
    A. perpetual   B. permanent   C. chronic   D. sustained

Section C Use the proper form of the following words given in the brackets to fill in the blanks.

1. Once we plant the seeds of concurrency in these base courses, we then could expand on them throughout the _____. (curricular)
2. He says the group used a million-and-a-half-dollar _____ from the Nike Foundation to expand the program to cricket players in India. (donate)
3. Like most Americans, Laura and I have been following the television _____ from Haiti. (cover)
4. Sudan even threatened to _____ in response to the ultimatums. (mobilization)
5. She was told her sister died of acute bacterial meningitis with a contributing factor of _____. (nutrition)
6. The judge awarded the costs of the case to the _____. (petition)
7. _____ by mental illness, he was unable to make good decisions about his healthcare. (ravage)
8. In Nigeria, the federal government tries to _____ the agenda of the United Nations. (perpetual)
9. The surviving victim' immune systems have been weakened, leading to chronic respiratory disorders and a _____ to diabetes. (susceptible)
10. The GOJ Schools Internet Project introduced in 1998 is another strategy implemented to _____ learning achievement. (facilitator)

Section D Use the proper form of the following phrases if necessary to fill in the blanks.

| in a quest to | in effect | deprived of | go through |
| as intended | at its roots | expose to | tailor to |

1. In the mid-90s, _____ foreign support, the Cambodian communist movement gradually fell apart.
2. But despite the selfishness that is _____, what Jesus is asking us to recognize is that it's not a sin, it's not evil.
3. Now, We _____ the city, to the culture, and we learn from our competition.
4. Last week, Ms. Merkel and French President Nicolas Sarkozy proposed tighter policy coordination between euro-zone states, _____ reassure markets about the cohesion and survival of the currency bloc.
5. The prime minister, it is argued, should rise above the fray and refuse to _____ himself _____ unnecessary risks.
6. If NPV is _____, Obama would not necessarily be awarded California's 55

electoral votes.
7. "In 12 years, a lot of stuff can _____ your head," he said.
8. The firm's tests also indicated that some back-up control system components did not perform _____.

II Grammar
Choose the best answer to complete the following sentence from the respective four choices.
1. Time _____, the celebration will be held as scheduled.
   A. permit   B. permitting   C. permitted   D. permits
2. The country's chief exports are coal, cars and cotton goods, cars _____ the most important of these.
   A. have been   B. are   C. being   D. are being
3. They overcame all the difficulties and completed the project two months ahead of time, _____ is something we had not expected.
   A. which   B. it   C. that   D. what
4. He is _____ as a "bellyacher" — he's always complaining about something.
   A. who is known   B. whom is known
   C. what is known   D. which is known
5. The team can handle whatever _____.
   A. that needs handling   B. which needs handling
   C. it needs handling   D. needs to be handled
6. This may have preserved the elephant from being wiped out as well as other animals _____ in Africa.
   A. hunted   B. hunting   C. that hunted   D. are hunted
7. Belarus' system of entrance exams to its universities does not consider the special needs of a person _____ disabilities.
   A. of   B. with   C. in   D. around
8. If you explained the situation to your solicitor, he _____ able to advise you much better than I can.
   A. would be   B. will have been   C. was   D. were
9. It is also a place _____ children can be children again.
   A. which   B. that   C. it   D. Where
10. ChildFund has opened 13 CCSs _____ areas in the Philippines, but thousands of children still require psychosocial support to overcome trauma from the typhoon.
    A. impacting   B. impacted   C. to impact   D. have impacted

III Cloze

Decide which of the choices given below would best complete the passage if inserted in the corresponding blanks. Mark the best choice for each blank.

As end-of-the-year giving gets under way, some charities abandon disaster pictures and use gentler imagery to urge people to give "something that means something". While (1) _____ to United States charities topped $290 billion last year, Mr. Ottenhoff, chief executive of GuideStar USA noted that the barrier to giving was (2) _____ "because money is harder to come by, and consumers also want to see value. They want to know that they are (3) _____ a difference."

"A few years ago," he said, "the emphasis was (4) _____ accountability and transparency. Now that's a given, and the focus is on (5) _____. In other words: 'No impact, no giving.'"

(6) _____ a result, Scott Jackson, chief executive of Global Impact, which works with a (n) (7) _____ of 58 international charities based in the United States and (8) _____ two federal giving campaigns, says nonprofits "are trying to do a better job of telling their story, which is (9) _____ on emotion, but it can't just be a picture of a child or an animal. The message has to spell out the effectiveness."

The emphasis on results means "the giver is guaranteed that the gift will do something really important (10) _____ not end up in the bottom of the drawer," said Stephanie Kurzina, an Oxfam America spokeswoman.

One of its print ads, which are (11) _____ in magazines like *The New Yorker* and *The Washingtonian*, underscores the impact of such gifts with the line: "This season's must-have holiday (12) _____: Food and Water."

In addition to print, Oxfam America's "gift better" (13) _____ will be shown on CNN, CNBC and other networks. Ms. Johansson advises that she finds (14) _____ gifts of chickens, books or fruit trees more pleasing than being (15) _____ with unusable presents.

The American Red Cross 2011 (16) _____ is called "Give Something That Means Something." In advance of this season's campaign, a survey (17) _____ by the Red Cross found that eight in ten would rather someone give a donation to charity in their (18) _____ than receive another gift they would not use.

The campaign "was a great (19) _____ for the Red Cross to change the giving conversation," said John Osborn, chief executive of BBDO, "and create a sense of relevance and story for those who can't (20) _____ to leave anyone out."

1. A. allowances   B. contributions   C. distributions   D. gifts
2. A. rising   B. risen   C. raising   D. raised
3. A. bringing   B. making   C. giving   D. having
4. A. with   B. at   C. on   D. of
5. A. importance   B. impact   C. money   D. value

6. A. By	B. At	C. Beside	D. As
7. A. ally	B. alliance	C. cooperation	D. negotiation
8. A. manages	B. to manage	C. managed	D. managing
9. A. base	B. bases	C. based	D. Basing
10. A. but	B. and	C. however	D. if
11. A. aroused	B. arousing	C. appearing	D. appeared
12. A. gift	B. gifts	C. gifting	D. gifted
13. A. appeal	B. sign	C. need	D. print
14. A. unique	B. uncommon	C. charitable	D. expensive
15. A. showered	B. shower	C. showering	D. to shower
16. A. sport	B. event	C. campaign	D. activity
17. A. commissioned	B. commission	C. commissioning	D. will commission
18. A. life	B. name	C. value	D. sign
19. A. purpose	B. situation	C. opportunity	D. possibility
20. A. bear	B. beat	C. bite	D. bend

IV Translation

Section A Translate the following Chinese sentences into English.

1. 那条法律把我的最基本权利都剥夺了。(deprive)
2. 一个高效而可持续发展的交通系统的创建是非常重要的。(sustainable)
3. 在你入睡之前，下意识地去想你希望梦到的某件事情，或是某个人。(dream about)
4. 企业没有良好的管理不会兴旺。(thrive)
5. 世界银行肯定并非一家典型的银行，但在这方面它也遵循这种规范。(in this respect)
6. 毕竟，有很多方法可以减轻这种焦虑，而不用把所有钱都藏在床垫底下。(turn down)
7. 领导艺术是关于给予员工最大的支持，开发他们最大的潜能，调动他们对工作的最大动力和积极性去完成好工作。(to one's fullest potential)
8. 她说："在受到考验的时候，坚定自己的信仰是相当重要的。"(be grounded in)
9. 请正确处理电池，不要把它们置于高温中。(expose to)
10. 他们要尽一切力量弥补这些经济损失。(make up)

Section B Translate the following English paragraph into Chinese.

Andrew Carnegie, known as the King of Steel, built the steel industry in the United States, and, in the process, became one of the wealthiest men in America. Carnegie believed that individuals should progress through hard work, but he also felt strongly that the wealthy should use their fortunes for the benefit of society. He opposed charity, preferring instead to provide educational opportunities that would allow others to help themselves. "He who dies rich, dies disgraced," he often said. Among his more noteworthy contributions to society are those that bear his name, including the Carnegie Institute of Pittsburgh, which has a library, a museum of fine arts, and a museum of national history. He also founded a school of technology that is now part of Carnegie-Mellon University. Other philanthropic gifts are the Carnegie Endowment for International Peace to promote understanding between nations, the Carnegie Institute of Washington to fund scientific research, and Carnegie Hall to provide a center for the arts. Few Americans have been left untouched by Andrew Carnegie's generosity.

V Topic for Discussion

Some people believe that charity organizations should give the aid to those who are in great needs all around the world, some people think that charity organizations should concentrate on helping people who live in their own country. Discuss both views and give your opinion.

VI Written Work

Write a short essay of about 200 words on the following topic. You are required to choose a title by yourselves.

Chenshou in the Western Jin Dynasty once said, "We must do good rather than evil, on however humble a scale." How far do you agree with this philosophy?

Text B

Stop Telling Rich Folks to Give More to Charity
——Walmart and the Rise of Philanthro-shaming

Benjamin Soskis

1 By now, the Walton family, the nation's richest through its ownership stake in Walmart, must have developed a pretty thick hide. They have long been subjected to intense criticism regarding the massive retailer's allegedly exploitative labor practices. But this month, they absorbed a blow at a particularly sensitive spot: their philanthropic self-regard.

2 In a report entitled "The Phony Philanthropy of the Walmart Heirs," a union-backed group, Walmart 1 Percent, argued that the enormous size of the Walton Family Foundation — it can claim total assets of $2 billion and was recently ranked as one of the top foundations in terms of annual giving — should not be taken as a measure of the family's generosity.

3 Nearly all the foundation's resources come from a handful of trusts set up with assets provided by Sam Walton, Walmart's founder, his wife Helen, his son John, or their estates. The next generation of living heirs has done little to add to its coffers. According to the report, based on analysis of 23 years of tax returns, the heirs have donated to the family foundation a mere .04 percent of their present net worth of some $140 billion. As the nation's richest family, the report says, the Waltons "have enough wealth and power to literally change the world." And they haven't — at least not for the better. (The Walton Family Foundation has responded by claiming that the entire family participated in decisions regarding the family's wealth and that it does not make sense to categorize the contributions generationally.)

4 The report represents a new phenomenon of this latest Gilded Age: the rise of philanthro-shaming. Blame the convergence of two related trends: a faith in philanthropy to render lasting social change and an uneasiness with the oversized fortunes concentrated at the cloud-covered apex of the income scale. Combined, they have led the public to scrutinize more carefully the charitable pretensions of the nation's richest citizens. Philanthro-shaming suggests the promise — but also some of the perils — of this new regime of philanthropic accountability.

5 The nation experienced its first major bout of philanthro-shaming during the original Gilded Age, at the turn of the last century. The creation of massive industrial fortunes led to intense public focus on the responsibilities of great wealth. And a heightened sensitivity to inequality placed an even greater burden on large-scale giving. Enterprising journalists began compiling lists of the nation's millionaires and determining who donated the most — and the least. And some of them began to issue demands that these philanthropic slackers shape up. Such calls bumped up against an older, biblically-rooted mode of voluntary giving, one that had prioritized discreet, warm-hearted charity — the kind in which the right hand had little idea what the left was doing. But the new imperatives for philanthropic accountability challenged this tradition.

6 "It is a hopeful sign of the times," declared *the Boston Globe* in 1892, "that many rich men, who are not naturally generous or beneficent, are being forced by a healthy public sentiment to gifts, which they would not donate through the natural promptings of their own hearts."

7 That same tension, between a spirit of private voluntarism and public coercion, runs through these latest efforts to goad billionaires into greater acts of giving. Earlier this year, for instance, salesforce.com founder Marc Benioff called out his fellow tech billionaires for their lack of generosity to Bay Area anti-poverty programs. He's urged every major company in the San Francisco area to pledge $500,000 to a local philanthropy, and has signaled his willingness to expose those CEOs who have been slow to reach into their pockets.

8 In March, Inside Philanthropy, an online industry publication, compiled a list of tech giving based on relative generosity — overall giving relative to net worth — and made sure to tabulate the least generous tech moguls, too (Amazon's Jeff Bezos and Google's Larry Page were among those singled out). Then there's the Giving Pledge, the campaign championed by Bill Gates and Warren Buffett to convince their fellow billionaires to join them in committing at least half their wealth to philanthropy. Although Gates and Buffett have shied away from applying public pressure to potential signatories, the campaign has established a benchmark to which those wealthy citizens who lack strong public philanthropic identities can be, and have been, held to account.

9 Today, much like during the last Gilded Age, some worry that philanthro-shaming could do damage to the voluntarist roots of philanthropy — and might, for that reason, actually deter giving in the long run. Critics have also pointed out that these shaming campaigns ignore less publicity-oriented acts of giving that might not have caught the media's attention. The authors of the Walton "Phony Philanthropy" report concede this point, acknowledging the "limitations" of their data, since they rely on the assumption that the Walmart heirs chose their family foundation as the primary vehicle through which to contribute to charity. If the Walton heirs made significant donations outside their family foundation, the report would have substantially underestimated their total giving — although the report's authors claim that they have not uncovered any such gifts in any of their investigations that would force them to revise their calculations. The Walton Family Foundation had no comment on this question.

10 This indeed represents a serious methodological shortcoming. But the real problem with philanthro-shaming is not that it demands too much of the nation's wealthiest citizens, but that it threatens to demand too little. It frames the responsibilities of wealth as a matter of bookkeeping. But philanthropic accountability is more than balance sheets; its imperatives are not satisfied merely by knowing how much billionaires give but in scrutinizing the objects of that largest.

11 Ironically enough, the Walton Family Foundation certainly appreciates this distinction. The foundation is one of the leading champions of education reform, spending hundreds of millions of dollars over the last decade to transform public education through the elixir of market-based mechanisms. This program has earned the ire of labor; one has to assume that the folks behind the Walmart 1 Percent campaign wouldn't really be thrilled if Walton family members took their chastisement to heart and decided to channel much more of their personal wealth to their family foundation so it could increase its spending on charter schools and the promotion of merit-based teacher pay. Around the same time as the "Phony Philanthropy" report came out on June 3, more than half of the New York City Council signed a "cease-and-desist" letter addressed to Walmart and the Walton Family Foundation demanding that it stop sending its "dangerous dollars" to local nonprofits. The council members assumed that the

donations represented a "cynical public-relations campaign" to buy support for the introduction of a Walmart mega-store in the city. After this week, you could forgive the Waltons for feeling that they were damned if they gave, and damned if they didn't.

12   Which is not to suggest that the public should stop philanthro-shaming; it can be a useful tool for shining a light on the giving priorities of the nation's wealthiest citizens. And though it might bruise some egos, it's unlikely that such attention will discourage giving in the long run. If anything, appreciating that the public really does take their philanthropic commitments seriously should inspire more giving, and giving that is more closely attuned to the nation's needs. But philanthro-shaming should be the beginning — and not the end — of a civil and engaged conversation about philanthropic means and ends. The flowering of that sort of "healthy public sentiment" from 1892 — that really would be a hopeful sign of the times.

Notes

1. About the author.

Mr. Soskis holds a PhD in history from Columbia University, with a focus on philanthropy. He is a fellow at the Center for Nonprofit Management, Philanthropy and Policy at George Mason University. He is currently writing a book on the history of the critique of philanthropy.

2. ... **the Walton family**, the nation's richest through its ownership stake in **Walmart**... (Para. 1)

The Walton family is among the richest families in the world. Their wealth is inherited from Bud and Sam Walton, founders of the world's largest retailer, Walmart. The three most prominent living members (Jim, Rob and Alice) have consistently been in the top ten of the *Forbes* 400 since 2001, as were John (d. 2005) and Helen (d. 2007) prior to their deaths. Christy Walton took her husband John's place after his death. Collectively, the Waltons own over 50% of the company, and are worth a combined total of $175 billion (as of January 2015). In 2010, six members of the Walton family had the same net worth as either the bottom 28% or 41% of American families combined (depending on how it is counted).

Wal-Mart Stores, Inc. is an American multinational retail corporation that operates a chain of discount department stores and warehouse stores. Headquartered in Bentonville, Arkansas, the company was founded by Sam Walton in 1962 and incorporated on October 31, 1969. It has over 11,000 stores in 27 countries, under a total 71 different brands. Walmart is the world's largest company by revenue, according to the Fortune Global 500 list in 2014, the biggest private employer in the world with over two million employees, and the largest retailer in the world. Walmart is a family-owned business, as the company is controlled by the Walton family, who own over 50 percent of Walmart through their holding company, Walton Enterprises. It is also one of the world's most valuable companies (in terms of market value), and is also the largest grocery retailer in the US. In 2009, it generated 51 percent of its US $258 billion (equivalent to $284 billion in 2015) sales in the US from grocery business. It also owns and operates the Sam's Club retail warehouses in North America.

3. In a **report** entitled "The Phony Philanthropy of the Walmart Heirs," … (Para. 2)

The report was released on June 3, 2014 by The Walmart 1 Percent. It exposes how the richest family in America uses their private foundation to mislead the public and increase their wealth. According to this report, the Waltons — America's richest family — have contributed almost none of their own wealth to the Walton Family Foundation and use the Foundation to avoid an estimated $3 billion in estate taxes. Based on an analysis of 23 annual tax returns filed by the Walton Family Foundation, the report shows that, if the Foundation is their primary vehicle for giving, the Waltons give much less generously than their billionaire peers and ordinary Americans. Following is the Link of the report: http://walmart1percent.org/files/2014/06/PhonyPhilanthropy.pdf

4. The report represents a new phenomenon of this latest **Gilded Age**: … (Para. 4)

The Gilded Age in United States history is the late 19th century, from the 1870s to about 1900. The term was coined by writer Mark Twain in *The Gilded Age: A Tale of Today* (1873), which satirized an era of serious social problems masked by a thin gold gilding

5. … the rise of **philanthro-shaming**… (Para 4)

Charitable giving is an honored tradition in American culture. Nearly 80% of Americans, many without extensive means to do so, donate annually. Those with the means and the will to give substantially are deemed "philanthropists" and treated with great deference in the public sphere. While giving to charity is a note-worthy gesture, regardless of the amount, this report shows that not all "philanthropists" actually give in ways that most Americans would recognize as charitable. The report, based on an analysis of 23 annual tax returns filed by the Walton Family Foundation, shows that, if the Foundation is their primary vehicle for charitable giving, the Waltons give much less generously than other Americans — including both their billionaire peers and ordinary, middle class Americans. Additionally, the report outlines the wealth management and tax avoidance schemes that lie at the heart of the family's philanthropic enterprise.

6. … declared *the* **Boston Globe** in 1892… (Para. 6)

The Boston Globe is an American daily newspaper based in Boston, Massachusetts. Founded in 1872 by Charles H. Taylor, it was privately held until 1973, when it went public as Affiliated Publications. *The Boston Globe* has been awarded 23 Pulitzer Prizes since 1966, and its chief print rival is the Boston Herald.

7. ... the campaign championed by Bill Gates and **Warren Buffett** to... (Para. 8)

Warren Edward Buffett (born on August 30, 1930) is an American business magnate, investor and philanthropist. He was the most successful investor of the 20th century. Buffett is the chairman, CEO and largest shareholder of Berkshire Hathaway, and consistently ranked among the world's wealthiest people. He was ranked as the world's wealthiest person in 2008 and as the third wealthiest in 2011. In 2012 *Time* named Buffett one of the world's most influential people.

8. ... signed a "**cease-and-desist**" letter addressed to Walmart... (Para. 11)

A cease and desist letter, also known as "infringement letter" or "demand letter," is a document sent to an individual or business to halt purportedly-unlawful activity ("cease") and not take it up again later ("desist"). The letter may warn that if the recipient by deadlines set in the letter does not cease and desist specified conduct, or take certain actions, that party may be sued.

Questions for Discussion

1. What do you think goads billionaires into greater acts of giving?
2. How do you understand "Philanthro-shaming could actually deter giving in the long run"?
3. Why does the author say "that 'healthy public sentiment' from 1892 would be a hopeful sign of the times"?

Memorable Quotes

1. Love is not patronizing and charity isn't about pity, it is about love. Charity and love are the same — with charity you give love, so don't just give money but reach out your hand instead.

    — Mother Teresa

2. As you grow older, you will discover that you have two hands, one for helping yourself and the other for helping others.

    — Sam Levenson

3. A bone to the dog is not charity. Charity is the bone shared with the dog, when you are just as hungry as the dog.

    — Jack London

4. Every man must decide whether he will walk in the light of creative altruism or in the darkness of destructive selfishness.

    — Martin Luther King Jr.

5. In charity to all mankind, bearing no malice or ill will to any human being, and

even compassionating those who hold in bondage their fellow men, not knowing what they do.

— John Quincy Adams

6. No one has ever become poor by giving.

— Anne Frank

Further Readings

1. Jac Depczyk, *Looking Good by Doing Good*
2. Robert Reich, *Rich People's Idea of Charity*
3. John Carnwath, *The Deduction for Charitable Contributions: The Sacred Cow of the Tax Code*

Unit 9

Pre-reading Questions

1. Can you name some famous black people (athletes/politicians/writers. etc.)? In your opinion, who is the greatest black people ever in the world?
2. What makes the success of black people?
3. How much do you know about racism?

Text A
The Story Behind the Amazing Success of Black Athletes

Jon Entine

The Race to the Swift or the Swift to the Race

1 Here's a safe prediction: all of the athletes who line up at the final of the men's 100-meter sprint in Sydney trace their ancestry to West Africa. It's also unlikely that any sprinter other than one with West African roots will ever again hold the unofficial title of "world's fastest human." Even more startlingly, athletes who trace their ancestry to Africa, home to roughly 1 in 8 of the world population, or 800 million people, dominate elite sprinting and road racing: an athlete of African origin holds every major world running record.

2 The controversial question is why?

3 To many sociologists, the answer is "racism". "What really is being said in a kind of underhanded way," comments Harry Edwards of University of California/Berkeley, "is that blacks are closer to beasts and animals in terms of their genetic and physical and anatomical make up than they are to the rest of humanity. And that's where the indignity comes in."

4 Most hard scientists take a different view. "If you can believe that individuals of recent African ancestry are not genetically advantaged over those of European and Asian ancestry in certain athletic endeavors," says biological anthropologist Vincent Sarich, also of Berkeley, "then you could probably be led to believe just about anything."

5 What are the scientific facts? What is behind the extraordinary reality that over the past 30 years, as equality of opportunity has steadily increased in sports, spreading to vast sections of Asia and Africa, equality of results on the playing field has actually declined. Greater opportunity has led to greater inequality in performance at the elite level between ethnic groups in a range of sports.

- Blacks of exclusively West African ancestry make up 13 percent of the North American and Caribbean population but 40 percent of Major League baseball players, 70 percent of the NFL, and 85 percent of professional basketball.
- Nigeria, Cameroon, Tunisia, and South Africa have emerged as soccer powers. Africans have also become fixtures in Europe's top clubs even with sharp restrictions on signing foreign players. In England, which was slow to allow foreigners and has a black population of less than 2 percent, one in five soccer players in the Premiership is black.

- From Wales to South Africa, rugby has been played almost exclusively by whites because of historical social restrictions and taboos — except in New Zealand where Maori and Pacific Islanders have risen to the top ranks far out of proportion to their numbers. Maori women have also become the stars in netball, which demands extraordinary quickness.
- The outsized success of Australian athletes with primarily Aboriginal genes in running, tennis, boxing, and rugby and a recent six-fold surge in the number of Aboriginal players in the Australian Football League.

6   Are these purely cultural phenomena as socially-acceptable wisdom suggests? And why is this subject so taboo?

Rethinking RACE, SCIENCE, & SPORTS

7   Athletic achievement has long been a Catch-22 for blacks. When an athlete lost a running, it encouraged racist notions that blacks were an inferior race, too frail to handle the challenge and not smart enough to plan a race strategy. But winning only reinforced the equally pernicious stereotype that blacks were less evolved than whites or Asians. That is the fate that befell Jesse Owens after he shocked the 1936 Olympics, held in the capital of Hitler's Germany. His four gold medals were subtly devalued as a product of his "natural" athleticism.

8   The racist stereotype of the "animalistic black" is rooted in hundreds of years of colonialism, slavery, and racism. In the nineteenth century, white Europeans were enraptured by pseudosciences such as phrenology. Racial and ethnic groups were ranked by skull size that supposedly proved that white males were intellectually superior. Jews, blacks, and other minorities were targets of the most egregious generalizations, usually associated with physical characteristics and intellectual prowess.

9   Since World War II, in an understandable reaction to extremist race theories that provided intellectual fuel for Nazism, it has been widely held that the very concept of race is a meaningless social construct. "Race science" as it was then called, was based largely on the notion of skin color, which scientists had come to realize explained only a tiny fraction of the evolutionary history of the genes that make us human. And since the world's major populations separated only an eye blink of historical time ago — from 5,000 to 100,000 years ago — many scientists also came to believe that natural selection could not have generated anything more than superficial differences like skin color. Those beliefs fed the stereotype that athletic success was entirely social and cultural — the product of hard work and opportunity, with population genetics playing no significant role.

10   Now science can definitively state that the post WWII anthropological orthodoxy — what is referred to as environmental determinism — is clearly wrong. The

genetics revolution now sweeping the world has decisively overturned this belief that all humans are created with equal potential, a tabula rasa for experience to write upon. Evidence spilling forth from the Human Genome Project shows that some functional characteristics do differentiate population clusters — most clearly in the proclivity to certain diseases and in athletic ability — although the classic racial trichotomy of sub-Saharan black/European white/Asian is indeed fuzzy around the edges and potentially misleading.

11　How have racial differences evolved?

12　Although the move out of Africa by modern humans to Europe and Asia occurred rather recently in evolutionary time, scientists now know that in relatively few generations, even small, chance mutations can trigger a chain reaction with cascading consequences resulting in significant racial differences or possibly even the creation of new species. Economic ravages, natural disasters, genocidal pogroms, and geographical isolation caused by mountains, oceans, and deserts, have deepened these differences over time. This is the endless loop of genetics and culture, nature and nurture.

13　Genetically linked, highly heritable characteristics such as skeletal structure, the distribution of muscle fiber types, reflex capabilities, metabolic efficiency, lung capacity, and the ability to use energy more efficiently are not evenly distributed among populations and cannot be explained by known environmental factors. Scientists are just beginning to isolate the genetic links to biologically-based differences, most notably in isolating the causes of population specific diseases such as Tay-Sachs, which afflicts Jews, and sickle cell, which targets blacks.

14　Popular thinking still lags this genetic revolution. "Differences among athletes of elite caliber are so small," notes Robert Malina, a Michigan State University physical anthropologist and editor of the Journal of Human Genetics, "that if you have a physique or the ability to fire muscle fibers more efficiently that might be genetically based ... it might be very, very significant. The fraction of a second is the difference between the gold medal and fourth place."

15　Although scientists are just beginning to isolate the genetic links to those biologically-based differences, it is indisputable that they exist. Each sport demands a slightly different mix of biomechanical, anaerobic, and aerobic abilities. Athletes from each region of the world tend to excel in specific events as a result of evolutionary adaptations to extremely different environments that became encoded in the genes.

16　Whites of Eurasian ancestry, who have, on average, more natural upper-body strength, predictably dominate weightlifting, wrestling and all field events, such as the shot-put and hammer (whites hold 46 of the top 50 throws). Evolutionary forces in this northern clime have shaped a population with a mesomorphic body type — large and muscular, particularly in the upper body, with relatively short arms and legs and thick torsos. These proportions tend to be an advantage, particularly in sports in which strength rather than speed is at a premium.

17 East Asians tend to be small with relatively short extremities, long torsos, and a thicker layer of fat, evolutionary adaptations to harsh climes encountered by Homo sapiens who migrated to Northeast Asia about 40,000 years ago. As a result, athletes from this region are somewhat slower and less strong than whites or blacks, but more flexible on average — a key potential advantage in diving and some events in gymnastics (hence the term "Chinese splits") and figure skating. That anthropometric reality severely hampers Asians from being great sprinters or leapers: not one Asian male or female high jumper makes the top 50 all-time. It should come as no surprise that the world's most remarkable ultra-endurance runners, the 4,000 or so Native American Tarahumara of Mexico, have East Asian ancestry.

18 The cluster of islands that straddle the international date line in the South Pacific, including Samoa and American Samoa, have funneled hundreds of players into American football and Australian rugby. Polynesia is a hotbed of human biodiversity. More than likely, its inhabitants trace their ancestry to southern Asia by way of Africa. Polynesians, especially the Samoans, are amongst the world's most mesomorphic body types. A number of studies have shown that muscle bulk and the degree of muscularity especially in the thigh and buttock are important predictors of success in rugby players whereas the opposite applies in such sports as distance running. This genetic admixture helps in part explain why athletes from this region are large, agile, and fast.

19 Whether or not genes confer a competitive advantage on blacks when it comes to stealing bases, running with the football, shooting hoops, or jumping hurdles remains the question. Since the first known study of differences between blacks and white athletes in 1928, the data have been remarkably consistent: in most sports, African-descended athletes have the capacity to do better with their raw skills than whites. Blacks with a West African ancestry generally have: relatively less subcutaneous fat on arms and legs and proportionately more lean body and muscle mass, broader shoulders, larger quadriceps, and bigger, more developed musculature in general; denser, shallower chests; higher center of gravity, generally shorter sitting height, narrower hips, and lighter calves; longer arm span and "distal elongation of segments" — the hand is relatively longer than the forearm, which in turn is relatively longer than the upper arm; the foot is relatively longer than the tibia (leg), which is relatively longer than the thigh; faster patellar tendon reflex; greater body density, which is likely due to higher bone mineral density and heavier bone mass at all stages in life, including infancy (despite evidence of lower calcium intake and a higher prevalence of lactose intolerance, which prevents consumption of dairy products); modestly, but significantly, higher levels of plasma testosterone (3-19 percent), which is anabolic, theoretically contributing to greater muscle mass, lower fat, and the ability to perform at

a higher level of intensity with quicker recovery; a higher percentage of fast-twitch muscles and more anaerobic enzymes, which can translate into more explosive energy.

20 Relative advantages in these physiological and biomechanical characteristics are a gold mine for athletes who compete in such anaerobic activities as football, basketball, and sprinting, sports in which West African blacks clearly excel. However, they also pose problems for athletes who might want to compete as swimmers (heavier skeletons and smaller chest cavities could be drags on performance) or in cold-weather and endurance sports. Central West African athletes are more susceptible to fatigue than whites and East Africans, in effect making them relatively poor candidates for aerobic sports.

21 White athletes appear to have a physique between central West Africans and East Africans. They have more endurance but less explosive running and jumping ability than West Africans; they tend to be quicker than East Africans but have less endurance.

22 Still, it should not be forgotten that ancestry is not destiny. "From a biomechanical perspective, the answer is 'yes,' race and ethnicity do matter," says Lindsay Carter, a physical anthropologist at San Diego State University who has studied thousands of Olympic-level athletes over the years. "All of the large-scale studies show it, and the data goes back more than a hundred years." But he adds a critical caveat. It is critical to remember that no individual athlete can succeed without the X factor — the lucky spin of the roulette wheel of genetics matched with considerable dedication and sport smarts. "There are far too many variables to make blanket statements about the deterministic quality of genetics," Carter says. "Nature provides an average advantage, yes. But that says nothing about any individual competitor."

Glossary

aboriginal [ˌæbəˈrɪdʒɪnəl] n.   native; belonging or relating to the Australian Aborigines 澳大利亚土著的
aerobic [eəˈrəʊbɪk] a.   需氧的；增氧健身法的
afflict [əˈflɪkt] v.   cause bodily suffering to and make sick or indisposed
agile [ˈædʒaɪl] a.   moving quickly and lightly
animalistic [ˌænɪməˈlɪstɪk] a.   relating to, or resembling an animal or animals
anatomical [ˌænəˈtɒmɪkəl] n.   relating to the structure of the bodies of people and animals
anthropologist [ˌænθrəˈpɒlədʒɪst] n. 人类学家
anthropological [ˌænθrəpəˈlɒdʒɪkəl] a. of or concerned with the science of anthropology
anaerobic [ˌæneəˈrəʊbɪk] a.   （生物或过程）厌氧的

Unit 9

athleticism	[æθˈletɪsɪzəm] n.	someone's fitness and ability to perform well at sports or other physical activities
befall	[bɪˈfɔːl] v.	become of; happen to
biomechanical	[baɪəʊməˈkænɪkəl] n.	生物力学
biodiversity	[baɪəʊdaɪˈvɜːsɪtɪ] n.	生物多样性
bulk	[bʌlk] n.	the main part
buttock	[ˈbʌtək] n.	either of the two large fleshy masses of muscular tissue that form the human rump
cascade	[kæsˈkeɪd] v.	rush down in big quantities, like a cascade
caveat	[ˈkævɪæt] n.	a warning against certain acts
caliber	[ˈkælɪbə] n.	a degree or grade of excellence or worth
cluster	[ˈklʌstə] n.	a grouping of a number of similar things
colonialism	[kəˈləʊnɪəlɪzəm] n.	the practice by which a powerful country directly controls less powerful countries and uses their resources to increase its own power and wealth 殖民主义
controversial	[kɒntrəˈvɜːʃəl] a.	marked by or capable of arousing controversy
confer	[kənˈfɜː] v.	present; have a conference to talk sth. over
determinism	[dɪˈtɜːmɪnɪzəm] n.	the belief that all actions and events result from other actions, events, or situations, so people cannot in fact choose what to do 决定论
differentiate	[dɪfəˈrenʃɪeɪt] v.	mark as different
egregious	[ɪˈgriːdʒəs] a.	very bad and offensive
elite	[eɪˈliːt] n.	a group or class of persons enjoying superior intellectual or social or economic status
encode	[ɪnˈkəʊd] v.	convert ordinary language into code
endeavor	[ɪnˈdevə] n.	effort; trial; a purposeful or industrious undertaking (especially one that requires effort or boldness)
endurance	[ɪnˈdjuərəns] n.	the power to withstand hardship or stress
enrapture	[ɪnˈræptʃə] v.	hold spellbound
enzyme	[ˈenzaɪm] n.	[生化] 酶
Eurasian	[juəˈreɪʃən] n. a.	a person of mixed European and Asian descent relating to, or coming from, Europe and Asia
excel	[ɪkˈsel] v.	distinguish oneself
extremity	[ɪksˈtremɪtɪs] n.	an external body part that projects from the body
fixture	[ˈfɪkstʃə] n.	a regular patron; a object firmly fixed in place (especially in a household)
-fold	[fəʊld] suff.	表示"倍","重";表示"由…部分构成"

frail	[freɪl] a.	physically weak
fraction	[ˈfrækʃən] n.	a component of a mixture that has been separated by a fractional process; a small part or item forming a piece of a whole
funnel	[ˈfʌnl] v.	通过漏斗或烟囱等；使成漏斗形
genetic	[dʒɪˈnetɪk] a.	tending to occur among members of a family usually by heredity
generalization	[dʒenərəlaɪˈzeɪʃən] n.	a statement that seems to be true in most situations or for most people, but that may not be completely true in all cases
genocidal	[dʒenəˈsaɪdl] a.	种族灭绝的
hamper	[ˈhæmpə] v.	prevent the progress or free movement of
heritable	[ˈherɪtəbl] a.	that can be inherited
humanity	[hjuːˈmænətɪ] n.	the quality of being humane; the quality of being human; all of the living human inhabitants of the earth
hotbed	[ˈhɔtbed] n.	a situation that is ideal for rapid development (especially of something bad)
indignity	[ɪnˈdɪgnətɪ] n.	an affront to one's dignity or self-esteem
indisputable	[ɪndɪsˈpjuːtəbl] a.	impossible to doubt or dispute
inequality	[ɪnɪˈkwɔlətɪ] n.	lack of equality
lag	[læg] v.	hang (back) or fall (behind) in movement, progress, development, etc.
loop	[luːp] n.	圈
mesomorphic	[mesəʊˈmɔːfɪk] a.	（具有）体育型体质
metabolic	[metəˈbɔlɪk] a.	of or relating to metabolism 新陈代谢的
minority	[maɪˈnɔrətɪz] n.	a group of people who differ racially or politically from a larger group of which it is a part
muscularity	[mʌskjuˈlærətɪ] n.	possessing muscular strength
mutation	[mjuːˈteɪʃən] n.	a change or alteration in form or qualities
netball	[ˈnetbɔːl] n.	a team game similar to basketball, played mainly by women
notably	[ˈnəʊtəblɪ] ad.	to a notable extent
notion	[ˈnəʊʃən] n.	a general inclusive concept
nurture	[ˈnɜːtʃə] n.	the properties acquired as a consequence of the way you were treated as a child
orthodoxy	[ˈɔːθədɒksɪ] n.	a belief or orientation agreeing with conventional standards
outsized	[ˈaʊtsaɪzd] a.	larger than normal for its kind

overturn	[ˌəʊvəˈtɜːn] v.	turn from an upright or normal position
premiership	[prɪˈmɪəʃɪp] n.	the office of premier; the period of time during which they are the leader
pernicious	[pəˈnɪʃəs] a.	exceedingly harmful
pseudosciences	[ˈsjuːdəʊsaɪəns] n.	an activity resembling science but based on fallacious assumptions
phrenology	[frɪˈnɒlədʒɪ] n.	颅相学，骨相学
pogrom	[ˈpɒgrəm] n.	organized persecution of an ethnic group (especially Jews) 大屠杀
Polynesia	[ˌpɒlɪˈniːzjə] n.	玻利尼西亚（中太平洋的岛群）
proclivity	[prəˈklɪvɪtɪ] n.	a natural inclination; a tendency to behave in a particular way or to like a particular thing, often a bad way or thing
prowess	[ˈpraʊɪs] n.	a superior skill that you can learn by study and practice and observation
racism	[ˈreɪsɪzəm] n.	racial discrimination; the prejudice that members of one race are intrinsically superior to members of other races
racist	[ˈreɪsɪst] n.	a person with a prejudiced belief that one race is superior to others
ravage	[ˈrævɪdʒ] n.	(usually plural) a destructive action
roulette	[ruːˈlet] n.	a gambling game 轮盘赌
sociologist	[ˌsəʊsɪˈɒlədʒɪst] n.	a social scientist who studies the institutions and development of human society
sprinter	[ˈsprɪntə] n.	someone who runs a short distance at top speed
sprint	[sprɪnt] n.	a quick run
	v.	run very fast, usually for a short distance
straddle	[ˈstrædəl] v.	sit or stand astride of
startlingly	[ˈstɑːtlɪŋlɪ] ad.	surprisingly; alarmingly; in a startling manner
stereotype	[ˈsterɪəʊtaɪp] n.	a conventional or formulaic conception or image
sub-Saharan	[ˌsʌbsəˈhɑːrən] a.	撒哈拉沙漠以南的
surge	[sɜːdʒ] n.	a sudden large increase in something that has previously been steady, or has only increased or developed slowly
taboo	[təˈbuː] a.	excluded from use or mention
Tarahumara	[ˌtɑːrəhuːˈmɑːrə] n.	塔拉乌马拉人（墨西哥北部印第安部族）
Tay-Sachs	[ˈteɪsæks] n.	家族黑蒙性白痴
torso	[ˈtɔːsəʊ] n.	the body excluding the head and neck and limbs
trichotomy	[traɪˈkɒtəmɪ] n.	三分法

underhanded [ˌʌndəˈhændɪd] a.　　marked by deception; with hand brought forward and up from below shoulder level

variable [ˈveərɪəbəl] n.　　[数] 变量；可变物，可变因素

Notes

1. About the author and the text.

Jon Entine (1952—), born in Philadelphia, Pennsylvania, is an American author and science journalist. Entine is a senior research fellow at the Center for Health & Risk Communication at George Mason University and founder and executive director of the Genetic Literacy Project, a biotechnology and genetics outreach organization affiliated with Sense About Science-United States. He is also a senior fellow at the Institute for Food and Agricultural Literacy at the University of California, Davis. After working as a network news writer and producer for NBC News and ABC News, Entine moved into scholarly research and print journalism. Entine has written seven books and is a contributing columnist to multiple newspapers and magazines; he is also a commentator on radio and television news programs. His works include, *Taboo: Why Black Athletes Dominate Sports and Why We're Afraid to Talk About It* (2000), *Pension Fund Politics: The Dangers of Socially Responsible Investing* (2005), *Scared to Death: How Chemophobia Threatens Public Health* (2011), *Let Them Eat Precaution: How Politics is Undermining the Genetic Revolution* (2006), *Abraham's Children: Race, Identity and the DNA of the Chosen People* (2008), *No Crime But Prejudice: Fischer Homes, the Immigration Fiasco, and Extrajudicial Prosecution* (2009), *Crop Chemophobia: Will Precaution Kill the Green Revolution?* (2011).

This article is the first part of two analyses on the amazing success of black athletes.

2. … comments **Harry Edwards** of University of California/Berkeley … (Para. 3)

Harry Edwards is an African-American sociologist who took his PhD at Cornell University and is Professor Emeritus of Sociology at the University of California, Berkeley. Edwards' career has focused on the experiences of African-American athletes and he is a strong advocate of black participation in the management of professional sports. He has served as a staff consultant to the San Francisco 49ers football team and to the Golden State Warriors basketball team. He has also been involved in recruiting black talent for front-office positions in major league baseball.

3. … but 40 percent of **Major League baseball** players… (Para. 5)

Major League Baseball (MLB), founded in Cincinnati in 1869, is a professional baseball organization that constitutes one of the four major professional sports leagues in North America. It is the oldest league of the four. In 2000, the leagues merged into a single organization led by the Commissioner of Baseball. The organization oversees minor league baseball leagues, which operate about 240 teams affiliated with the major-league clubs. With the International Baseball Federation, the league also manages the international World Baseball Classic tournament.

4. ... 70 percent of the **NFL**... (Para. 5)

The National Football League (NFL), formed in 1920, is a professional American football league consisting of 32 teams, divided equally between the National Football Conference (NFC) and the American Football Conference (AFC). The NFL is one of the four major professional sports leagues in North America, and the highest professional level of American football in the world.

5. ... in the number of Aboriginal players in the **Australian Football League**... (Para. 5)

The Australian Football League (AFL) is the highest-level professional competition in the sport of Australian rules football. Through the AFL Commission, the AFL also serves as the sport's governing body, and is responsible for controlling the Laws of the Game.

6. Athletic achievement has long been a **Catch-22** for blacks. (Para. 7)

If you describe a situation as a Catch-22, you mean it is an impossible situation because you cannot do one thing until you do another thing, but you cannot do the second thing until you do the first thing. 相互矛盾的困窘

7. ... the fate that befell **Jesse Owens** after... (Para. 7)

James Cleveland "Jesse" Owens (September 12, 1913 — March 31, 1980) was an American track and field athlete and four-time Olympic gold medalist. Owens specialized in the sprints and the long jump and was recognized in his lifetime as "perhaps the greatest and most famous athlete in track and field history". His achievement of setting three world records and tying another in less than an hour at the 1935 Big Ten track meet has been called "the greatest 45 minutes ever in sport" and has never been equaled. At the 1936 Summer Olympics in Berlin, Germany, Owens won international fame with four gold medals: 100 meters, 200 meters, long jump, and 4 × 100 meter relay. He was the most successful athlete at the games and as such has been credited with "single-handedly crush[ing] Hitler's myth of Aryan supremacy." The Jesse Owens Award, USA Track and Field's highest accolade for the year's best track and field athlete, is named after him, and he was ranked by ESPN as the sixth greatest North American athlete of the twentieth century and the highest-ranked in his sport.

8. ... that provided intellectual fuel for Nazism... (Para. 9)

Nazism or National Socialism, is the ideology and practice of the German Nazi Party and state. It is sometimes applied to other far-right groups. Usually characterized as a form of fascism that incorporates scientific racism and antisemitism, Nazism arose from pan-Germanism, the Völkisch German nationalist movement and the anti-communist Freikorps after World War I. Nazism subscribed to theories of racial hierarchy and social Darwinism. Germanic peoples (called the Nordic race) were depicted as true "Aryans", and the "master race". Opposed to both capitalism and Marxism, it aimed to overcome social divisions, with all parts of a homogeneous society seeking national unity, and what it viewed as historically German territory as well as additional lands for expansion.

9. "**Race science**" as it was then called, ... (Para. 9)

Scientific racism is the use of scientific techniques and hypotheses to support or justify the belief in racism, racial inferiority, or racial superiority, or alternatively the practice of classifying individuals of different phenotypes into discrete races.

10. ... a **tabula rasa** for experience to write upon. (Para. 10)

It means a young mind not yet affected by experience (according to John Locke); an opportunity to start over without prejudice.

11. Evidence spilling forth from the **Human Genome Project** shows that... (Para. 10)

The Human Genome Project (HGP) is an international scientific research project with the goal of determining the sequence of chemical base pairs which make up human DNA, and of identifying and mapping all of the genes of the human genome from both a physical and functional standpoint. It remains the world's largest collaborative biological project. The project was proposed and funded by the US government; planning started in 1984, the project got underway in 1990, and was declared complete in 2003. The Human Genome Project originally aimed to map the nucleotides contained in a human haploid reference genome (more than three billion). The "genome" of any given individual is unique; mapping "the human genome" involves sequencing multiple variations of each gene. The project did not study the entire DNA found in human cells; some heterochromatic areas (about 8% of the total genome) remain unsequenced.

12. ... encountered by **Homo sapiens** who... (Para. 17)

The only surviving hominid; species to which modern man belongs; bipedal primate having language and ability to make and use complex tools; brain volume at least 1400 cc. 智人（现代人的学名）；人类

13. ... hence the term "**Chinese splits**" ... (Para. 17)

A split (commonly referred to as "splits" or "the splits") is a physical position in which the legs are in line with each other and extended in opposite directions. Splits are performed in various athletic activities, including dance, figure skating, gymnastics, martial arts, contortionism, synchronized swimming, cheerleading and yoga. A person who has assumed a split position is said to be "in a split" or "doing the splits". When executing a split, the lines defined by the inner thighs of the legs form an angle of approximately 180 degrees. This large angle significantly stretches, and thus demonstrates excellent flexibility of, the hamstring and iliopsoasmuscles. Consequently, splits are often used as a stretching exercise to warm up and enhance the flexibility of leg muscles.

  14. ... in diving and some events in gymnastics (hence the term "Chinese splits") and **figure skating**. (Para. 17)
  花式溜冰
  15. ... including Samoa and **American Samoa**... (Para. 18)
  a United States territory on the eastern part of the island of Samoa 美属萨摩亚

Comprehension Questions

Answer the following questions after reading the text.

1. What does Vincent Sarich mean by saying "If you can believe that individuals of recent African ancestry are not genetically advantaged over those of European and Asian ancestry in certain athletic endeavors, then you could probably be led to believe just about anything"?
2. What does the author try to imply by telling "Greater opportunity has led to greater inequality in performance at the elite level between ethnic groups in a range of sports"?
3. What are the racist notions people have on the blacks in terms of running?
4. Can you list some examples to show biologically-based differences?
5. What does it mean by Carter's saying "Nature provides an average advantage, yes. But that says nothing about any individual competitor."?

Exercises

I Vocabulary

Section A Paraphrase the sentences chosen from the text.

1. It's also unlikely than any sprinter other than one with West African roots will ever again hold the unofficial title of "world's fastest human." (Para. 1)
2. Even more startlingly, athletes who trace their ancestry to Africa, home to roughly 1 in 8 of the world population, or 800 million people, dominate elite sprinting and road racing: an athlete of African origin holds every major world running record. (Para. 1)
3. Since the world's major populations separated only an eye blink of historical time ago — from 5,000 to 100,000 years ago — many scientists also came to believe that natural selection could not have generated anything more than superficial differences like skin color. (Para. 9)
4. Those beliefs fed the stereotype that athletic success was entirely social and cultural

— the product of hard work and opportunity, with population genetics playing no significant role. (Para. 9)
5. Athletes from each region of the world tend to excel in specific events as a result of evolutionary adaptations to extremely different environments that became encoded in the genes. (Para. 15)

Section B There are ten sentences in this section. Beneath each sentence there are four words or phrases marked A, B, C and D. Choose one word or phrase that best completes the sentence.

1. Its strange way of making a nest _____ this bird from others.
   A. differs   B. distinguishes   C. differentiates   D. discriminates
2. Without my glasses I can hardly _____ what has been written in the letter.
   A. make for   B. make up   C. make out   D. make over
3. Prejudice sometimes _____ a person from doing the right thing.
   A. bars   B. obstructs   C. blocks   D. hampers
4. Her first born is not the only one in her family who is good at handwriting; in fact, all her children _____ calligraphy.
   A. are fond of   B. are tired of   C. excel at   D. go in for
5. The job candidates' main _____ was that he'd never held a job for more than eight months.
   A. illusion   B. indignation   C. endurance   D. liability
6. A university education usually follows an educational scheme that _____ a degree in a particular field of study.
   A. ends to   B. reaches to   C. gives to   D. leads to
7. _____, there has grown up in the postwar years what is sometimes referred to as the "DIY Movement".
   A. At once   B. As a result   C. As a result of   D. Resulting in
8. When a person has in infectious disease, he is usually _____.
   A. isolated   B. invited   C. managed   D. secured
9. Montgomery believed in assembling an overwhelming force and then _____ a crushing blow on his opponent.
   A. affiliating   B. conflicting   C. afflicted   D. inflicting
10. He was _____ with the power of acute observation.
    A. conferred   B. endowed   C. equipped   D. bestowed

Section C Use the proper form of the following words given in the brackets to fill in the blanks.

1. You sold your _____ for nothing but an illusion. (human)
2. In Ohio, another comedian, Drew Hastings, a _____ on "Comedy Central," became mayor of tiny Hillsboro. (fix)
3. She presents her _____ drawings as traditional Chinese scroll paintings — but

the themes they express are universal. (size)
4. My mother spoke of her kindly, not infrequently mentioning the tragedy that had _____ her, with the death of her young husband. (fall)
5. The ultimate victims of the death sentence are the backward, the _____ and the weak. (minor)
6. "We found that finger length was 70 percent _____ with little influence of the womb environment," he said. (heritage)
7. The growing pains _____ the U.S. Mars program are partly due to it being a victim of its own success. (afflict)
8. They _____ the other automakers in the fierce competition. (lag)
9. Parents can teach their children how to _____ fears in their heads from actual danger. (different)
10. Other _____ similarities suggested they all had a single, common ancestor about 300 years ago. (gene)

Section D Use the proper form of the following phrases if necessary to fill in the blanks.

in terms of	come in	as a result of	spill forth
in a range of	out of proportion to	than any ... other than ...	emerge as

1. China sends more students to colleges and universities in the United States _____ country _____ India.
2. "It does have an effect _____ emotional and mental health," he added.
3. That's where the trouble often _____.
4. Bank Indonesia is targeting inflation this year _____ 4% to 6%.
5. Creativity must _____ a top down, bottom up competency within leading companies.
6. But anxiety can become a problem when it becomes persistent or is _____ the situation.
7. Hell, itself, is poised to _____ into your world like a tidal wave of blood and nightmares.
8. _____ new technology and an awareness of green growth, all garbage recycling facilities in Beijing have now adopted this technique.

II Grammar

Choose the best answer to complete the following sentence from the respective four choices.

1. Have you ever been in a situation _____ you know the other person is right yet you cannot agree with him?
   A. by which   B. that   C. in where   D. where
2. He is quite worn out from years of hard work. He is not the man _____ he was

twenty years ago.

   A. which   B. that   C. who   D. whom
3. Congratulations _____ your successful adaptation _____ a tough rule for you to comply with.

   A. on... to   B. to... on   C. on... in   D. to... with
4. _____, there is no place like home.

   A. Humble as it may be   B. As it may be humble
   C. It may as be humble   D. Humble it may be
5. We left the meeting, there obviously _____ no point in staying.

   A. was   B. being   C. to be   D. having
6. Just as the value of a telephone network increases with each new phone _____ to the system, so does the value of a computer system increase with each program that turns out.

   A. adding   B. to be added   C. added   D. to add
7. He wasn't asked to take on the chairmanship of the society, _____ insufficiently popular with all members.

   A. being considered   B. being considering
   C. to be considered   D. has considered
8. Anna was reading a piece of science fiction, completely _____ to the outside world.

   A. losing   B. lose   C. lost   D. being lost
9. A large part of a person's memory is _____ words and combination of words.

   A. by means of   B. in terms of
   C. in connection with   D. by way of
10. Chance mutations can trigger a chain reaction with cascading consequences _____ significant racial differences.

   A. as a result of   B. as a result   C. resulted in   D. resulting in

III Fast Reading (Skimming and Scanning)

In this part, you will have 15 minutes to go over the passages quickly and answer the questions. For questions 1-7, choose the best answer from the four choices marked A. B. C. D. For questions 8-10, complete the sentences with the information given in the passage.

Obama's Success Isn't all Good News for Black Americans

AS ERIN WHITE watched the election results head towards victory for Barack Obama, she felt a burden lifting from her shoulders. "In that one second, it was a validation for my whole race," she recalls.

"I've always been an achiever," says White, who is studying for an MBA at

Vanderbilt University in Nashville, Tennessee. "But there had always been these things in the back of my mind questioning whether I really can be who I want. It was like a shadow, following me around saying you can only go so far. Now it's like a barrier has been let down."

White's experience is what many psychologists had expected — that Obama would prove to be a powerful role model for African Americans. Some hoped his rise to prominence would have a big impact on white Americans, too, challenging those who still harbour racist sentiments. "The traits that characterize him are very contradictory to the racial stereotypes that black people are aggressive and uneducated," says Ashby Plant of Florida State University. "He's very intelligent and eloquent."

Sting in the tail

Ashby Plant is one of a number of prescient psychologists who seized on Obama's candidacy to test hypotheses about the power of role models. Their work is already starting to reveal how the "Obama effect" is changing people's views and behaviour. Perhaps surprisingly, it is not all good news: there is a sting in the tail of the Obama effect.

But first the good news. Barack Obama really is a positive role model for African Americans, and he was making an impact even before he got to the White House. Indeed, the Obama effect can be surprisingly immediate and powerful, as Ray Friedman of Vanderbilt University and his colleagues discovered.

They tested four separate groups at four key stages of Obama's presidential campaign. Each group consisted of around 120 adults of similar age and education, and the test assessed their language skills. At two of these stages, when Obama's success was less than certain, the tests showed a clear difference between the scores of the white and black participants — an average of 12.1 out of 20, compared to 8.8, for example. When Obama fever was at its height, however, the black participants performed much better. Those who had watched Obama's acceptance speech as the Democrats' presidential candidate performed just as well, on average, as the white subjects. After his election victory, this was true of all the black participants.

Dramatic shift

What can explain this dramatic shift? At the start of the test, the participants had to declare their race and were told their results would be used to assess their strengths and weaknesses. This should have primed the subjects with "stereotype threat" — an anxiety that their results will confirm negative stereotypes, which has been shown to damage the performance of African Americans.

Obama's successes seemed to act as a shield against this. "We suspect they felt inspired and energized by his victory, so the stereotype threat wouldn't prove a distraction," says Friedman.

Lingering racism

If the Obama effect is positive for African Americans, how is it affecting their white compatriots? Is the experience of having a charismatic black president modifying lingering racist attitudes? There is no easy way to measure racism directly; instead psychologists assess what is known as "implicit bias", using a computer-based test that measures how quickly people associate positive and negative words — such as "love" or "evil" — with photos of black or white faces. A similar test can also measure how quickly subjects associate stereotypical traits — such as athletic prowess or mental ability — with a particular group.

In a study that will appear in *the Journal of Experimental Social Psychology*, Plant's team tested 229 students during the height of Obama-mania. They found that implicit bias had fallen by as much as 90 percent compared with the level found in a similar study in 2006. "That's an unusually large drop," Plant says.

While the team can't be sure their results are due solely to Obama, they also showed that those with the lowest bias were likely to subconsciously associate black skin colour with political words such as "government" or "president". This suggests that Obama was strongly on their mind, says Plant.

Drop in bias

Brian Nosek of the University of Virginia in Charlottesville, who runs a website that measures implicit bias using similar tests, has also observed a small drop in bias in the 700,000 visitors to the site since January 2007, which might be explained by Obama's rise to popularity. However, his preliminary results suggest that change will be much slower coming than Plant's results suggest.

Talking honestly

"People now have the opportunity of expressing support for Obama every day," says Effron. "Our work raises the concern that people may now be more likely to raise negative views of African Americans." On the other hand, he says, it may just encourage people to talk more honestly about their feelings regarding race issues, which may not be such a bad thing.

Another part of the study suggesting far more is at stake than the mere expression of views. The Obama effect may have a negative side. Just one week after Obama was elected president, participants were less ready to support policies designed to address racial inequality than they had been two weeks before the election.

Huge obstacles

It could, of course, also be that Obama's success helps people to forget that a disproportionate number of black Americans still live in poverty and face huge obstacles when trying to overcome these circumstances. "Barack Obama's family is such a salient image, we generalise it and fail to see the larger picture — that there's injustice in every aspect of American life," Kaiser says. "For a lot of people, his tale reinforces the protestant work ethic," she adds. "But they fail to see that society might stop others from having their talent recognised." Those trying to address issues of racial inequality need to constantly remind people of the inequalities that still exist to counteract the Obama effect, she says.

Though Plant's findings were more positive, she too warns against thinking that racism and racial inequalities are no longer a problem. "It's not the time to be complacent — the last thing I want is for people to think everything's solved."

These findings do not only apply to Obama, or even just to race. They should hold for any role model in any country. "There's no reason we wouldn't have seen the same effect on our views of women if Hillary Clinton or Sarah Palin had been elected," says Effron. So the election of a female leader might have a downside for other women.

Beyond race

We also don't yet know how long the Obama effect — both its good side and its bad — will last. Political sentiment is notoriously fickle: what if things begin to go wrong for Obama, and his popularity slumps?

And what if Americans become so familiar with having Obama as their president that they stop considering his race altogether. "Over time he might become his own entity," says Plant. This might seem like the ultimate defeat for racism, but ignoring the race of certain select individuals — a phenomenon that psychologists call subtyping — also has an insidious side. "We think it happens to help people preserve their beliefs, so they can still hold on to the previous stereotypes." That could turn out to be the cruellest of all the twists to the Obama effect.

1. How did Erin White feel upon seeing Barack Obama's victory in the election?
   A. Excited.   B. Victorious.   C. Anxious.   D. Relieved.
2. Before the election, Erin White has been haunted by the question of whether ____.
   A. she could obtain her MBA degree
   B. she could go as far as she wanted in life
   C. she was overshadowed by her white peers
   D. she was really an achiever as a student
3. What is the focus of Ashby Plant's study?
   A. Racist sentiments in America.
   B. The power of role models.

C. Personality traits of successful Blacks.

D. The dual character of African Americans.

4. In their experiments, Ray Friedman and his colleagues found that _____.

   A. Blacks and whites behaved differently during the election

   B. Whites' attitude towards blacks has dramatically changed

   C. Obama's election has eliminated the prejudice against blacks

   D. Obama's success impacted blacks' performance in language tests

5. What do Brian Nosek's preliminary results suggest?

   A. The change in bias against blacks is slow in coming.

   B. Bias against blacks has experienced an unusual drop.

   C. Website visitor's opinions are far from being reliable.

   D. Obama's popularity may decline as time passes by.

6. A negative side of the Obama effect is that _____.

   A. more people have started to criticise President Obama's racial policies

   B. relations between whites and African Americans may become tense again

   C. people are now less ready to support policies addressing racial inequality

   D. white people are likely to become more critical of African Americans

7. Cheryl Kaiser holds that people should be constantly reminded that _____.

   A. Obama's success is sound proof of Blacks' potential

   B. Obama is but a rare example of Blacks' excellence

   C. racial inequality still persists in American society

   D. Blacks still face obstacles in political participation

8. According to Effron, if Hillary Clinton or Sarah Palin had been elected, there would also have been a negative effect on _____.

9. It is possible that the Obama effect will be short-lived if there is a change in people's _____.

10. The worst possible aspect of the Obama effect is that people could ignore his race altogether and continue to hold on to their old racial _____.

IV Translation

Section A Translate the following Chinese sentences into English.

1. 人均猪肉消费比其他任何国家都多（除了德国）。(than any... other than...)
2. 伦敦的创造性与艺术热忱在我眼中引人注目。(in terms of)
3. 那时正值人们的态度开始变化，许多新思想正在流行。(come in)
4. 她应该通过离婚的方式来离开他。(by way of)
5. 你的价值所在就存在于你是谁，而不是你在做什么。(be rooted in)
6. 幸运的是，现在越来越多的人已经认识到吸烟的危害。(come to realize)
7. 法律应该是人民意志的反映。(reflex)

8. 招聘经理经常首先会直截了当地询问面试者的经历、对公司的了解及在岗位上超水平发挥的能力。（excel in）
9. 要懂得，你值得拥有生活所提供的最好的东西，并且你有那么多的东西贡献给这个世界。（contribute to）
10. 看一下董事会的组成，并不惊讶他们中的许多人都有失职。（it should come as no surprise that ...）

Section B Translate the following English paragraph into Chinese.

A Marxist sociologist has argued that racism stems from the class struggle that is unique to the capitalist system — that racial prejudice is generated by capitalists as a means of controlling workers. His thesis works relatively well when applied to discrimination against Blacks in the United States, but his definition of racial prejudice as "racially-based" negative prejudgments against a group generally accepted as a race in any given region of ethnic competition, can be interpreted as also including hostility toward such ethnic groups as the Chinese in California and the Jews in medieval Europe. However, since prejudice against these latter peoples was not inspired by capitalists he has to reason that such antagonisms were not really based on race. He disposes thusly (albeit unconvincingly) of both the intolerance faced by Jews before the rise of capitalism and the early twentieth-century discrimination against Oriental people in California, which, inconveniently, was instigated by workers.

V Topic for Discussion

Racism is a phenomenon that our society is constantly struggling with. However, it seems that this problem cannot be completely eliminated, since some people just have strong inner beliefs and attitude towards people of another race, sex, age, etc. Your main task is to prove that racism is fundamentally wrong. You have to prove that this phenomenon is the cause of numerous conflicts and disagreements in the society.

VI Written Work

Write a short argumentative essay of about 200 words on the following topic. You are required to choose a title by yourselves.

"Can Racial Discrimination Be Eliminated Completely?"

Text B
Why the Story of Muhammad Ali's Rebellion Matters Today

Dave Kreissman

"I am America. I am the past you won't recognize; but get used to me. Black, confident, cocky. My name, not yours. My religion, not yours. My goal, my own. Get used to me."

— *Muhammad Ali*

1   In 1908, Jack Johnson shook up world of boxing, becoming the first African-American heavyweight champion of the world. Determined to prove "that a white man is better than a Negro", former heavyweight champion Jim Jeffries came out of retirement just to fight him. Johnson demolished his opponent, causing riots to break out across the country. No racial event until the assassination of Martin Luther King Jr. would have such a violent reaction. As a black man with unrepentant masculinity and confident assertion of superiority, Johnson embodied the fear of White America. Subsequent African-American boxing champions such as Joe Louis and Floyd Patterson were careful to present themselves as clean, patriotic and non-threatening black men. Louis in particular was beloved by White America for his humility and service in World War II. But Johnson represented the potential that boxing had to shake the racial hierarchy, a potential that would not be realized until Muhammad Ali.

2   The 1960's were a time of tremendous social upheaval in the United States, especially for an African-American man. In addition to the Civil Rights Movement, the Vietnam War had a profound impact on Black America. While blacks only made up 11 percent of the total population, they accounted for 27 percent of those who died in the war. The war was unpopular, but it would be Muhammad Ali, already the most controversial heavyweight champion in history, who would take a stand.

3   Muhammad Ali was the 1960s reincarnation of the ever-feared Jack Johnson and represented an attitude and perspective that has revolutionized American social consciousness through the 1960s to the present day. His radical decisions, particularly his draft refusal, caused much of White America, as well as the black establishment, to portray the boxer as un-American. On the other hand, liberal elites and other radical African-American leaders rallied behind Ali, lauding him as a hero and a martyr. He was considrerd as divisive within the black community. But Ali, through self-discipline and force of personality, forged a new black identity: entitled to agency and confidence. Ali had a singular impact on how Black America came to view itself, and

how White America perceived African Americans and their role in the United States.

4   On January 17, 1942, Cassius Marcellus Clay was born to Odessa O'Grady Clay and Cassius Marcellus Clay. In 1954, at the age of twelve, young Cassius, who had his bike stolen by a local bully, decided to pick up boxing in order to fight back. But it was the murder of Emmett Till in 1955 that left the greatest impression on the young boxing prodigy. As Ali reflected in his later years, seeing the grotesque image of Emmett Till's open casket profoundly scarred the 13-year-old. Furthermore, it was the murder of Emmett Till that forced the young Cassius Clay to recognize the discrimination that he faced and would face as a black man living in Louisville, Kentucky. He was disgusted that a fellow teenage African-American boy living only a few hundred miles away could be brutalized for next to nothing. His mother later maintained that this disgust would bring about a desire for radical change within her eldest son. The treatment of blacks in his hometown and neighboring states convinced Clay that boxing "was the fastest way for a black person to make it in the Unites States". Clay pushed on with his highly promising boxing career, winning many local and regional amateur fights. Yet it would be the call to Rome in 1960 which would set off a course of events that would completely redefine the young boxer and the image of the black man in America.

5   Clay's Olympic journey foreshadowed his future outspokenness. Before departing for the Olympics, 18-year-old Cassius Clay ventured to New York City. In New York's Harlem neighborhood, Clay, for the first time in his life, would witness an African-American man standing in the center of a crowd, advocating for the resistance to White America. It was like nothing the young Kentuckian had seen in all his teenage years. Despite his growing awareness of discrimination within the United States, Clay arrived in Rome proud of his country and ready to compete. He would go on to defeat his Polish opponent, Tadeusz Walasek, in the ring for the light-heavyweight gold medal. Clay was met with resounding applause in both Rome and at a brief stop in New York City. But it was the reaction in his hometown of Louisville that most shocked the 18-year-old. Clay believed for much of his young life that success within the ring would translate to respect when the gloves were off. He received a parade on his return to Louisville, but this glory would be short-lived. Later, Clay and a friend of his sat down at a local restaurant counter only to be threatened: "I done told you. We don't serve no niggers!" It was this event that would bring the young Clay to realize a sense of betrayal at the contradictions of the American dream; he struggled to represent and have pride for a nation which had no respect for him.

6   Soon after his return from Rome, Clay left Louisville to begin working with famed boxing trainer Angelo Dundee. While the young boxer had lived in a black neighborhood in Louisville for his entire life, he had never experienced anything like Overtown in Miami, where Dundee had arranged for his young trainee to board. In the

words of Marvin Dunn, author of *Black Miami in the 1920's*: "Anything you could find in Harlem, you could find in Overtown." This African-American section of Miami was, in fact, a center of black culture and education, as well as a progressive force in the Civil Rights Movement. While racial segregation in Miami was not as harsh as in other Southern urban centers, it was still very much present. Yet with a resource such as Overtown, African-Americans were able to respond to the injustices of segregation in a much more radical way than could the less organized and more repressed blacks of Louisville. Miami, and specifically Overtown, was where Cassius Clay began his transformation into Muhammad Ali and where the radicalization that would lead the boxer to reject his call to fight the war truly took form.

7 Clay's new celebrity also provided him the resources that he needed to experiment with a new persona. At 19, Clay met renowned wrestler "Gorgeous" George Raymond Wagner at a Las Vegas radio station. The then forty-six year-old gaudy professional wrestler ranted about how he would kill his opponent and tear him limb from limb. He then shared a word of advice for the young boxer whose boastfulness at the time paled in comparison: "A lot of people will pay to see someone shut your mouth. So keep on bragging, keep on sassing, and always be outrageous." And young Cassius Clay immediately took these words to heart. This loud and pompous attitude served at first to promote his fights and sell tickets for Cassius Clay, but it would later give Muhammad Ali the voice to challenge authority on the social and racial issues of the era.

8 Cassius Clay continued his training in Miami and both his boxing career and involvement with black activism steadily evolved. From October 29, 1960 to June 18, 1963, the young boxing prodigy managed to win his first nineteen professional fights without tremendous opposition and often with authority. These nineteen victories became the ticket for the rising star to have his true shot at glory and boxing immortality, a shot at the heavyweight title belt. Outside of the ring, Clay's life began a change that many whites and blacks would view as disturbingly radical. Louis Farrakhan stated that it was his album, *A White Man's Heaven Is a Black Man's Hell*, that truly pushed the boxer to seriously consider the Black Muslim movement. In addition, the Kentucky native was now surrounded by a much more urbanized Miami where the Black Muslims had an environment to thrive. Like the Black Muslims, and unlike the National Association for the Advancement of Colored People (NAACP) Cassius did not want to overcome someday, he desired to overcome yesterday. And what had the most profound impact on Clay's conversion to Islam, and perhaps the most tremendous influence of his life, was a minister of the Nation of Islam, Malcolm X.

9 Malcolm X completely transformed Clay's belief system, political intelligence, and ultimately his name. Malcolm served as more than just a mentor and religious leader for the former Olympic champion, but also acted as an older sibling. While they were both astonishingly charismatic, the thirty-seven year-old Omaha, Nebraska native

possessed a certain wisdom and poise that genuinely attracted the young Cassius. Furthermore, the sense of freedom that was to be attained by joining the Black Muslim cause was tremendously appealing for the soon-to-be Muhammad Ali. He dreamed throughout his teenage years that success in the ring would ultimately lead to respect wherever he traveled, but the reality was that no black man, even if he were an Olympic gold medalist, could sit down at a Louisville lunch counter and order a burger and fries. Clay recognized that White American society often repressed him, and he sought a way to rise up. He found this in the Nation of Islam. Under the wing of Malcolm X and Nation of Islam leader Elijah Muhammad, Cassius began to believe that Christianity contributed to constraining the black man in the United States; Christianity turned Africans into slaves while Islam could change slaves into powerful black people. Furthermore, an exclusively black group that preached black supremacy and that African-Americans should be proud of themselves, would be extremely appealing to the young Clay who felt like he had been grossly mistreated. Needless to say, the Black Muslims seemed like a tremendous threat to white society and the work of NAACP as well. As Clay's bout against the then-heavyweight champion of the world Sonny Liston approached, the status of the contender's political and religious ideology came into question. He would soon shock the world, both within and outside of the boxing ring.

10   As the loudmouth Clay garnered attention for his upcoming fight with the seemingly unbeatable Sonny Liston, the social and racial turmoil of the Civil Rights Movement erupted on a whole new scale. April 1963 saw massive demonstrations in Birmingham, Alabama, resulting in the arrest of Martin Luther King and thousands of other blacks protesting segregation. August of that year saw the historic march on Washington, attracting a quarter of a million people from all over the country. The march pushed President John Fitzgerald Kennedy toward support for broad Civil Rights legislation. In November, Lee Harvey Oswald assassinated the forty-six year-old President while in Dallas, Texas. It was impossible, especially as an African-American at this time, to not have been profoundly affected by the turbulence of events unfolding throughout 1963 and 1964. This chaos was the background for the soon-to-be historic Cassius Clay vs Sonny Liston match.

11   Clay's patrons at the Louisville Sponsoring Group, which had underwritten his professional career, advised their star to keep his passion for Islam out of the press. Yet rumors of Cassius's connection to the movement, as well as his friendship with Malcolm X, continuously swirled in anticipation of the Liston fight. Many of the young boxer's patrons believed that the discovery of Clay's religious affiliation might offend White America and cause the fight to be called off. However, Cassius never confirmed his involvement, and February 25, 1964 arrived without a cancellation of the big fight. Clay entered the weigh-in with the utmost bombasity on the morning of February the 25th. He had displayed playful immaturity and ridiculous banter in his early career and

leading up to the fight, but even in the face of Liston, hours before the biggest fight of his life, Cassius Clay was as convincingly mad and dangerously outrageous as he had ever been. At this point, the entire United States was his stage, and he responded by building up his act even more. He shouted at Liston, predicting that the heavyweight champion would hang up the gloves after six rounds. He ranted to the press, proclaiming that he had to be restrained as his staff held him back. His attitude was unlike anything that America, much less the boxing world, had ever seen from a black man, and Clay gleamed in the spotlight. He entered boxing at a time when a black fighter was expected to behave himself with complete obedience to white sensibilities, but he could not have been further from the expectation bestowed upon him.

12 The general consensus heading into the fight was that Liston, nicknamed the Bear, would easily finish off the Louisville Lip without much contention. However, after seven rounds of sweat and surprise in the ring, Clay emerged as the victor by way of technical knockout. This nearly unparalleled underdog victory catapulted the soon-to-be Muhammad Ali to a level of fame, both in America and internationally, that he had never experienced before. It would not be the only time he would "shake up the world", the phrase he hollered into a camera broadcasting nationally seconds after the conclusion of the fight.

13 While the match to this day stands as one of the most significant in the history of boxing, the press conference the day after had a much more profound cultural impact. After his defeat of Sonny Liston, the masses and the media could not dismiss the young Cassius Clay as an overly hyped up loudmouth in the same way they could before the fight. While this one fight may not have been Liston's best performance, the kid from Kentucky looked like a legitimate champion. The heavyweight title belt allowed Clay to take the stage and announce to the press that he did indeed have affiliations with the Nation of Islam and that he had changed his name from Cassius Marcellus Clay to Cassius X, which served as a temporary moniker until Elijah Muhammad bequeathed to him the name Muhammad Ali. Later, when asked about his name, Ali informed the press: "Cassius Clay is my slave name! Clay means dirt. I didn't choose it and I don't want it. I am Muhammad Ali, a free name — Muhammad means free and Ali means most high." He asked the press to respect his name change and to refer to him as Muhammad Ali in the future. But he would soon learn that "Muhammad Ali" would transcend a mere name; it would instead have serious racial and social implications for both White and Black America.

Notes

1. About the author and the text.

Dave Kreissman, grown up in a New York sports family and New York Sports world, and educated at Northwestern University, is an award winning sports analyst and a contributing Writer at *the Huffington Post* since July 2013. He publishes columns regularly on sports and political topics. He was selected to write for *HuffPo Teen*, later promoted to Sports and Politics areas on main site. Articles are frequently retweeted and cited in other media. (http://www.huffingtonpost.com/dave-kreissman)

As we recognize that American sports and culture are not a "post-racial society" after all, it's important to look back at the '60s, the era where there was perhaps the greatest change in the relationship between African-Americans and White America. This article is the first and second of several about the meaning of Muhammad Ali in America and the world. Furthermore, Ali's embrace of Islam resonates in light of today's confrontations.

2. **Civil Rights Movement** (Para. 2)

The African-American Civil Rights Movement or 1960s Civil Rights Movement encompasses social movements in the United States whose goals were to end racial segregation and discrimination against black Americans and to secure legal recognition and federal protection of the citizenship rights enumerated in the Constitution and federal law. This article covers the phase of the movement between 1954 and 1968, particularly in the South.

The movement was characterized by major campaigns of civil resistance. Between 1955 and 1968, acts of nonviolent protest and civil disobedience produced crisis situations and productive dialogues between activists and government authorities. Federal, state, and local governments, businesses, and communities often had to respond immediately to these situations that highlighted the inequities faced by African Americans. Forms of protest and/or civil disobedience included boycotts such as the successful Montgomery Bus Boycott (1955 — 1956) in Alabama; "sit-ins" such as the influential Greensboro sit-ins (1960) in North Carolina; marches, such as the Selma to Montgomery marches (1965) in Alabama; and a wide range of other nonviolent activities.

3. **The Vietnam War** (Para. 2)

The Vietnam War, also known as the Second Indochina War, and also known in Vietnam as Resistance War Against America or simply the American War, was a Cold War-era proxy war that occurred in Vietnam, Laos, and Cambodia from 1 November 1955 to the fall of Saigon on 30 April 1975. This war followed the First Indochina War (1946 — 1954) and was fought between North Vietnam — supported by the Soviet Union, China and other communist allies — and the government of South Vietnam — supported by the United States and other anti-communist allies.

Direct U.S. military involvement ended on 15 August 1973 as a result of the Case-Church Amendment passed by the U.S. Congress. The capture of Saigon by the North Vietnamese Army in April 1975 marked the end of the war, and North and South

Vietnam were reunified the following year. The war exacted a huge human cost in terms of fatalities. Estimates of the number of Vietnamese service members and civilians killed vary from 800,000 to 3.1 million. Some 200,000 — 300,000 Cambodians, 20,000 — 200,000 Laotians, and 58,220 U.S. service members also died in the conflict.

4. **Jack Johnson** (Para. 3)

John Arthur "Jack" Johnson (March 31, 1878 — June 10, 1946), was an American boxer, who — at the height of the Jim Crow era — became the first African American world heavyweight boxing champion (1908 — 1915). Johnson was faced with much controversy when he was charged with violating the Mann Act in 1912, even though there was an obvious lack of evidence and the charge was largely racially based. In a documentary about his life, Ken Burns notes that "for more than thirteen years, Jack Johnson was the most famous and the most notorious African-American on Earth".

5. **Cassius Marcellus Clay** (Para. 4)

Muhammad Ali (born Cassius Marcellus Clay, Jr.; January 17, 1942) is an American former professional boxer, generally considered among the greatest heavyweights in the sport's history. A controversial and polarizing figure during his early career, Ali is today widely regarded for the skills he displayed in the ring plus the values he exemplified outside of it: religious freedom, racial justice and the triumph of principle over expedience. He is one of the most recognized sports figures of the past 100 years, crowned "Sportsman of the Century" by Sports Illustrated and "Sports Personality of the Century" by the BBC.

6. **Emmett Till** (Para. 4)

Emmett Louis Till (July 25, 1941 — August 28, 1955) was an African-American teenager who was murdered in Mississippi at the age of 14 after reportedly flirting with a white woman. Till was from Chicago, Illinois, visiting his relatives in Money, Mississippi, in the Mississippi Delta region, when he spoke to 21-year-old Carolyn Bryant, the married proprietor of a small grocery store there. Several nights later, Bryant's husband Roy and his half-brother J. W. Milam went to Till's great-uncle's house. They took Till away to a barn, where they beat him and gouged out one of his eyes, before shooting him through the head and disposing of his body in the Tallahatchie River, weighting it with a 70-pound (32 kg) cotton gin fan tied around his neck with barbed wire. Three days later, Till's body was discovered and retrieved from the river. Till's body was returned to Chicago. His mother, who had raised him mostly by herself, insisted on a public funeral service with an open casket to show the world the brutality of the killing. "The open-coffin funeral held by Mamie Till Bradley exposed the world to more than her son Emmett Till's bloated, mutilated body. Her decision focused attention not only on American racism and the barbarism of lynching but also on the limitations and vulnerabilities of American democracy." The trial attracted a vast amount of press attention. In September 1955, Bryant and Milam were acquitted of Till's kidnapping and murder. Protected against double jeopardy, Bryant and Milam publicly admitted in an interview with *Look* magazine that they killed Till. Till's murder is noted as a pivotal event motivating the African-American Civil Rights Movement.

7. **George Raymond Wagner** (Para. 7)

George Raymond Wagner (March 24, 1915 — December 26, 1963) was an American professional wrestler best known by his ring name Gorgeous George. In the United States, during the First Golden Age of Professional Wrestling in the 1940s — 1950s, Gorgeous George gained mainstream popularity and became one of the biggest stars of this period, gaining media attention for his outrageous character, which was described as flamboyant and charismatic. He was inducted into Professional Wrestling Hall of Fame in 2002 and the WWE Hall of Fame as part of the Class of 2010.

8. **Louis Farrakhan** (Para. 8)

Louis Farrakhan Muhammad, Sr. (born Louis Eugene Wolcott; May 11, 1933, and formerly known as Louis X) is the leader of the religious group Nation of Islam (NOI). He served as the minister of major mosques in Boston and Harlem, and was appointed by the longtime NOI leader, Elijah Muhammad, as the National Representative of the Nation of Islam. Farrakhan is a black religious and social leader. Farrakhan has been both praised and widely criticized for his often controversial political views and outspoken rhetorical style. He has been criticized for remarks that have been perceived as antisemitic, anti-white and prejudiced against gays. Over recent years, however, Farrakhan has been very active, including delivering weekly online sermons throughout 2013 as well as speaking at both large public NOI events as well as smaller venues.

9. **NAACP** (Para. 8)

The National Association for the Advancement of Colored People (NAACP) is an African-American civil rights organization in the United States, formed in 1909. Its mission is "to ensure the political, educational, social, and economic equality of rights of all persons and to eliminate racial hatred and racial discrimination".

10. **Malcolm X** (Para. 8)

Malcolm X (May 19, 1925 — February 21, 1965), born Malcolm Little, was an African-American Muslim minister and a human rights activist. To his admirers he was a courageous advocate for the rights of blacks, a man who indicted white America in the harshest terms for its crimes against black Americans; detractors accused him of preaching racism and violence. He has been called one of the greatest and most influential African Americans in history. In 1946, at age 20, he went to prison for larceny and breaking and entering. While in prison he became a member of the Nation of Islam, and after his parole in 1952 he quickly rose to become one of its leaders. For a dozen years he was the public face of the controversial group; in keeping with the Nation's teachings he espoused black supremacy, advocated the separation of black and white Americans and scoffed at the civil rights movements emphasis on integration. In February 1965, shortly after repudiating the Nation of Islam, he was assassinated by three of its members. *The Autobiography of Malcolm X*, published shortly after his death, is considered one of the most influential nonfiction books of the 20th century.

11. **Elijah Muhammad** (Para. 9)

Elijah Muhammad (born Elijah Robert Poole; October 7, 1897 — February 25, 1975) was an African-American religious leader, who led the Nation of Islam (NOI) from 1934 until his death in 1975. He was a mentor to Malcolm X, Louis Farrakhan, Muhammad Ali, and his son, Warith Deen Muhammed.

12. **Sonny Liston** (Para. 9)

Charles L. "Sonny" Liston (died on December 30, 1970) was an American professional boxer known for his toughness, punching power and intimidating appearance. He became World Heavyweight Champion in 1962 by knocking out Floyd Patterson in the first round. The two fights between Muhammad Ali and Sonny Liston for boxing's World Heavyweight Championship were among the most anticipated, watched and controversial fights in the sport's history. The first bout was held in February 1964 in Miami Beach, Florida. Ali (then Clay) won when Liston gave up at the opening of the seventh round (after being clearly dominated in the sixth). Their second fight was in May 1965 in Lewiston, Maine.

13. **Martin Luther King** (Para. 10)

Martin Luther King, Jr., (January 15, 1929 — April 4, 1968) was an American pastor, activist, humanitarian, and leader in the African-American Civil Rights Movement. He is best known for his role in the advancement of civil rights using nonviolent civil disobedience based on his Christian beliefs. In 1968, King was planning a national occupation of Washington, D. C., to be called the Poor People's Campaign, when he was assassinated on April 4 in Memphis, Tennessee. His death was followed by riots in many U. S. cities. Allegations that James Earl Ray, the man convicted of killing King, had been framed or acted in concert with government agents persisted for decades after the shooting.

14. President **John Fitzgerald Kennedy** (Para. 10)

John Fitzgerald Kennedy (May 29, 1917 — November 22, 1963), commonly known as Jack Kennedy or by his initials JFK, was an American politician who served as the 35th President of the United States from January 1961 until his assassination in November 1963. Notable events that occurred during his presidency included the Bay of Pigs Invasion, the Cuban Missile Crisis, the Space Race — by initiating Project Apollo (which later culminated in the moon landings), the building of the Berlin Wall, the African-American Civil Rights Movement, and the increased US involvement in the Vietnam War. Kennedy was assassinated in Dallas, Texas on November 22, 1963. Lee Harvey Oswald was arrested that afternoon and charged with the crime that night. Jack

Ruby shot and killed Oswald two days later, before a trial could take place. The FBI and the Warren Commission officially concluded that Oswald was the lone assassin. The United States House Select Committee on Assassinations (HSCA) agreed with the conclusion that Oswald fired the shots which killed the president, but also concluded that Kennedy was probably assassinated as the result of a conspiracy.

Questions for Discussion

1. What has the story of Muhammad Ali's rebellion enlightened you?
2. In 1950s, what forced the young Cassius Clay to recognize the discrimination that he faced?
3. Who influenced Ali's belief system and political intelligence in 1960s?
4. Why did Ali change his name from Cassius Marcellus Clay to Muhammad Ali?

Memorable Quotes

1. I refuse to accept the view that mankind is so tragically bound to the starless midnight of racism and war that the bright daybreak of peace and brotherhood can never become a reality… I believe that unarmed truth and unconditional love will have the final word.

    — Martin Luther King, Jr.

2. Hating people because of their color is wrong. And it doesn't matter which color does the hating. It's just plain wrong.

    — Muhammad Ali

3. No human race is superior; no religious faith is inferior. All collective judgments are wrong. Only racists make them.

    — Elie Wiesel

4. Ignorance and prejudice are the handmaidens of propaganda. Our mission, therefore, is to confront ignorance with knowledge, bigotry with tolerance, and isolation with the outstretched hand of generosity. Racism can, will, and must be defeated.

    — Kofi Annan

5. The white man's happiness cannot be purchased by the black man's misery.

    — Frederick Douglas

6. That's just how white folks will do you. It wasn't merely the cruelty involved; I was learning that black people could be mean and then some. It was a particular brand of arrogance, an obtuseness in otherwise sane people that brought forth our bitter laughter. It was as if whites didn't know they were being cruel in the first place. Or at least thought you deserved of their scorn.

    — Barack Obama

7. However much history may be invoked in support of these policies (affirmative action), no policy can apply to history but can only apply to the present or the future. The past may be many things, but it is clearly irrevocable. Its sins can no more be purged than its achievements can be expunged. Those who suffered in centuries past are as much beyond our help as those who sinned are beyond our retribution.

— Thomas Sowell

Further Readings

1. Alan Marsh et Melahat Sahin-Dikmen, the Eruope Opinion Research Group (EEIG), *Discrimination in Europe*
2. Vanessa Chuaa, *Can Prejudice Ever Be Eliminated?*
3. Matt Novak, *Oregon Was Founded as a Racist Utopia*
4. Barack Obama, *Dreams from My Father: A Story of Race and Inheritance*

Unit 10

Pre-reading Questions
1. Does the human body have anything to do with politics?
2. What do you think is body politics?
3. What do you think of the slogan "The personal is the political"?

Text A

Body Politics

Anonymous

1. The term "body politics" refers to the practices and policies through which powers of society regulate the human body, as well as the struggle over the degree of individual and social control of the body. The powers at play in body politics include institutional power expressed in government and laws, disciplinary power exacted in economic production, discretionary power exercised in consumption, and personal power negotiated in intimate relations. Individuals and movements engage in body politics when they seek to alleviate the oppressive effects of institutional and interpersonal power on those whose bodies are marked as inferior or who are denied rights to control their own bodies.

2. Scholarly research on body politics was greatly influenced by French philosopher Michel Foucault (*Discipline and Punish*, 1977), who used the terms "biopower" and "anatomo-politics" to refer to the insinuation of governmental and institutional power into people's everyday activities. He argued that such power shapes people's subjectivity — their sense of themselves as persons. From Foucault's point of view, disciplinary mechanisms such as prisons, as well as medical knowledge and the education system, provide the discourse, ideas, resources, and procedures through which individuals come to know who they are and through which they learn to conform to the social and political order. What begins as externally imposed discipline becomes internalized, such that individuals become their own disciplinarians. Even though Foucault's work represents human subjectivity as caught in the thrall of discourses that impose meaning and shape action, inherent in body politics is the optimistic possibility that by changing the body's relationship to power, one might change the expression of power in society. Using the concept of body politics, scholars have studied the status of women and racial minorities, and somatic or body norms generated in particular cultures (and individuals' appropriation or rejection of them), as well as the regulation of the body through hygiene, medicine, law, and sports.

Feminism and Body Politics

3. Body politics was first used in this sense in the 1970s, during the "second wave" of the feminist movement in the United States. It arose out of feminist politics and the abortion debates. Body politics originally involved the fight against objectification of the female body, and violence against women and girls, and the

campaign for reproductive rights for women. "The personal is the political" became a slogan that captured the sense that domestic contests for equal rights in the home and within sexual relationships are crucial to the struggle for equal rights in the public. This form of body politics emphasized a woman's power and authority over her own body. Many feminists rejected practices that draw attention to differences between male and female bodies, refusing to shave their legs and underarms and rejecting cosmetics and revealing, form-fitting clothing. The book *Our Bodies, Our Selves*, published in 1973, aimed to widen and deepen women's knowledge of the workings of the female body, thus allowing women to be more active in pursuit of their sexual pleasure and reproductive health.

  4 Second-wave feminist body politics promoted breaking the silence about rape, sexual abuse, and violence against women and girls, which many interpreted as extreme examples of socially sanctioned male power. The feminists who followed at the end of the twentieth century accepted this stance on rape and violence against women and girls, but they found the gender ideals of second-wave feminists too confining. Members of this generation, sometimes called third-wave feminists or post-feminists, endorse a range of body modification and gender practices that include butch-fem gender roles, gender-blending, transgender lifestyles, transsexual surgeries, body piercing, and tattoos.

  5 Women's bodies were the political battleground of the abortion debates. A protracted struggle to establish a woman's right to terminate her pregnancy was won when the U. S. Supreme Court upheld the right to abortion in the case of Roe v. Wade in 1974. Almost immediately after that decision, anti-abortion (also called pro-life) activists began protesting against this extension of women's reproductive rights. Anti-abortion advocates likened aborting a fetus to murder, while pro-abortion advocates (also called pro-choice) pointed to the legion of women who had died in illegal abortions, and to the many more who would doubtlessly follow them if abortion were to become illegal again. In that adversaries square off over the issue of individual versus social control of a woman's pregnancy, the abortion debates are prime examples of body politics.

  6 Debates about laws and women's bodies sparked the interests of other groups of women who felt that government or institutional power had unfairly exercised control over their bodies or that society should take greater responsibility for the care and protection of women and children. Noting that the abortion debates were about whether or not to have a child, activists pointed to policies and practices that denied reproduction to women in minority communities, especially the forced sterilization of Native Americans. Activists from both sides of the abortion debates joined in to press for employment rights for pregnant women and for maternity and paternity leave for new parents. Arguing that the laws and ethics governing commercial sex transactions were outdated, organizations

of prostitutes argued for decriminalization of their work.

Racial Body Politics

7 The study of colonial policies and practices has been a particularly prolific area of scholarship on body politics. Colonialism produced body politics intended to create acquiescent subjects, and it was, in part, successful. But colonialism also inspired resistance and revolution. The bodies of colonial subjects built the colonial infrastructure, fueled its economy, and bought its products. Clothing, in specified styles and patterns, and soaps and oils advertised and sold by colonizers pulled colonized bodies into the moral and aesthetic spheres of the colonizers. Colonized people were often treated as disease vectors, necessitating residential segregation and public health programs to ensure the health and well-being of the colonizers. Colonial administrations grouped colonized people according to race and tribe and used these distinctions to control their access to rights and resources. In some cultures, body politics took a supernatural turn, as the spirits of colonizers were believed to take over the bodies of former colonial subjects. This spirit possession highlights cultural memory and the embodiment of political power. Anti-colonial movements rejected colonial rules of deference, fought for political sovereignty, revived older demonstrations of respect, and instituted new policies and practices to regulate the human body.

8 The attribution of ethical, moral, temperamental, and social characteristics to individuals or populations based on skin color, facial features, body types, and sexual anatomy figure prominently in racial body politics. This practice is most pronounced in the United States in racism against African Americans. As African people were turned into commodities in the Atlantic slave trade, western countries used bodily differences to justify African subjugation. According to racist logic, dark skin was at the negative pole in the dichotomy of white and good versus black and evil, broad facial features denote licentiousness and lack of intelligence, and the brawny bodies of black men and women cry out for hard labor. Other populations have also been subject to negative characterizations. For example, the bodies of Mexicans are supposedly built low for farm labor, while the "delicate, nimble" fingers of Asian women supposedly suit them for fine work such as computer-chip manufacture.

9 Because body politics covers the power to control bodies on the one hand, and resistance and protest against such powers on the other hand, body politics can both uphold and challenge racism. In the United States, the civil rights movement unseated the predominant racial body politics in abolishing Jim Crow laws and abating racial segregation. The slogan "Black is Beautiful" heralded a moment in the 1960s when African Americans pointedly attributed positive values to black physical features. Body politics during that time included wearing hair in a natural, unprocessed "Afro" and donning African-inspired clothing. Remnants of this politics remain in those who

attribute positive social and psychological qualities to melanin, the pigment that causes dark skin.

10 A major challenge to racial body politics came from within the feminist movement. In the 1970s, Black, Latina, Native American, and Asian feminists insisted that an inclusive feminism examine and redress the historic evaluations of bodily difference that structured oppression of women according to race. Women of color objected to the narrow construction of gender politics by white feminists, and they moved to include the differences that race, class, and sexuality make in women's position in society. The welfare mothers' movement, radical lesbians of color, and black feminist theorists were among those to call attention to the ways in which race inflected feminism. The 1981 anthology *This Bridge Called My Back* captured the physical nature of the social and cultural experience of women of color who tried to bridge the gap between nationalist movements where sexism flourished and the feminist movement's singular concentration on gender. The editors, Cherie Moraga and Gloria Anzaldúa (1942—2004) are celebrated writers, theorists, and activists, who in this influential, transformative volume brought together poetry, critical and reflective essays, and photographs of artwork by noted women of color. *This Bridge Called My Back* contained the first publication of Audre Lorde's (1934—1992) essay, "The Master's Tools Will Never Dismantle the Master's House," which, along with her essays on breaking silence and the erotic as power, were crucial in forging a language of body politics for women of color and lesbian feminists. This push within the feminist movement contributed to the inclusive politics of diversity and multiculturalism in the United States.

Notes

1. About the text.

This article is taken from Online Encyclopedia and the author is anonymous.

2. Scholarly research on body politics was greatly influenced by French philosopher **Michel Foucault** (*Discipline and Punish*, 1977), who used the terms "bio-power" and "anatomo-politics" to refer to the insinuation of governmental and institutional power into people's everyday activities. (Para. 2)

Michel Foucault was a French philosopher, historian of ideas, social theorist, philologist and literary critic. His theories addressed the relationship between power and knowledge, and how they are used as a form of social control through societal institutions. Though often cited as a post-structuralist and postmodernist, Foucault rejected these labels, preferring to present his thought as a critical history of modernity. His thought has been highly influential for both academic and activist groups.

Discipline and Punish, a book by Michel Foucault, is an analysis of the social and theoretical mechanisms behind the massive changes that occurred in Western penal systems during the modern age and it focuses on historical documents from France. Foucault argues against the idea that the prison became the consistent form of punishment due mainly to the humanitarian concerns of reformists. He traces the cultural shifts that led to the prison's dominance, focusing on the body and questions of power. Prison is a form used by the "disciplines", a new technological power, which can also be found, according to Foucault, in places such as schools, hospitals, and military barracks.

3. Body politics was first used in this sense in the 1970s, during the "second wave" of the **feminist** movement in the United States. (Para. 3)

Feminism is a collection of movements and ideologies that share a common stated aim: to define, establish, and defend equal political, economic, cultural, and social rights for women.

The history of the modern western feminist movements is divided into three "waves". Each wave dealt with different aspects of the same feminist issues. The first wave comprised women's suffrage movements of the nineteenth and early twentieth centuries, promoting women's right to vote. The second wave was associated with the ideas and actions of the women's liberation movement beginning in the 1960s. The second wave campaigned for legal and social equality for women. The third wave is a continuation of, and a reaction to, the perceived failures of second-wave feminism, beginning in the 1990s.

4. "**The personal is the political**" became a slogan that captured the sense that domestic contests for equal rights in the home and within sexual relationships are crucial to the struggle for equal rights in the public. (Para. 3)

The personal is political, also termed the private is political, is a political argument used as a rallying slogan of student movement and second-wave feminism from the late 1960s. It underscored the connections between personal experience and larger social and political structures. In the context of the feminist movement of the 1960s and 1970s, it was a challenge to the nuclear family and family values. The phrase has been repeatedly described as a defining characterization of second-wave feminism, radical feminism, Women's Studies, or feminism in general. It differentiated the second-wave feminism of the 1960s and 1970s from the early feminism of the 1920s, which was concerned with achieving the right to vote for women.

5. The book *Our Bodies, Our Selves*, published in 1973, aimed to widen and deepen women's knowledge of the workings of the female body, thus allowing women to be more active in pursuit of their sexual pleasure and reproductive health. (Para. 3)

Our Bodies, Our Selves is a book about women's health and sexuality produced by the nonprofit organization Our Bodies Ourselves (originally called the Boston Women's Health Book Collective). First published in 1971, it contains information related to many aspects of women's health and sexuality, including sexual health, sexual orientation, gender identity, birth control, abortion, pregnancy and birth, violence and abuse and menopause.

6. Members of this generation, sometimes called third-wave feminists or post-feminists, endorse a range of body modification and gender practices that include **butch-fem** gender roles, gender-blending, transgender lifestyles, transsexual surgeries, body piercing, and tattoos. (Para. 4)

Butch-fem, also butch and femme, is a term used to describe individual gender identities in the lesbian, gay, bisexual, transgender and cross-dressing subcultures to ascribe or acknowledge a masculine (butch) or feminine (femme) identity with its associated traits, behaviors, styles, self-perception and so on.

7. A protracted struggle to establish a woman's right to terminate her pregnancy was won when the U. S. Supreme Court upheld the right to abortion in the case of **Roe v. Wade** in 1974. (Para. 5)

The case of Roe v. Wade: the American Supreme Court issued its decision on January 22, 1973, with a 7-to-2 majority vote in favor of Roe. Burger and Douglas' concurring opinions and White's dissenting opinion were issued along with the Court's opinion in Doe v. Bolton (announced on the same day as Roe v. Wade). The Court deemed abortion a fundamental right under the United States Constitution, thereby subjecting all laws attempting to restrict it to the standard of strict scrutiny.

8. In the United States, the civil rights movement unseated the predominant racial body politics in abolishing **Jim Crow** laws and abating racial segregation. (Para. 9)

Jim Crow laws were racial segregation laws enacted after the Reconstruction period in Southern United States, at state and local levels, and which continued in force until 1965, which mandated the racial segregation in all public facilities in Southern states of the former Confederacy, with, starting in 1890, a "separate but equal" status for African Americans. The separation in practice led to conditions for African Americans that were inferior to those provided for white Americans, systematizing a number of economic, educational and social disadvantages.

9. The 1981 anthology *This Bridge Called My Back* captured the physical nature of the social and cultural experience of women of color who tried to bridge the gap between nationalist movements where sexism flourished and the feminist movement's singular concentration on gender. (Para. 10)

This Bridge Called My Back: *Writings by Radical Women of Color* is a feminist anthology edited by Cherie Moraga and Gloria Anzaldúa. It centered on the experiences of women of color, offering a serious challenge to white feminists who made claims to solidarity based on sisterhood. Writings in the anthology, along with works by other prominent feminists of color, call for a greater prominence within feminism for race-related subjectivities, and ultimately laid the foundation for third wave feminism.

10. *This Bridge Called My Back* contained the first publication of **Audre Lorde's**

(1934—1992) essay, "The Master's Tools Will Never Dismantle the Master's House," which along with her essays... (Para. 10)

Audre Lorde was a Caribbean-American writer, radical feminist, womanist, lesbian, and civil rights activist. Lorde served as an inspiration to women worldwide, one of her most notable efforts being her activist work with Afro-German women in the 1980s. Her identity as a black lesbian gave her work a novel perspective and put her in a unique position to speak on issues surrounding civil rights, feminism, and oppression. Her work gained both wide acclaim and wide criticism, due to the elements of social liberalism and sexuality presented in her work and her emphasis on revolution and change.

In her 1984 essay "The Master's Tools Will Never Dismantle the Master's House", Lorde attacked underlying racism within feminism, describing it as unrecognized dependence on the patriarchy. She argued that, by denying difference in the category of women, white feminists merely passed on old systems of oppression and that, in so doing, they were preventing any real, lasting change. Her argument aligned white feminists with white male slave-masters, describing both as "agents of oppression".

Glossary

abate [ə'beɪt] v.	make less active or intense
abortion [ə'bɔːʃn] n.	termination of pregnancy; failure of a plan
acquiescent [ækwɪ'esnt] a.	willing to carry out the orders or wishes of another without protest
alleviate [ə'liːvɪeɪt] v.	make easier
anatomy [ə'nætəmɪ] n.	the branch of morphology that deals with the structure of animals
appropriation [əprəʊprɪ'eɪʃn] n.	a deliberate act of acquisition of something, often without the permission of the owner
brawny ['brɔːnɪ] a.	possessing physical strength and weight; rugged and powerful
butch-fem n.	See note "butch and femme"
cosmetics [kɒz'metɪks] n.	a toiletry designed to beautify the body
decriminalization n.	legislation that makes something legal that was formerly illegal
deference ['defərəns] n.	a disposition or tendency to yield to the will of others
dichotomy [daɪ'kɒtəmɪ] n.	being twofold; a classification into two opposed parts or subclasses
disciplinarian [dɪsəplɪ'neərɪən] n.	someone who demands exact conformity to rules and forms

disciplinary [ˈdɪsəplɪnərɪ] a.   designed to promote discipline
discretionary [dɪˈskreʃənərɪ] a.   having or using the ability to act or decide according to your own discretion or judgment
dismantle [dɪsˈmæntl] v.   take off or remove
don v.   put clothing on one's body
embodiment [ɪmˈbɒdɪmənt] n.   giving concrete form to an abstract concept
endorse [ɪnˈdɔːs] v.   give support or one's approval to
erotic [ɪˈrɒtɪk] a.   giving sexual pleasure; sexually arousing
exact [ɪgˈzækt] v.   claim as due or just;
extension [ɪkˈstenʃn] n.   the spreading of something (a belief or practice) into new regions
fetus [ˈfiːtəs] n.   an unborn or unhatched vertebrate in the later stages of development showing the main recognizable features of the mature animal
flourish [ˈflʌrɪʃ] v.   grow vigorously; make steady progress; be at the high point in one's career
hygiene [ˈhaɪdʒiːn] n.   a condition promoting sanitary practices
inclusive [ɪnˈkluːsɪv] a.   including much or everything; and especially including stated limits
inflect [ɪnˈflekt] v.   turn from a course or a specified alignment; bend
infrastructure [ˈɪnfrəstrʌktʃə] n.   the basic structure or features of a system or organization
insinuation [ɪnsɪnjuˈeɪʃn] n.   the act of gaining acceptance or affection for yourself by persuasive and subtle blandishments
institute [ˈɪnstɪtjuːt] v.   set up or lay the groundwork for
institutional [ɪnstɪˈtjuːʃnl] a.   relating to or constituting or involving an institution
legion [ˈliːdʒən] n.   a large military unit
lesbian [ˈlezbɪən] n.   a female homosexual
licentious [laɪˈsenʃəs] a.   lewd and lascivious
liken [ˈlaɪkən] v.   consider or describe as similar, equal, or analogous
maternity [məˈtɜːnətɪ] n.   the state of being pregnant; the period from conception to birth when a woman carries a developing fetus in her uterus
melanin [ˈmelənɪn] n.   insoluble pigments that account for the color of e. g. skin and scales and feathers
necessitate [nəˈsesɪteɪt] v.   make sth. necessary
nimble [ˈnɪmbl] a.   moving quickly and lightly
objectify [əbˈdʒektɪfaɪ] a.   make impersonal or present as an object
pigment [ˈpɪgmənt] n.   any substance whose presence in plant or animal

	tissues produces a characteristic color
pregnancy ['pregnənsɪ] n.	the state of being pregnant
protract [prə'trækt] v.	lengthen in time; cause to be or last longer
redress [rɪ'dres] v.	make reparations or amends for
revealing [rɪ'viːlɪŋ] a.	showing one's body
sanction ['sæŋkʃn] v.	give authority or permission to
singular ['sɪŋgjələ] a.	being a single and separate person or thing; unusual or striking
somatic [səʊ'mætɪk] a.	affecting or characteristic of the body as opposed to the mind or spirit
sovereignty ['sɒvrəntɪ] n.	royal authority; the dominion of a monarch
stance [stæns] n.	a rationalized mental attitude
sterilization [sterəlaɪ'zeɪʃn] n.	the act of making an organism barren or infertile (unable to reproduce)
subjugation [sʌbdʒʊ'geɪʃn] n.	the act of subjugating by cruelty
temperamental a.	relating to or caused by temperament
thrall [θrɔːl] n.	the state of being under the control of another person
transgender n.	involving a partial or full reversal of gender
unseat v.	remove from political office
uphold [ʌp'həʊld] v.	keep or maintain in unaltered condition; support

Comprehension Questions

Answer the following questions after reading the text.

1. How does the disciplinary power relate to people's sense of themselves, according to Michel Foucault?
2. What are the differences between the second-wave and the third-wave feminist body politics?
3. What do you think of the statement that women's bodies were the political battleground of the abortion debates?
4. How does body politics interact with racism?
5. What is the major challenge to racial body politics which came from within the feminist movement?

Exercises

I Vocabulary
Section A Paraphrase the following sentences chosen from the text.
1. The powers at play in body politics include institutional power expressed in

government and laws, disciplinary power exacted in economic production, discretionary power exercised in consumption, and personal power negotiated in intimate relations. (Para. 1)

2. Even though Foucault's work represents human subjectivity as caught in the thrall of discourses that impose meaning and shape action, inherent in body politics is the optimistic possibility that by changing the body's relationship to power, one might change the expression of power in society. (Para. 2)
3. Anti-abortion advocates likened aborting a fetus to murder, while pro-abortion advocates (also called pro-choice) pointed to the legion of women who had died in illegal abortions, and to the many more who would doubtlessly follow them if abortion were to become illegal again. (Para. 5)
4. The attribution of ethical, moral, temperamental, and social characteristics to individuals or populations based on skin color, facial features, body types, and sexual anatomy figure prominently in racial body politics. (Para. 8)
5. *This Bridge Called My Back* contained the first publication of Audre Lorde's essay, "The Master's Tools Will Never Dismantle the Master's House," which along with her essays on breaking silence and the erotic as power were crucial in forging a language of body politics for women of color and lesbian feminists. (Para. 10)

Section B There are ten sentences in this section. Beneath each sentence there are four words or phrases marked A, B, C and D. Choose one word or phrase that best completes the sentence.

1. This unexpected _____ deprived the unfortunate mother of her chance of being a mother.
   A. abortion   B. miscarriage   C. delivery   D. birth
2. Alcohol functions as the medicine which can only _____ his pain but cannot cure his illness.
   A. activate   B. alleviate   C. mediate   D. deteriorate
3. She took much pleasure in his _____ to almost all her wishes.
   A. homage   B. deference   C. deterrence   D. inference
4. The academic commission has _____ power to award extra funds to any scholar or researcher it supports.
   A. discretionary   B. discretional   C. discrete   D. recreational
5. _____ knowledge is the precondition to be a qualified scholar.
   A. Expansive   B. Intensive   C. Extensive   D. Pervasive
6. The dinosaur, which once _____ on this planet, was a magnificent species and dominated the earth for a quite long time.
   A. thrived   B. swelled   C. prospered   D. flourished
7. In Chinese culture, a wedding invitation, also addressed as a "red bomb", is an _____ invitation for cash gift.

A. inclusive   B. exclusive   C. ingenious   D. implicit
8. To _____ the suspense, Mr. Hong paused for a considerable period of time before telling us the result of the singing competition.
   A. contract   B. protract   C. retract   D. distract
9. The church did not _____ the king's second marriage, which definitely intensified their relationship.
   A. agree with   B. sanction   C. approve of   D. confirm
10. There are different types of affixes or morphemes. The affix "ed" in the word "learned" is known as a (n) _____.
   A. derivational morpheme   B. free morpheme
   C. inflectional morpheme   D. free form

Section C Use the proper form of the following words given in the brackets to fill in the blanks.

1. The muted _____ of the local administration irritated the public, who started to demonstrate against the government's improper act. (acquiescent)
2. He tried his best and successfully brought home the bacon by getting a sizable _____ for his company. (appropriate)
3. His stance on the _____ of prostitution incurred widespread disapproval and fierce criticism. (criminalize)
4. Aphrodite is believed to be the _____ of love and beauty. (embody)
5. She kept _____ to us that we moved her cheese, which bothered us a lot. (insinuation)
6. He is all that is worst in the aristocracy: profligate, _____ and godless. (licentiousness)
7. The development of this new economic zone _____ a greater supply of raw materials and skilled workers. (necessitation)
8. They are convinced of the _____ of their good taste. (singular)
9. Some veteran professors also note a strong cultural gap in _____ and outlook between themselves and the new faculty members. (temperamental)
10. It is understandable that certain groups seek to _____ others militarily or economically. (subjugation)

Section D Use the proper form of the following phrases to fill in the blanks.

be at play	figure in	in pursuit of
conform to	press for	be crucial to
square off	arise out of	in that

1. The scientists checked the data for all possible natural influences such as the lunar cycle as well as random variations but found neither to _____.
2. He doesn't _____ the usual stereotype of math teacher with clear logic and

rational mind.
3. It is a challenge for the artists to figure out a way to avoid boredom _____ repetition in their artistic creation.
4. The data collected _____ naval engineers trying to predict the vessel's likely shifts of position.
5. A perfectionist is a person who is always unsatisfied with the status quo and always _____ the perfection.
6. The boy's request is rejected by his parents outright _____ they are too poor to afford such an expensive toy.
7. The public would like to see the two candidates _____ on camera and then gave their vote according to their performance.
8. The whole world _____ the severe punishment of that belligerent country in the form of economic sanction and political isolation.
9. "Do I still _____ your plan"? asked the girl earnestly.

II Grammar

Choose the best answer to complete the following sentence from the respective four choices.

1. If not _____ with the respect he feels due to him, Jack gets very ill-tempered and grumbles all the time.
   A. being treated   B. treated
   C. be treated   D. having been treated
2. _____, some rare species were discovered, which amazed other scientists.
   A. Exploring this uninhabited area
   B. While exploring this uninhabited area
   C. These biologists were exploring this uninhabited area
   D. These biologists exploring this uninhabited area
3. The Minister of Finance is believed _____ of imposing new taxes to raise extra revenue.
   A. that he is thinking   B. to be thinking
   C. that he is to think   D. to think
4. Which of the following sentences does not have a logic subject?
   A. It is foolish of you to make your weakness known to your rivalry.
   B. I don't mind your telling him the news.
   C. There being nothing more for discussion, the meeting was over.
   D. It was once thought that the earth was the center of the universe.
5. What's the chance of _____ a timely rain after such a prolonged drought?
   A. there being   B. there to be   C. there be   D. there going to be
6. It is not uncommon for there _____ problems of communication between the old

and the young.

    A. being   B. would be   C. be   D. to be

7. What a nice day! How about the three of us _____ a walk in the park nearby?

    A. to take   B. take   C. taking   D. to be taking

8. Which of the following prepositional phrases is an adverbial of concession?

    A. Are you sure *of Simon's disappearance*?

    B. The man *with a beard* is talking to the manager.

    C. Every precaution was taken *against the failure of the plan*.

    D. *Despite the rain*, everyone enjoyed the trip.

9. Which of the following contains an adverbial clause of cause?

    A. I got a job as soon as I left university.

    B. As there was no answer, I wrote again.

    C. You must do the exercises as I show you.

    D. Wealthy as he is, Mark is not a happy man.

10. _____ he wanted to hang out with his friends at the weekend, he had to stay at home to finish his assignment.

    A. Much though   B. Much as   C. As much   D. Though much

11. I enjoyed myself so much _____ I visited my friends in Paris last year.

    A. when   B. which   C. that   D. where

12. _____, I'll marry him all the same.

    A. Was he rich or poor   B. Whether rich or poor

    C. Were he rich or poor   D. Be he rich or poor

13. Fool _____ Jane is, she could not have done such a thing.

    A. who   B. as   C. that   D. Like

14. _____ the claim about the threat from China, as a matter of fact, China has a long history of peace loving.

    A. To give   B. Given   C. Giving   D. Having given

15. I am extremely disappointed _____ my job is boring and not promising at all.

    A. that you should think   B. by what you are thinking

    C. that you would think   D. with what you were thinking

III Cloze

Fill in the blanks with words from the following list. Use the words in their proper form. Pay attention each word is used only once.

astounding	brain	candidate	confront
debate	failed	frustrated	graft
health	liking	majority	minimum
premium	prescription	pressure	proposal
rational	reversing	superb	uplifting

In the last 40 years, only one Democrat has been elected and re-elected to the American presidency: Bill Clinton. And during the same period, only one Republican has (1) _____ to win re-election: George H. W. Bush. These are (2) _____ facts, given that during those same years, whenever registered Democrats and Republicans were not in roughly equal numbers in the United States, Democrats were in the (3) _____, as they are today.

Democratic voters are confused and (4) _____. What's the matter with Kansas, they ask? Why do blue-collar workers consistently vote for wealthy Republicans who staunchly oppose increasing the (5) _____ wage while giving themselves a $70 billion tax cut?

Because Democrats are starting from the wrong vision of mind and (6) _____: a dispassionate vision, which suggests that if you just marshal the right facts and figures, policies and position statements, voters will compare the (7) _____ on "the issues" and choose the one who maximizes their rational self-interest. The problem is that that's not how the mind and brain work at all.

Consider a populist appeal made by Al Gore in a presidential (8) _____ with then-governor George W. Bush. When asked what older voters could expect from the two candidates on (9) _____ care, Gore offered this response: "Under the Governor's plan, if you kept the same fee for service that you have now under Medicare, your (10) _____ would go up by between 18 and 47 per cent, and that is the study of the Congressional plan that he's modeled his (11) _____ on by the Medicare actuaries. Let me give you one quick example. There is a man here tonight named George McKinney from Milwaukee. He's 70 years old, has high blood (12) _____, his wife has heart trouble. They have an income of $25,000 a year. They can't pay for their (13) _____ drugs. They're some of the ones that go to Canada regularly in order to get their prescription drugs."

What's wrong with that response?

If voters were calculators, this would have been a (14) _____ response. It was an appeal to reason — followed by an attempt at a personal story (15) _____ on to the "real message", which sounded like some consultant told him, "You have to throw in a story for the voters who don't think. Give them a story — they like stories." But that's not how voters' minds work. Educated voters are no more (16) _____ than their less educated or politically interested peers. The most politically aware voters tend to be the most partisan — and the most partisan voters are the least likely to listen to reasoned arguments. Instead, as our research using brain scanning has shown, when (17) _____ with information they don't like, partisans simply change their interpretation of the information until it's more to their (18) _____ — and then their brains get a jolt of dopamine, a neural "fix" that reinforces their failure to take data seriously.

If Gore wanted to appeal to real human brains, not the idealized minds of rational decision-makers, he needed to start by (19) _____ the sequence of his answer, drawing voters in with an emotionally compelling story that would tell them why they should care about his facts and figures. If you study the "syntax" of the speeches and debate responses of the most emotionally intelligent American politician in our lifetimes, Bill Clinton, you almost always find him leading with something emotionally compelling; following it with a description of what the problem is, why his opponent's approach won't solve it, and why his will; and "closing the argument" with something powerful, (20) _____, or moving that lets voters know he was going to do something about it — that his heart was truly in it.

IV Translation

Section A Translate the following Chinese sentences into English.

1. 年轻人喜欢戴着耳机听音乐来缓解等候所带来的无聊。(alleviate)
2. 大部分亚洲人属于服从型的而不是好斗型的。(acquiescent)
3. 我们正在全世界范围内建立新的伙伴关系，以挫败、摧毁和战胜国际恐怖组织。(dismantle)
4. 她的经纪人不支持她对这一毫无根据的谣言进行回应。(endorse)
5. 虚拟物流配送模式的实现需要构建一个由中央、区域性和次级区域性虚拟物流配送组成的配送网络体系。(necessitate)
6. 父权压迫妇女，即压迫柔情，压迫美貌，压迫母性。(maternity)
7. 与此同时，各学校正采取措施纠正教学与科研不平衡的状况。(redress)
8. 我面对的最至关重要、最痛苦的决定来自于情感关系。(crucial)
9. 这两位科学家理论不一致，因此停止了合作。(conform)
10. 在追求成功的过程中忽略了一切道德约束是不可取的。(in pursuit of)

Section B Translate the following English paragraphs into Chinese.

I am speaking not as a Briton, not as a European, not as a member of a western democracy, but as a human being, a member of the species Man, whose continued existence is in doubt. The world is full of conflicts: Jews and Arabs; Indians and Pakistanis; White men and Negroes in Africa; and, overshadowing all minor conflicts, the titanic struggle between communism and anticommunism.

Almost everybody who is politically conscious has strong feelings about one or more of these issues; but I want you, if you can, to set aside such feelings for the moment and consider yourself only as a member of a biological species which has had a remarkable history and whose disappearance none of us can desire. I shall try to say no single word which should appeal to one group rather than to another. All, equally, are in peril, and if the peril is understood, there is hope that they may collectively avert it. We have to learn to think in a new way. We have to learn to ask ourselves not what steps can be taken to give military victory to whatever group we prefer, for there no longer are such steps. The question we have to ask ourselves is: What steps can be taken to prevent a military contest of which the issues must be disastrous to all sides?

V Topic for Discussion

There is no such thing as an objective point of view. No matter how much we may try to ignore it, human communication always takes place in a context, through a medium, and among individuals and groups who are situated historically, politically, economically, and socially. This state of affairs is neither bad nor good. It simply is. Bias is a small word that identifies the collective influences of the entire context of a message.

Politicians are certainly biased and overtly so. Journalists, too, speak from political positions but usually not overtly so. The press is often thought of as a unified voice with a distinct bias (right or left depending on the critic).

For citizens and information consumers (which are one in the same today), it is important to develop the skill of detecting bias. Remember: Bias does not suggest that a message is false or unfair. You should apply other techniques to determine if a message is fallacious.

What do you think of this phenomenon? What attitude should we take toward the political bias on media?

VI Written Work

Write a short essay of about 200 words on the following topic.

Some people hold that politics has little to do with each individual's life and that one can live a good life without any involvement in politics at all. What do you think of this opinion? Put your opinion into an essay based on the following title: Does politics really mean much to us?

Text B
The Moral Causes of Europe's Predicament

Bill Muehlenberg

1 Back in 1948, T. S. Eliot wrote about "the common tradition of Christianity which has made Europe what it is". In his essay, the American-British poet and critic argued that if we lose Christianity, we lose Europe. He is worth quoting at length.

2 He wrote: "It is in Christianity that our arts have developed; it is in

Christianity that the laws of Europe have — until recently — been rooted. It is against a background of Christianity that all our thought has significance. An individual European may not believe that the Christian Faith is true, and yet what he says, and makes, and does, will all spring out of his heritage of Christian culture and depend upon that culture for its meaning.

3　"Only a Christian culture could have produced a Voltaire or a Nietzsche. I do not believe that the culture of Europe could survive the complete disappearance of the Christian faith. And I am convinced of that, not merely because I am a Christian myself, but as a student of social biology.

4　"If Christianity goes, the whole of our culture goes. Then you must start painfully again, and you cannot put on a new culture ready made. You must wait for the grass to grow to feed the sheep to give the wool out of which your new coat will be made. You must pass through many centuries of barbarism. We should not live to see the new culture, nor would our great-great-great-grandchildren: and if we did, not one of us would be happy in it."

5　He had it exactly right, and now, some 60 years on, we see the very thing he warned about. Europe has abandoned its Christian roots and is now paying the price for it. And it is not just the economic collapse which is engulfing so much of Europe.

6　The continent is in a moral and spiritual freefall, and whether it can ever recover remains to be seen. Of interest, today I came upon three different articles, all looking at the European condition, but from slightly different perspectives. One is rather pessimistic, one is rather optimistic, and a third is somewhere in the middle.

7　All three pieces offer some insightful and helpful thoughts on the situation in Europe. So let me discuss each one, beginning with a more negative assessment. The Rev. Dr Peter Mullen of the United Kingdom echoes the thoughts of Eliot in his article, "If Christianity goes, so does Europe".

8　He writes: "Whatever the future holds, we need to understand that the economic collapse is not the main crisis which engulfs Europe. More significantly, we see the EU developing into the ever-tighter totalitarianism which was envisaged from its inception."

9　The founding fathers of the EU never foresaw a democratic union. The founders of the project, such as Coundenhove-Kalergi and Jean Monnet, always assumed there would be government not by elected statesmen but by technocrats. This is indeed what we have seen recently in the appointment of such men to supreme power in Greece and Italy.

10　But this creeping totalitarianism is not the root of our problem. Our crisis is a spiritual crisis, a crisis of identity. As the philosopher and former President of the Italian Senate, Professor Marcello Pera, said, "Christianity is so consubstantial with the West, that any surrender on its part would have devastating consequences." But all references to Europe's Christian character have been expunged by the EU bureaucrats. Europe is now officially secular.

11   Pope Benedict XVI identified our real crisis with terrifying clarity: "The EU is godless. But then it is unthinkable that the EU could build a common European house while ignoring Europe's identity. Europe is a historical, cultural and moral identity before it is a geographic, economic or political reality. It is an identity built on a set of values which Christianity played a part in moulding."

12   He concludes, "If Christianity goes, the lot goes. As T. S. Eliot said back in 1934, 'Such attainments as you can boast in the way of polite society will hardly survive the faith to which they owe their significance'." (*The Telegraph*, UK, December 1, 2011).

13   Jeff Fountain of the Schuman Centre for European Studies takes a somewhat less pessimistic look at modern-day Europe. He reports on an address recently given by a leading Polish Christian:

14   "Christians had a special responsibility in moments such as Europe's current crisis, President Jerzy Buzek of the European Parliament told participants of the European Prayer Breakfast in Brussels last week. Today's crisis was one of values, not economics, he added. Material development had not been accompanied by spiritual development. Yet competitiveness needed justice. Jobs needed a work ethic. Welfare required values and responsibility.

15   "Without love, we were just clanging gongs, clashing cymbals, he said, quoting the Apostle Paul. 'Our special responsibility as Christians is to be salt and light,' he urged his listeners gathered from the political world across Europe, adding, 'and we must promote this idea.'

16   "Buzek came to the breakfast straight from a meeting of EU leaders on the monetary crisis. 'There is a real difference in the atmosphere here!' he remarked on arrival. 'Here you are looking to God!' Referring to his Lutheran affiliation, the president said he had always been a strong supporter of ecumenical initiatives.

17   "The year 2013 would mark the 1700th anniversary of the Edict of Milan, he reminded his audience. That event had been a turning point bringing freedom of religion to the Roman Empire. Christianity from then on had become the main driving force shaping Europe. While over the centuries Christianity had produced both good and bad experiences, the former Polish prime minister conceded, it had bequeathed to Europe a rich heritage of values and beliefs....

18   "Fascism and communism had strongly challenged this heritage in the 20th century, he recalled, both of which had tried to change the face of Europe. But their demise had resulted in Europe's reunification and in unprecedented growth. This must not be forgotten as we faced today's challenges, said Buzek, a professor of chemical engineering. The question today was if the Christian heritage was still valid — or was it

simply a respectable but useless historical culture? The answer in his opinion was that it was this heritage that had produced tolerance and openness for understanding.

19　"'If we give it up, it will be replaced by a spiritual emptiness corroded by nationalism and particularism (self-interest),' he added. Then, addressing the relationship between church and state, he explained that both were autonomous domains. 'But autonomy is not separation. Cooperation is important for a fair and just society.'

20　"Yet Europe was being weakened by an aggressive secularism with a negative tolerance, he continued. It wanted to lock faith away into a small box of privacy. If unchecked, it would undo the tolerance won in 313 with the Edict of Milan, he warned." (*Weekly Word*, December 5, 2011).

21　Finally, two Spanish academics, Alejo José G. Sison and Juncal Cuñado, offer some hope regarding the state of faith in Europe. They argue that it is not quite as secular and godless as many believe.

22　They write: "Europeans no longer believe in God or go to church anymore. They don't even consider themselves to be religious at all. It is clear, therefore, that Europe is a secularised continent. Or is it, really? The European Values Study 2005 — 2008 presents a much more nuanced picture. In half of the surveyed countries, the majority of the people, sometimes an overwhelming one, found the statement 'There is a personal God' as that which comes closest to their belief, while in the other half, the statement 'There is some God, spirit or life force' was chosen.

23　"The statement 'I don't know if there is a God, spirit or life force' was second choice for France and the Russian Federation, and the option 'There is no God, spirit or life force' always came in last, even for France where it was chosen by 15 per cent of the population, the highest percentage among the different countries. Believers, therefore, still vastly outnumber non-believers, despite the variance in the object of their belief.

24　"As for religious practice, the same study affords us an equally varied panorama. Although in most countries, the majority of the population never attends religious services, in ten, the majority of the population attends religious services once a week. On the aggregate, half of all Europeans pray or meditate at least once a week, and even in a country known for its liberal tradition such as the Netherlands, one-fourth of its inhabitants attends church. So despite the decrease in church attendance and religious practice through the years, a considerable number of Europeans still engage in them, albeit with varying frequency."

25　Of course, religion and spirituality are not identical to biblical Christianity, but the survey results do reveal a Europe which still clings to some faith and some belief, despite such a lengthy period of secularism and anti-Christian agendas at work there.

26 So we have three somewhat differing takes on the situation in Europe. Whether we should be utterly pessimistic regarding its direction, or quite optimistic, or somewhere in between, depends on various factors. But we can all keep praying for the continent, and hope that Christians there will seek to reclaim Europe for Christ.

Notes

1. Back in 1948 **T. S. Eliot** wrote about "the common tradition of Christianity which has made Europe what it is". (Para. 1)

T. S. Eliot was a publisher, playwright, literary and social critic and "arguably the most important English-language poet of the 20th century". Although he was born an American, he moved to the United Kingdom in 1914 and was naturalised as a British subject in 1927 at age 39.

Paragraphs 2 – 4 are quoted from T. S. Eliot's essay, *Notes Towards a Definition of Culture*, 1948.

2. More significantly, we see the EU developing into the ever-tighter **totalitarianism** which was envisaged from its inception. (Para. 8)

Totalitarianism is a political system where the state holds total authority over the society and seeks to control all aspects of public and private life wherever necessary.

3. "Our special responsibility as Christians is to be **salt and light**," he urged his listeners gathered from the political world across Europe, adding, "and we must promote this idea." (Para. 15)

The idea of Salt and Light is taken from the Bible, Matthew 5: 13-16:

You are the salt of the earth. But if the salt loses its saltiness, how can it be made salty again? It is no longer good for anything, except to be thrown out and trampled underfoot.

You are the light of the world. A town built on a hill cannot be hidden. Neither do people light a lamp and put it under a bowl. Instead they put it on its stand, and it gives light to everyone in the house. In the same way, let your light shine before others, that they may see your good deeds and glorify your Father in heaven.

4. **Buzek** came to the breakfast straight from a meeting of EU leaders on the monetary crisis. (Para. 16)

Jerzy Karol Buzek is a Polish engineer, academic lecturer and politician who was the ninth post-Cold War Prime Minister of Poland from 1997 to 2001. He has been a member of the European Parliament since 13 June 2004, and he was elected as President of the European Parliament on 14 July 2009.

5. The year 2013 would mark the 1700th anniversary of **the Edict of Milan**, ... (Para. 17)

The Edict of Milan was granted by Emperor Constantine the Great in the West and

Licinius Augustus in the East in 313 granting religious freedom throughout the Roman Empire. In addition, the Edict of Milan ordered the restitution of property confiscated from Christians.

6. Yet Europe was being weakened by an aggressive **secularism** with a negative tolerance, he continued. (Para. 20)

Secularism: In one sense, secularism may assert the right to be free from religious rule and teachings, and the right to freedom from governmental imposition of religion upon the people within a state that is neutral on matters of belief. In another sense, it refers to the view that human activities and decisions, especially political ones, should be unbiased by religious influence. Some scholars are now arguing that the very idea of secularism will change.

Question for Discussion

Religious belief is regarded as very important for human beings. Yet, more and more modern people find that religion is farther from their life. What, do you think, causes this situation?

Memorable Quotes

1. Tranquil pleasures last the longest; we are not fitted to bear the burden of great joy.
   — Bovee, Christian Nevell
2. The trouble with this country is that there are too many politicians who believe, with a conviction based on experience, that you can fool all of the people all of the time.
   — Franklin P. Adams
3. Politics, as a practice, whatever its professions, has always been the systematic organization of hatreds.
   — Henry Brooks Adams

Further Readings

1. Gayatri Chakravorty Spivak, *In Other Worlds: Essays in Cultural Politics*
2. Aristotle, *Politics*

Unit 11

Pre-reading questions
1. What is beauty in your mind and what do you think beauty consists in?
2. Will you define a person's beauty from two aspects, "inside" & "outside"?
3. Why do you think women are described as being "beautiful" while men are described as being "handsome"?

Text A

Beauty

Susan Sontag

1 For the Greeks, beauty was a virtue: a kind of excellence. Persons then were assumed to be what we now have to call — lamely, enviously — whole persons. If it did occur to Greeks to distinguish between a person's "inside" and "outside", they still expected that inner beauty would be matched by the beauty of the other kind. The well-born young Athenians who gathered around Socrates found it quite paradoxical that their hero was so intelligent, so brave, so honorable, so seductive — and so ugly. One of Socrates' main pedagogical acts was to be ugly and teach those innocent, no doubt splendid-looking disciples of his how full of paradoxes life really was.

2 They may have resisted Socrates' lesson. We do not. Several thousand years later, we are more wary of the enchantments of beauty. We not only split off — with the greatest facility — the "inside" (character, intellect) from the "outside" (looks), but we are actually surprised when someone who is beautiful is also intelligent, talented, good.

3 It was principally the influence of Christianity that deprived beauty of the central place it had in classical ideals of human excellence. By limiting excellence (*virtus* in Latin) to *moral* virtue only, Christianity set beauty adrift — as an alienated, arbitrary, superficial enchantment. And beauty has continued to lose prestige. For close to two centuries it has become a convention to attribute beauty to only one of the two sexes: the sex which, however Fair, is always Second. Associating beauty with women has put beauty even further on the defensive, morally.

4 A beautiful woman, we say in English, but a handsome man. "Handsome" is the masculine equivalent of — and refusal of — a compliment which has accumulated certain demeaning overtones, by being reserved for women only. That one can call a man "beautiful" in French and in Italian suggests that Catholic countries — unlike those countries shaped by the Protestants version of Christianity — still retain some vestiges of the pagan admiration for beauty. But the difference, if one exists, is one of degree only. In every modern country that is Christian or post-Christian, women are the beautiful sex — to the detriment of the notion of beauty as well as of women.

5 To be called beautiful is thought to name something essential to women's character and concerns. (In contrast to men — whose essence is to be strong, or effective, or competent.) It does not take someone in the throes of advanced feminist awareness to perceive that the way women are taught to be involved with beauty

encourages narcissism, reinforces dependence and immaturity. Everybody (women and men) knows that. For it is "everybody", a whole society, that has identified being feminine with caring about how one looks. (In contrast to being masculine — which is identified with caring about what one is and does and only secondarily, if at all, about how one looks.) Given these stereotypes, it is no wonder that beauty enjoys, at best, a rather mixed reputation.

6 It is not, of course, the desire to be beautiful that is wrong but the obligation to be — or to try. What is accepted by most women as a flattering idealization of their sex is a way of making women feel inferior to what they actually are — or normally grow to be. For the ideal of beauty is administered as a form of self-oppression. Women are taught to see their bodies in parts, and to evaluate each part separately. Breasts, feet, hips, waistline, neck, eyes, nose, complexion, hair and so on — each in turn is submitted to an anxious, fretful, often despairing scrutiny. Even if some pass muster, some will always be found wanting. Nothing less than perfection will do.

7 In men, good looks is a whole, something taken in at a glance. It does not need to be confirmed by giving measurements of different regions of the body. Nobody encourages a man to dissect his appearance, feature by feature. As for perfection, that is considered trivial — almost unmanly. Indeed, in the ideally good-looking man a srnall imperfection or Hemish is considered positively desirable. According to one movie critic (a woman) who is a declared Robert Redford fan, it is having that cluster of skin-colored moles on one cheek that saves Redford from being merely a "pretty face". Think of the depreciation of women — as well as of beauty — that is implied in that judgment.

8 "The privileges of beauty are immense," said Cocteau. To be sure, beauty is a form of power. And deservedly so. What is lamentable is that it is the only form of power that most women are encouraged to seek. This power is always conceived in relation to men; it is not the power to do but the power to attract. It is a power that negates itself. For this power is not one that can be chosen freely — at least, not by women — or renounced without social censure.

9 To preen, for a woman, can never be just a pleasure. It is a duty. It is her work. If a woman does real work — and even if she has clambered up to a leading position in politics, law, medicine, business, or whatever — she is always under pressure to confess that she still works at being attractive. But in so far as she is keeping up as one of the Fair Sex, she brings under suspicion her very capacity to be objective, professional, authoritative, thoughtful. Damned if they do — women are. And damned if they don't.

10 One could hardly ask for more important evidence of the dangers of considering persons as split between what is "inside" and what is "outside" than that interminable half-comic half tragic tale, the oppression of women. How easy it is to start

off by defining women as caretakers of their surfaces, and then to disparage them (or find them adorable) for being "superficial". It is a crude trap, and it has worked for too long. But to get out of the trap requires that women get some critical distance from that excellence and privilege which is beauty, enough distance to see how much beauty itself has been abridged in order to prop up the mythology of the "feminine". There should be a way of saving beauty from women — and for them.

Notes

1. About the author.

Susan Sontag: (January 16, 1933 — December 28, 2004) was an American writer and filmmaker, literary icon, and political activist. Beginning with the publication of her 1964 essay "Notes on 'Camp'" Sontag became a life-long international cultural and intellectual celebrity. Sontag was often photographed and her image became widely recognized even in mainstream society. Her works include *On Photography*, *Against Interpretation*, *The Way We Live Now*, and *Regarding the Pain of Others*.

In "Beauty", first published in *Vogue* magazine in 1975, Sontag traces the history of a word which was once defined as general excellence but which has often been used to characterize female appearance.

2. **Socrates** (Para. 2)

Socrates was a classical Greek Athenian philosopher. Credited as one of the founders of Western philosophy, he is an enigmatic figure known chiefly through the accounts of later classical writers, especially the writings of his students Plato and Xenophon, and the plays of his contemporary Aristophanes. Many would claim that Plato's dialogues are the most comprehensive accounts of Socrates to survive from antiquity.

Through his portrayal in Plato's dialogues, Socrates has become renowned for his contribution to the field of ethics, and it is this Platonic Socrates who also lends his name to the concepts of Socratic irony and the Socratic method, or *elenchus*. The latter remains a commonly used tool in a wide range of discussions, and is a type of pedagogy in which a series of questions are asked not only to draw individual answers, but also to encourage fundamental insight into the issue at hand. It is Plato's Socrates that also made important and lasting contributions to the fields of epistemology and logic, and the influence of his ideas and approach remains strong in providing a foundation for much western philosophy that followed.

3. **Robert Redford** (Para. 7)

Robert Redford (1936—), U. S. actor, began to go into movies in 1965. He first made an impression as an accomplished performer with open good looks in *The Chase*

(1966), and played the title role in *The Great Gatsby* (1974).

4. Jean Cocteau (Para. 8)

Jean Cocteau (1880—1963), French poet, novelist, dramatist, essayist, film writer, and director. Cocteau's versatility in the arts is unrivalled in the twentieth century. He experimented audaciously in almost every artistic medium, becoming a leader of the French avant-garde in the 1920's.

Glossary

Athenian [ə'θi:njəns] n.	雅典人
adrift [ə'drɪft] a.	aimlessly drifting; afloat on the surface of a body of water
ad.	floating freely; wandering aimlessly
alienated ['eɪljənetɪd] a.	sociallydisoriented; caused to be unloved
arbitrary ['ɑ:bɪtrərɪ] a.	based on or subject to individual discretion or preference or sometimes impulse or caprice
attribute [ə'trɪbju:t] v.	credit to; decide as to where something belongs in a scheme
blemish ['blemɪʃ] n.	a mark or flaw that spoils the appearance of something (especially on a person's body)
censure ['senʃə] n.	an expression of blame or disapproval
clamber ['klæmbə] v.	climb awkwardly, as if by scrambling
disciple [dɪ'saɪpl] n.	someone who believes and helps to spread the doctrine of another
deprive [dɪ'praɪv] v.	keep from having, keeping or obtaining
demeaning [dɪ'minɪŋ] a.	causing awareness of your shortcomings
despairing [dɪ'speərɪŋ] a.	arising from or marked by despair or loss of hope
detriment ['detrɪmənt] n.	a damage or loss
disparage [dɪ'spærɪdʒ] v.	express a negative opinion of
dissect [dɪ'sekt] n.	cut open or cut apart
depreciation [dɪpri:ʃɪ'eɪʃən] n.	decrease in value of an asset due to obsolescence or use
enchantment [ɪn'tʃɑ:ntmənt] n.	a feeling of great liking for something wonderful and unusual
fretful ['fretful] a.	nervous and unable to relax; habitually complaining
interminable [ɪn'tɜ:mɪnəbl] a.	tiresomely long; seemingly without end
lamely ['lemlɪ] ad.	in a weak and unconvincing manner
muster ['mʌstə] v.	gather or bring together; call to duty, military service, jury duty, etc.

narcissism ['nɑːsɪsɪzəm] n.　　an exceptional interest in and admiration for yourself
negate [nɪ'geɪt] v.　　prove negative; show to be false
overtone ['əʊvətəʊn] n.　　an ulterior implicit meaning or quality
paradoxical [pærə'dɒksɪkəl] a.　seemingly contradictory but nonetheless possibly true
pagan ['peɪgən] n.　　a person who does not acknowledge your god
preen [priːn] v.　　dress or groom with elaborate care
pedagogical [pedə'gɒdʒɪkəl] a.　of or relating to pedagogy or teaching method
renounce [rɪ'naʊns] v.　　give up, such as power, as of monarchs and emperors, or duties and obligations
scrutiny ['skruːtənɪi] n.　　the act of examining something closely; a prolonged intense look
seductive [sɪ'dʌktɪv] a.　　tending to entice into a desired action or state
split [splɪt] v.　　separate into parts or portions
submit [səb'mɪt] v.　　yield to the control of another
throes [θrəʊ] n.　　violent pangs of suffering
vestiges ['vestɪdʒz] n.　　an indication that something has been present

Comprehension Questions

Answer the following questions after reading the text.

1. How does the notion of beauty held by the ancient Greeks basically differ from the modern one?
2. Did the limitation Christianity placed on the meaning of the word "beauty" give it any sexual bias?
3. What does Sontag mean by "And beauty has continued to lose prestige" (Para. 3)?
4. Why does Sontag think that regarding women as the beautiful sex is detrimental to both the notion of beauty and that of women (Para. 4)?
5. What does Sontag refer to by "stereotypes" in the last sentence of Para. 5? And what have they to do with the "mixed reputation" beauty enjoys?
6. Do you think (Sontag's) society is fair in its expectations of men and women with regard to their looks by contrasting Para. 6 with Para. 7?
7. What/Who has made it a woman's duty to preen? If a woman succeeds in keeping herself look nice, how would she expect society in general to assess her?
8. To get women out of the trap they are caught in, Sontag suggests that they "get some critical distance from that excellence and privilege which is beauty" (Para. 10). What do you think this means?
9. What does "the mythology of the feminine" (Para. 10) mean?
10. How do you interpret the last sentence of the essay?
11. Is there a sentence in the essay that contains the thesis statement? If not, where in

the essay is Sontag's point made especially clear?
12. Do you agree that "beauty" is also a topic through which the author is actually exploring very much a feminist issue that demands public attention too?

Exercises

I Vocabulary

Section A Paraphrase the sentences chosen from the text.
1. One of Socrates' main pedagogical acts was to be ugly and teach those innocent, no doubt splendid-looking disciples of his how full of paradoxes life really was. (Para. 1)
2. We not only split off — with the greatest facility — the "inside" (character, intellect) from the "outside" (looks), but we are actually surprised when someone who is beautiful is also intelligent, talented, good. (Para. 2)
3. By limiting excellence to moral virtue only, Christianity set beauty adrift — as an alienated, arbitrary, superficial enchantment. (Para. 3)
4. It does not take someone in the throes of advanced feminist awareness to perceive that the way women are taught to be involved with beauty encouraged narcissism, reinforces dependence and immaturity. (Para. 5)
5. What is accepted by most women as a flattering idealization of their sex is a way of making women feel inferior to what they actually are — or normally grow to be. For the ideal of beauty is administered as a form of self-oppression. (Para. 6)
6. For this power is not one that can be chosen freely — at least, not by women — or renounced without social censure. (Para. 8)
7. If a woman does real work — and even if she has clambered up to a leading position in politics, law, medicine, business, or whatever — she is always under pressure to confess that she still works at being attractive. (Para. 9)
8. One could hardly ask for more important evidence of the dangers of considering persons as split between what is "inside" and what is "outside" than that interminable half-comic half tragic tale, the oppression of women. (Para. 10)

Section B Choose the word or phrase that best completes each sentence.
1. Is a woman to be more highly _____ for her talent or for her beauty?
   A. estimated   B. evaluated   C. esteemed   D. reckoned
2. Robert Smith's reputation was established with the publication of his first poem in 1938 and was _____ by his splendid short stories for children.
   A. reinforced   B. obscured   C. revived   D. enhanced
3. All living creature have some _____ that are passed on from one generation to the next.
   A. attributes   B. properties   C. aspects   D. faculties

4. Far worse are the sufferings of the dependents of gambling addicts because they are usually _____ of all material comforts.
   A. deprived   B. denied   C. robbed   D. refused
5. Germination of seeds begins with the absorption of water, the swelling of the _____ seed, and the cracking of the seed coat.
   A. stiff   B. damp   C. outer   D. whole
6. Professor Smith and Professor Brown will _____ in presenting the series of lectures on American literature.
   A. alter   B. alternate   C. substitute   D. exchange
7. His manner was so pleasant that Bolla felt at _____ with him at once.
   A. peace   B. large   C. ease   D. best
8. Despite their good service provided, most inns are less expensive than hotels of _____ standards.
   A. equivalent   B. likely   C. alike   D. uniform
9. Many automobile accidents were _____ careless driving.
   A. attributed to B. resulted in C. contributed to D. raised from
10. The patterns of spoken language are _____ from those of writing.
    A. distinct   B. distinctive C. distinguished D. distinguishing
11. Visitors to the zoo are _____ against teasing the tigers by climbing over the railings as they may fall victim to their hungry jaws.
    A. commanded   B. advised   C. notified   D. informed
12. The evening TV programme was suddenly interrupted for a news _____ that a jacana, a bird of the American tropics, had slashed a baby to death.
    A. signal   B. release   C. alarm   D. flash
13. Since Emily saw the programme about the knack for longevity, she has become _____ with physical fitness.
    A. obsessed   B. concentrated C. engrossed   D. occupied
14. It matters not to the koala whether the water was _____ by waste from the factory or not, as it is the only land animal that doesn't need water to supplement its food.
    A. putrefied   B. infected   C. infested   D. contaminated
15. In that country, guest tend to feel they are not highly _____ if the invitation to a dinner party is extended only three or four days before the party date.
    A. admired   B. regarded   C. expected   D. worshiped

Section C Use the proper form of the following words given in the brackets to fill in the blanks.

1. Catholic countries still retain some vestige of the pagan _____ (admire) for beauty.
2. One strategy is simply to persuade people to stay longer, which provides more time

for employers to spot and _____ (seductive) the best performers.
3. But Fox's home fans, could only be _____ (envy) of the report, because this car will not enter the home.
4. Such is the curse of self-consciousness: extraordinary insight whose companion are melancholy, _____ (alien) and paralysis.
5. On the whole, they are better procurement than at _____ (pedagogical), better at school-building than schooling.
6. Astronomers can _____ (scrutiny) the movements of faraway stars, watching for the telltale gravitational tug of orbiting planets.
7. Michael's mistakes may be simply due to his _____ (mature).
8. The smile of Yang Gui Fei was enough to _____ (enchantment) and enrapture the Emperor.
9. Capable as they are, these _____ (authority), thoughtful women in our firm are not placed on an equal footing with men.
10. On such occasions we were so moved that words failed to give the _____ (measure) of our gratitude.

Section D Use the proper form of the following phrases to fill in the blanks.

occur to	deprive of	attribute to	submit to
at best	in turn	prop up	split off
pass muster	on the defensive		

1. Those who can be _____ from the enemy camp should be won over, educated and helped.
2. The Internet society, like a goldfish bowl, may _____ the privacy of everyone.
3. Does it ever _____ you to use your sight to see into the inner nature of a friend or acquaintance?
4. We learn new words and phrases, and these _____ are used in our own writing.
5. My victory _____ the coach's patient instruction and the backup of my family and friends.
6. In this deep recession only the government can _____ demand and fend off economic disaster.
7. The consultants shall _____ the client a copy of their biographical data and a copy of a satisfactory health certificate for review and approval.
8. His English is very fluent, and his pronunciation just _____.
9. There is only, _____, random monitoring of waste water effluent by the pollution control agency.
10. She is not well-liked as she is always _____ about her mistake.

II Grammar

Choose the best answer to complete the following sentence from the respective four choices.

1. Which sentence of the following is correct?
    A. In this remote area can only a small farm be found with a limited number of sheep and cattle.
    B. In this remote area a small farm can only be found with a limited number of sheep and cattle.
    C. In this remote area only could a small farm found with a limited number of sheep and cattle.
    D. In this remote area could only be found a small arm with a limited number of sheep and cattle.
2. There is no reason they should limit how much vitamin you take, _____ they can limit how much water you drink.
    A. much more than   B. no more than
    C. no less than   D. any more than
3. Einstein won the Nobel Prize in 1921 and enjoyed great fame in Germany until the rise of Nazism _____ he was expelled from Germany because he was a Jew.
    A. when   B. who   C. then   D. which
4. My train arrives in Shenyang at seven o'clock tomorrow. The plane I would like to take from there _____ by then.
    A. would leave   B. will have left   C. has left   D. had left
5. _____, he does not love her.
    A. As he likes her very much   B. Though much he likes her
    C. Much although he likes her   D. Much though he likes her
6. Some companies have introduced flexible working time with less emphasis on pressure _____.
    A. than more on efficiency   B. and more on efficiency
    C. and more efficiency   D. than efficiency
7. Physics is the present-day equivalent of _____ used to be called natural philosophy, from which most of present day science arose.
    A. that   B. all   C. which   D. what
8. He often sat in a small bar drinking considerably more than _____.
    A. he was in good health   B. his health was good
    C. his good health was   D. was good for his health
9. It _____ five years since the famous singer left her hometown.
    A. was   B. is   C. has passed   D. had been
10. Which of the following sentences is NOT correct?
    A. You should apply in person.   B. He has applied to join the army.

C. She will apply a passport first.   D. I applied to a company after graduation.
11. It is only when you nearly lose someone _____ fully conscious of how much you value him.
   A. do you become   B. then you become
   C. that you become   D. have you become
12. The bank is reported in the local newspaper _____ in broad daylight yesterday.
   A. to be robbed   B. robbed
   C. to have been robbed D. having been robbed
13. While driving along the treacherous road, _____.
   A. my right rear tire blew out
   B. my right rear tire had a blowout
   C. I had my right rear tire been blowout
   D. I had a blowout on my right rear tire
14. Televisions enable us to see things happen almost at the exact moment _____.
   A. which they are happening   B. they are happening
   C. which they happen   D. they have happened
15. The student expected there _____ more reviewing classes before the final exams.
   A. is   B. being   C. have been   D. to be

III Cloze
Decide which of the choices given below would best complete the passage if inserted in the corresponding blanks. Mark the best choice for each blank.

Aesthetic thought of a distinctively modern bent emerged during the 18th century. The western philosophers and critics of this time devoted much attention to such matters (1) _____ natural beauty, the sublime, and representation — a trend reflecting the central position they had given to the philosophy of nature. (2) _____ that time, however, the philosophy of art has become ever more (3) _____ and has begun to (4) _____ the philosophy of nature. Various issues (5) _____ to the philosophy of art have had a (6) _____ impact (7) _____ the orientation of 20th century aesthetics. (8) _____ among these are problems relating to the theory of art as form and (9) _____ the distinction between representation and expression. Still another far-reaching question has to do with the value of art. Two opposing theoretical positions (10) _____ on this issue: one holds that art and its appreciation are a means to some recognized moral good, (11) _____ the other maintains that art is intrinsically valuable and is an end in itself. Underlying this whole issue is the concept of taste, one of the basic concerns of aesthetics. In recent years there has also been an increasing (12) _____ with art as the prime object of critical judgment. Corresponding to the trend in contemporary aesthetic thought, (13) _____ have followed (14) _____ of two approaches. In one, criticism is restricted to the analysis and interpretation of the work of art. (15) _____, it is devoted to articulating the response to the aesthetic object and to (16) _____ a particular way of perceiving it.

Over the years aesthetics has developed into a broad field of knowledge and inquiry. The concerns of contemporary aesthetics include such (17) _____ problems as the nature of style and its aesthetic significance; the relation of aesthetic judgment to culture; the (18) _____ of a history of art; the (19) _____ of Freudian psychology and other forms of psychological study to criticism; and the place of aesthetic judgment in practical (20) _____ in the conduct of everyday affairs.

1. A. for   B. as   C. to   D. with
2. A. Since   B. For   C. As   D. In
3. A. promotional   B. promissory   C. promiscuous   D. prominent
4. A. plant   B. supplant   C. transplant   D. replant
5. A. central   B. concentrating   C. focusing   D. centering
6. A. marking   B. remarking   C. marked   D. remarked
7. A. on   B. for   C. in   D. to
8. A. Foreboding   B. Foremost   C. Forethoughtful D. Foregone
9. A. at   B. for   C. to   D. on
10. A. have brought   B. have been brought
    C. have taken   D. have been taken
11. A. whereas   B. wherein   C. whereon   D. wherefore
12. A. preoccupancy   B. preoccupation   C. premonition   D. proportion
13. A. artists   B. writers   C. critics   D. analysts
14. A. all   B. either   C. neither   D. none
15. A. In the other manner   B. In the other way
    C. In another   D. In the other
16. A. justify   B. justified   C. justifying   D. having justified
17. A. diverse   B. divided   C. divine   D. dividable
18. A. vicinity   B. viability   C. villainy   D. visibility
19. A. reliance   B. reliability   C. relief   D. relevancy
20. A. reason   B. reasonableness C. reasoning   D. reasonability

IV Translation

Section A Translate the following Chinese sentences into English.

1. 条约声明放弃使用武力,并保证两国将进行合作。(renounce)
2. 看到公园里树上的花儿,就知道春天终于来了。(announce)
3. 对于我们的工作的看法,肯定一切或者否定一切,都是片面性的。(negate)
4. 他的书基调一贯是负面消极的,有时还有点儿傲慢自大,且常常流于肤浅。

(negative)
5. 国际货币基金组织往往要求这些国家采取措施减少进口，或者将他们的货币贬值。(depreciate)
6. 为了能与这庄严的气氛相一致，如果你能熄灭香烟的话，我将很高兴。(appreciate)
7. 路程好像是漫无尽头似的，沿途经过了不少住得拥挤不堪的用砖砌的矮房子。(interminable)
8. 一些批评家轻蔑地把精神分析学看作是伪科学。(disparage)
9. 只要露营者不引发荒原大火，不乱扔垃圾，不疏远那些住在乡村的人们，他们还是会受到当地人的欢迎。(alienate)
10. 若不建立国际性条约，一些国家则仍有机会偏袒其国内金融机构，这不利于国际社会。(to the detriment of)

Section B Translate the following English passages into Chinese.

Beauty is essentially a form of energy, something that radiates from a fine example of absolutely anything, whether a delightful taste or smell, or a gorgeous sight. This energy is in effect a form of information, nature's bar code telling us how healthy that attitude is, because health-bringing things increase the likelihood that we and our genes will survive.

Yet, the greatest source of beauty, for the sheer intensity and volume of positive emotion it brings to our lives, is the beautiful relationship — the one in which we can thrive and flourish and grow beyond ourselves. This fertile bond can exist between two living things, or a person and a place, or a person and a skill, and the world becomes only more beautiful the more deeply we understand it. Therefore, we will find profound happiness in nurturing and appreciating diverse beauties in whatever ways we can.

V Topics for Discussion

1. Judgment of beauty varies from person to person. As the saying goes, love is blind. Do you think there is any universally accepted criterion for judging beauty?
2. Sontag begins her essay by defining the ancient Greek's attitude toward beauty, and goes on in subsequent paragraphs to trace the changes in the meaning of the word. What can you infer from this etymological study of the word?

VI Written Work

Inner beauty is a much discussed topic and people hold widely different views. Some define it as a readiness to assist others; some term it as a strong sense of justice... Write a coherent passage, defining the term as you understand it and stating clearly your view on the issue.

Text B
Give Her a Pattern

D. H. Lawrence

1 The real trouble about women is that they must always go on to adapt themselves to men's theories of women, as they always have done. When a woman is thoroughly herself, she is being what her type of man wants her to be. When a woman is hysterical it's because she doesn't quite know what to be, which pattern to follow, which man's picture of woman to live up to.

2 For, of course, just as there are many men in the world, there are many masculine theories of what women should be. But men run to type, and it is the type, not the individual, that produces the theory, or "ideal" of woman. Those very grasping gentry, the Romans, produced a theory or ideal of the matron, which fitted in very nicely with the Roman property lust. "Caesar's wife should be above suspicion." — So Caesar's wife kindly proceeded to be above it, no matter how far below it the Caesar fell. Later gentlemen like Nero produced the "fast" theory of woman, and later ladies were fast enough for everybody. Dante arrived with a chaste and untouched Beatrice, and chaste and untouched Beatrices began to march self-importantly through the centuries. The Renaissance discovered the learned woman, and learned women buzzed mildly into verse and prose. Dickens invented the child-wife, so child-wives have swarmed ever since. He also fished out his version of the chaste Beatrice, a chaste but marriageable Agnes. George Eliot imitated this pattern, and it became confirmed. The noble woman, the pure spouse, the devoted mother took the field, and was simply worked to death. Our own poor mothers were this sort. So we younger men, having been a bit frightened of our noble mothers, tended to revert to the child-wife. We weren't very inventive. Only the child-wife must be a boyish little thing — that was the new touch we added. Because young men are definitely frightened of the real female. She's too risky a quantity. She is too untidy, like David's Dora. No, let her be a boyish little thing, it's safer. So a boyish little thing she is.

3 There are, of course, other types. Capable men produce the capable woman ideal. Doctors produce the capable nurse. Business men produce the capable secretary. And so you get all sorts. You can produce the masculine sense of honour (whatever that highly mysterious quantity may be) in women, if you want to.

4 There is, also, the eternal secret ideal of men — the prostitute. Lots of women live up to this idea: just because men want them to.

5 And so, poor woman, destiny makes away with her. It isn't that she hasn't got

a mind — she has. She's got everything that man has. The only difference is that she asks for a pattern. Give me a pattern to follow! That will always be woman's cry. Unless of course she has already chosen her pattern quite young, then she will declare she is herself absolutely, and no man's idea of women has any influence over her.

6   Now the real tragedy is not that women ask and must ask for a pattern of womanhood. The tragedy is not, even, that men give them such abominable patterns, child-wives, little-boy-baby-face girls, perfect secretaries, noble spouses, self-sacrificing mothers, pure women who bring forth children in virgin coldness, prostitutes who just make themselves low, to please the men; all the atrocious patterns of womanhood that men have supplied to woman; patterns all perverted from any real natural fullness of a human being. Man is willing to accept woman as an equal, as a man in skirts, as an angel, a devil, a baby-face, a machine, an instrument, a bosom, a womb, a pair of legs, a servant, an encyclopedia, an ideal or an obscenity; the one thing he won't accept her as is a human being, a real human being of the feminine sex.

7   And, of course, women love living up to strange patterns, weird patterns — the more uncanny the better. What could be more uncanny than the present pattern of the Eton-boy girl with flower-like artificial complexion? It is just weird. And for its very weirdness women like living up to it. What can be more gruesome than the little-boy-baby-face pattern? Yet the girls take it on with avidity.

8   But even that isn't the real root of the tragedy. The absurdity, and often, as in the Dante-Beatrice business, the inhuman nastiness of the pattern — for Beatrice had to go on being chaste and untouched all her life, according to Dante's pattern, while Dante had a cozy wife and kids at home — even that isn't the worst of it. The worst of it is, as soon as a woman has really lived up to the man's pattern, the man dislikes her for it. There is intense secret dislike for the Eton-young-man girl, among the boys, now that she is actually produced. Of course, she's very nice to show in public, absolutely the thing. But the very young men who have brought about her production detest her in private and in their private hearts are appalled by her.

9   When it comes to marrying, the pattern goes all to pieces. The boy marries the Eton-boy girl, and instantly he hates the *type*. Instantly his mind begins to play hysterically with all the other types, noble Agneses, chaste Beatrices, clinging Doras and lurid *filles de joie*. He is in a wild welter of confusion. Whatever pattern the poor woman tries to live up to, he'll want another. And that's the condition of modern marriage.

10   Modern woman isn't really a fool. But modern man is. That seems to me the only plain way of putting it. The modern man is a fool, and the modern young man a prize fool. He makes a greater mess of his women than men have ever made. Because he absolutely doesn't know what he wants her to be. We shall see the changes in the woman-pattern follow one another fast and furious now, because the young men

hysterically don't know what they want. Two years hence women may be in crinolines — there was a pattern for you! — or a bead flap, like naked negresses in mid-Africa — or they may be wearing brass armour, or the uniform of the Horse Guards. They may be anything. Because the young men are off their heads, and don't know what they want.

11   The women aren't fools, but they must live up to some pattern or other. They know the men are the fools. They don't really respect the pattern. Yet a pattern they must have, or they can't exist.

12   Women are not fools. They have their own logic, even if it's not the masculine sort. Women have the logic of emotion, men have the logic of reason. The two are complementary and mostly in opposition. But the woman's logic of emotion is no less real and inexorable than the man's logic of reason. It only works differently. And the woman never really loses it. She may spend years living up to a masculine pattern. But in the end, the strange and terrible logic of emotion will work out the smashing of that pattern, if it has not been emotionally satisfactory. This is the partial explanation of the astonishing changes in women. For years they go on being chaste Beatrices or child-wives. Then on a sudden — bash! The chaste Beatrice becomes something quite different, the child-wife becomes a roaring lioness! The pattern didn't suffice, emotionally.

13   Whereas men are fools. They are based on a logic of reason or are supposed to be. And then they go and behave, especially with regard to women, in a more-than-feminine unreasonableness. They spend years training up the little-boy-baby-face type, till they've got her perfect. Then the moment they marry her, they want something else. Oh, beware, young women, of the young men who adore you! The moment they've got you they'll want something utterly different. The moment they marry the little-boy-baby face, instantly they begin to pine for the noble Agnes, pure and majestic, or the infinite mother with deep bosom of consolation, or the perfect business woman, or the lurid prostitute on black silk sheets: or, most idiotic of all, a combination of all the lot of them at once. And that is the logic of reason! When it comes to women, modern men are idiots. They don't know what they want, and so they never want, permanently, what they get. They want cream cake that is at the same time ham and eggs and at the same time porridge. They are fools. If only women weren't bound by fate to play up to them!

14   For the fact of life is that women *must* play up to man's pattern. And she only gives her best to a man when he gives her a satisfactory pattern to play up to. But today, with a stock of ready-made, worn-out idiotic patterns to live up to, what can women give to men but the trashy side of their emotions? What could a woman possibly give to a man who wanted her to be a boy-baby face? What could she possibly give him but the dribblings of an idiot? — And, because women aren't fools, and aren't fooled even for very long at a time, she gives him some nasty cruel digs with her claws, and makes him cry for mother dear! — abruptly changing his pattern.

15   Bah! men are fools. If they want anything from women, let them give women a decent, satisfying idea of womanhood — not these trick patterns of washed-out idiots.

Notes

1. D. H. Lawrence's "Give Her a Pattern" was first published (under the title "Woman in Man's Image") in the U. S. in *Vanity Fair* (May 1929) and in the U. K. (as "Give Her a Pattern") in the *Daily Express* (June 1929). It appears in *Phoenix II: Uncollected, Unpublished, and Other Prose Works by D. H. Lawrence*, edited by Warren Roberts and Harry T. Moore (Viking, 1968).

2. Gaius Julius Caesar (Para. 2)

Gaius Julius Caesar (July 100 BC — 15 March 44 BC) was a Roman general and statesman and a distinguished writer of Latin prose. He played a critical role in the gradual transformation of the Roman Republic into the Roman Empire.

3. Nero (Para. 2)

Nero (15 December 37 — 9 June 68) was Roman Emperor from 54 to 68, and the last in the Julio-Claudian dynasty. Nero was adopted by his great-uncle Claudius to become his heir and successor, and succeeded to the throne in 54 following Claudius' death. During his reign, Nero focused much of his attention on diplomacy, trade, and enhancing the cultural life of the Empire. He ordered theaters built and promoted athletic games. During his reign, the redoubtable general Corbulo conducted a successful war and negotiated peace with the Parthian Empire. His general Suetonius Paulinus crushed a revolt in Britain and also annexed the Bosporan Kingdom to the Empire, beginning the First Roman-Jewish War.

4. Dante and Beatrice (Para. 2)

According to Dante, he first met Beatrice when his father took him to the Portinari house for a May Day party. At the time, Beatrice was eight years old, a year younger than Dante. Dante was instantly taken with her and remained so throughout her life even though she married another man, banker Simone dei Bardi, in 1287. Beatrice died three years later in June 1290 at the age of 24. Dante continued to hold an abiding love and respect for the woman after her death, even after he married Gemma Donati in 1285 and had children. After Beatrice's death, Dante withdrew into intense study and began composing poems dedicated to her memory. The collection of these poems, along with others he had previously written in his journal in awe of Beatrice, became *La Vita Nuova*.

Questions for Discussion

1. As Lawrence sketches some of the patterns on women by men through the ages,

whom does he regard as villain? Is there any evidence that he regards both men and women as victims of their culture?
2. What details provide the basis for the statement that the one thing man "won't accept her as, is a human being, a real human being of the feminine sex"?
3. Observe the repetition of the charge that modern men are fools. What does Lawrence mean by the statement "that women are bound by fate to play up to men"? How does he suggest that women are not as great fools as men?
4. What is the basis for his fatalistic attitude toward the possibility of real change in relationships between men and women?

Memorable Quotes

1. A girl should be two things: classy and fabulous.

— Coco Chanel

2. It is amazing how complete is the delusion that beauty is goodness.

— Leo Tolstoy

3. Everything has beauty, but not everyone sees it.

— Confucius

4. Youth is happy because it has the capacity to see beauty. Anyone who keeps the ability to see beauty never grows old.

— Franz Kafka

5. Think of all the beauty still left around you and be happy.

— Anne Frank

Further Readings

1. Nancy Etcoff, *Survival of the Prettiest: The Science of Beauty*
2. Naomi Wolf, *The Beauty Myth: How Images of Beauty Are Used Against Women*

Unit 12

Pre-reading Questions

1. Can you name some famous philosophers? Can you say something about their philosophical ideas?

2. How can philosophy benefit us?

3. Is it necessary for us to look up at the starry sky? Why or why not?

Text A

Plato

Jostein Gaarder

1 Hermes had already started to run toward the edge of the woods, and Sophie followed a few yards behind. Twice the dog turned around and growled, but Sophie was not to be deterred.

2 This time she was determined to find the philosopher — even if it meant running all the way to Athens.

3 The dog ran faster and suddenly turned off down a narrow path. Sophie chased him, but after a few minutes he turned and faced her, barking like a watchdog. Sophie still refused to give up, taking the opportunity to lessen the distance between them.

4 Hermes turned and raced down the path. Sophie realized that she would never catch up with him. She stood quite still for what seemed like an eternity, listening to him running farther and farther away. Then all was silent.

5 She sat down on a tree stump by a little clearing in the woods. She still had the brown envelope in her hand. She opened it, drew out several typewritten pages, and began to read:

Plato's Academy

6 Plato (428—347 B.C.) was twenty-nine years old when Socrates drank the hemlock. He had been a pupil of Socrates for some time and had followed his trial very closely. The fact that Athens could condemn its noblest citizen to death did more than make a profound impression on him. It was to shape the course of his entire philosophic endeavor.

7 To Plato, the death of Socrates was a striking example of the conflict that can exist between society as it really is and the true or ideal society. Plato's first deed as a philosopher was to publish Socrates' *Apology*, an account of his plea to the large jury.

8 As you will no doubt recall, Socrates never wrote anything down, although many of the pre-Socratics did. The problem is that hardly any of their written material remains. But in the case of Plato, we believe that all his principal works have been preserved. (In addition to Socrates' *Apology*, Plato wrote a collection of Epistles and about twenty-five philosophical Dialogues.) That we have these works today is due not least to the fact that Plato set up his own school of philosophy in a grove not far from Athens, named after the legendary Greek hero Academus. The school was therefore known as the Academy. (Since then, many thousands of "academies" have been established all over the world. We still speak of "academics" and "academic

subjects.")

9   The subjects taught at Plato's Academy were philosophy, mathematics, and gymnastics — although perhaps "taught" is hardly the right word. Lively discourse was considered most important at Plato's Academy. So it was not purely by chance that Plato's writings took the form of dialogues.

The Eternally True, Eternally Beautiful, and Eternally Good

10   In the introduction to this course I mentioned that it could often be a good idea to ask what a particular philosopher's project was. So now I ask: what were the problems Plato was concerned with?

11   Briefly, we can establish that Plato was concerned with the relationship between what is eternal and immutable, on the one hand, and what "flows", on the other. (Just like the pre-Socratics, in fact.) We've seen how the Sophists and Socrates turned their attention from questions of natural philosophy to problems related to man and society. And yet in one sense, even Socrates and the Sophists were preoccupied with the relationship between the eternal and immutable, and the "flowing". They were interested in the problem as it related to human morals and society's ideals or virtues. Very briefly, the Sophists thought that perceptions of what was right or wrong varied from one city-state to another and from one generation to the next. So right and wrong was something that "flowed". This was totally unacceptable to Socrates. He believed in the existence of eternal and absolute rules for what was right or wrong. By using our common sense we can all arrive at these immutable norms, since human reason is in fact eternal and immutable.

12   Do you follow, Sophie? Then along comes Plato. He is concerned with both what is eternal and immutable in nature and what is eternal and immutable as regards morals and society. To Plato, these two problems were one and the same. He tried to grasp a "reality" that was eternal and immutable.

13   And to be quite frank, that is precisely what we need philosophers for. We do not need them to choose a beauty queen or the day's bargain in tomatoes. (This is why they are often unpopular!) Philosophers will try to ignore highly topical affairs and instead try to draw people's attention to what is eternally "true", eternally "beautiful", and eternally "good".

14   We can thus begin to glimpse at least the outline of Plato's philosophical project. But let's take one thing at a time. We are attempting to understand an extraordinary mind, a mind that was to have a profound influence on all subsequent European philosophy.

The World of Ideas

15   Both Empedocles and Democritus had drawn attention to the fact that although in the natural world everything "flows", there must nevertheless be "something" that never changes. Plato agreed with the proposition as such — but in quite a different

way.

16 Plato believed that everything tangible in nature "flows". So there are no "substances" that do not dissolve. Absolutely everything that belongs to the "material world" is made of a material that time can erode, but everything is made after a timeless "mold" or "form" that is eternal and immutable.

17 You see? No, you don't.

18 Why are horses the same, Sophie? You probably don't think they are at all. But there is something that all horses have in common, something that enables us to identify them as horses. A particular horse "flows", naturally. It might be old and lame, and in time it will die. But the "form" of the horse is eternal and immutable.

19 That which is eternal and immutable, to Plato, is therefore not a physical "basic substance", as it was for Empedocles and Democritus. Plato's conception was of eternal and immutable patterns, spiritual and abstract in their nature that all things are fashioned after.

20 Let me put it like this: The pre-Socratics had given a reasonably good explanation of natural change without having to presuppose that anything actually "changed". In the midst of nature's cycle there were some eternal and immutable smallest elements that did not dissolve, they thought. Fair enough, Sophie! But they had no reasonable explanation for how these "smallest elements" that were once building blocks in a horse could suddenly whirl together four or five hundred years later and fashion themselves into a completely new horse. Or an elephant or a crocodile, for that matter. Plato's point was that Democritus' atoms never fashioned themselves into an "eledile" or a "crocophant". This was what set his philosophical reflections going.

21 If you already understand what I am getting at, you may skip this next paragraph. But just in case, I will clarify: You have a box of Lego and you build a Lego horse. You then take it apart and put the blocks back in the box. You cannot expect to make a new horse just by shaking the box. How could Lego blocks of their own accord find each other and become a new horse again? No, you have to rebuild the horse, Sophie. And the reason you can do it is that you have a picture in your mind of what the horse looked like. The Lego horse is made from a model which remains unchanged from horse to horse.

22 How did you do with the fifty identical cookies? Let us assume that you have dropped in from outer space and have never seen a baker before. You stumble into a tempting bakery — and there you catch sight of fifty identical gingerbread men on a shelf. I imagine you would wonder how they could be exactly alike. It might well be that one of them has an arm missing, another has lost a bit of its head, and a third has a funny bump on its stomach. But after careful thought, you would nevertheless conclude that all gingerbread men have something in common. Although none of them is perfect, you would suspect that they had a common origin. You would realize that all

the cookies were formed in the same mold. And what is more, Sophie, you are now seized by the irresistible desire to see this mold, because clearly, the mold itself must be utter perfection — and in a sense, more beautiful — in comparison with these crude copies.

23 If you solved this problem all by yourself, you arrived at the philosophical solution in exactly the same way that Plato did.

24   Like most philosophers, he "dropped in from outer space". He was astonished at the way all natural phenomena could be so alike, and he concluded that it had to be because there are a limited number of forms "behind" everything we see around us. Plato called these forms ideas. Behind every horse, pig, or human being, there is the "idea horse", "idea pig", and "idea human being". (In the same way, the bakery we spoke of can have gingerbread men, gingerbread horses, and gingerbread pigs, because every self-respecting bakery has more than one mold. But one mold is enough for each type of gingerbread cookie.)

25 Plato came to the conclusion that there must be a reality behind the "material world". He called this reality the world of ideas; it contained the eternal and immutable "patterns" behind the various phenomena we come across in nature. This remarkable view is known as Plato's theory of ideas.

True Knowledge

26 I'm sure you've been following me, Sophie dear. But you may be wondering whether Plato was being serious. Did he really believe that forms like these actually existed in a completely different reality?

27 He probably didn't believe it literally in the same way for all his life, but in some of his dialogues that is certainly how he means to be understood. Let us try to follow his train of thought.

28 A philosopher, as we have seen, tries to grasp something that is eternal and immutable. It would serve no purpose, for instance, to write a philosophic treatise on the existence of a particular soap bubble. Partly because one would hardly have time to study it in depth before it burst, and partly because it would probably be rather difficult to find a market for a philosophic treatise on something nobody has ever seen, and which only existed for five seconds.

29   Plato believed that everything we see around us in nature, everything tangible, can be likened to a soap bubble, since nothing that exists in the world of the senses is lasting. We know, of course, that sooner or later every human being and every animal will die and decompose. Even a block of marble changes and gradually disintegrates. (The Acropolis is falling into ruin, Sophie! It is a scandal, but that's the way it is.) Plato's point is that we can never have true knowledge of anything that is in a constant state of change. We can only have opinions about things that belong to the world of the senses, tangible things. We can only have true knowledge of things that

can be understood with our reason.

30 All right, Sophie, I'll explain it more clearly: a gingerbread man can be so lopsided after all that baking that it can be quite hard to see what it is meant to be. But having seen dozens of gingerbread men that were more or less successful, I can be pretty sure what the cookie mold was like. I can guess, even though I have never seen it. It might not even be an advantage to see the actual mold with my own eyes because we cannot always trust the evidence of our senses. The faculty of vision can vary from person to person. On the other hand, we can rely on what our reason tells us because that is the same for everyone.

31 If you are sitting in a classroom with thirty other pupils, and the teacher asks the class which color of the rainbow is the prettiest, he will probably get a lot of different answers. But if he asks what 8 times 3 is, the whole class will — we hope — give the same answer. Because now reason is speaking and reason is, in a way, the direct opposite of "thinking so" or "feeling". We could say that reason is eternal and universal precisely because it only expresses eternal and universal states.

32 Plato found mathematics very absorbing because mathematical states never change. They are therefore states we can have true knowledge of. But here we need an example.

33 Imagine you find a round pinecone out in the woods. Perhaps you say you "think" it looks completely round, whereas Joanna insists it is a bit flattened on one side. (Then you start arguing about it!) But you cannot have true knowledge of anything you can perceive with your eyes. On the other hand you can say with absolute certainty that the sum of the angles in a circle is 360 degrees. In this case you would be talking about an ideal circle which might not exist in the physical world but which you can clearly visualize. (You are dealing with the hidden gingerbread-man mold and not with the particular cookie on the kitchen table.)

34 In short, we can only have inexact conceptions of things we perceive with our senses. But we can have true knowledge of things we understand with our reason. The sum of the angles in a triangle will remain 180 degrees to the end of time. And similarly the "idea" horse will walk on four legs even if all the horses in the sensory world break a leg.

Notes

1. About the author.

Jostein Gaarder was born on 8 August 1952 in Oslo, Norway and is a Norwegian intellectual and author of several novels, short stories and children's books. Gaarder often writes from the perspective of children, exploring their sense of wonder about the world. He often uses metafiction in his works, writing stories within stories.

Gaarder was born into a pedagogical family. His best known work is the novel *Sophie's World*, subtitled *A Novel about the History of Philosophy*. This popular work has been translated into fifty-three languages.

2. **Plato** was twenty-nine years old when Socrates drank the hemlock. (Para. 6)

Plato was a Classical Greek philosopher, mathematician, student of Socrates, writer of philosophical dialogues, and founder of the Academy in Athens, the first institution of higher learning in the Western world. Along with his mentor, Socrates, and his student, Aristotle, Plato helped to lay the foundations of Western philosophy and science. Plato's sophistication as a writer is evident in his Socratic dialogues; thirty-six dialogues and thirteen letters have been ascribed to him. Plato's writings have been published in several fashions; this has led to several conventions regarding the naming and referencing of Plato's texts. Plato's dialogues have been used to teach a range of subjects, including philosophy, logic, ethics, rhetoric, and mathematics. Plato is one of the most important founding figures in Western philosophy.

3. Plato set up his own school of philosophy in a grove not far from Athens, named after the legendary Greek hero **Academus**. (Para. 8)

Academus was an Attic hero in Greek mythology. The tale traditionally told of him is that when Castor and Pollux invaded Attica to liberate their sister Helen, he betrayed to them that she was kept concealed at Aphidnae. For this reason the Tyndarids always showed him much gratitude, and whenever the Lacedaemonians invaded Attica, they always spared the land belonging to Academus which lay on the Cephissus, six stadia from Athens.

4. We've seen how the **Sophists** and Socrates turned their attention from questions of natural philosophy to problems related to man and society. (Para. 11)

The term "sophist" is derived from the Greek words sophos and sophia which are usually translated as "wise" and "wisdom". The Sophists were itinerant teachers who claimed to teach wisdom; more specifically, Protagoras, one of the first to willingly identify himself as a Sophist, stated that he taught one how to take "proper care of his personal affairs, so that he may manage his own household, and also of the State's affairs, so as to become a real power in the city, both as speaker and man of action." Socrates reinterprets Protagoras' statement as a claim to make students into good citizens, and Protagoras readily agrees.

5. Both **Empedocles** and **Democritus** had drawn attention to the fact that although in the natural world everything "flows," there must nevertheless be "something" that never changes. (Para. 15)

Empedocles (490—430 BC) was a Greek pre-Socratic philosopher. Empedocles' philosophy is best known for being the originator of the cosmogenic theory of the four Classical elements. He also proposed powers called Love and Strife which would act as forces to bring about the mixture and separation of the elements. These physical speculations were part of a history of the universe which also dealt with the origin and development of life. Influenced by the Pythagoreans, he supported the doctrine of reincarnation.

Democritus (460—370 BC) was an Ancient Greek philosopher born in Abdera, Thrace, Greece. He was an influential pre-Socratic philosopher and pupil of Leucippus, who formulated an atomic theory for the universe.

6. The **Acropolis** is falling into ruin, Sophie! It is a scandal, but that's the way it is. (Para. 29)

The Acropolis of Athens is an ancient citadel located on a high rocky outcrop above the city of Athens and containing the remains of several ancient buildings of great architectural and historic significance, the most famous being the Parthenon.

Glossary

absorbing [əb'sɔːbɪŋ] a.	capable of arousing and holding the attention
accord [ə'kɔːd] v.	harmony of people's opinions or actions or characters
assume [ə'sjuːm] v.	take to be the case or to be true; accept without verification or proof; take on titles, offices, duties, responsibilities
bubble ['bʌbl] v.	form, produce, or emit bubbles
clarify ['klærəfaɪ] v.	make clear and (more) comprehensible
clearing ['klɪərɪŋ] n.	a tract of land with few or no trees in the middle of a wooded area
condemn [kən'dem] v.	to express strong disapproval of
crude [kruːd] adj.	not carefully or expertly made
decompose [dɪkəm'pəʊz] v.	separate (substances) into constituent elements or parts
deter [dɪ'tɜː] v.	try to prevent; show opposition to
discourse ['dɪskɔːs] v.	carry on a conversation
disintegrate [dɪs'ɪntɪgreɪt] v.	break into parts or components or lose cohesion or unity
dissolve [dɪ'zɒlv] v.	cause to go into a solution
endeavor [ɪn'devə] n.	attempt by employing effort
epistle [ɪ'pɪsl] n.	a specially long, formal letter
erode [ɪ'rəʊd] v.	become ground down or deteriorate
eternity [ɪ'tɜːnətɪ] n.	time without end
faculty ['fækltɪɪ] n.	one of the inherent cognitive or perceptual powers of the mind
grove [grəʊv] n.	a small growth of trees without underbrush
growl [graʊl] v. & n.	to utter or emit low dull rumbling sounds
hemlock ['hemlɒk] n.	poisonous drug derived from an Eurasian plant of the

	genus Conium
identical [aɪˈdentɪkl] a.	exactly alike; incapable of being perceived as different
immutable [ɪˈmjuːtəbl] a.	not subject or susceptible to change or variation in form or quality or nature
irresistible [ɪrɪˈzɪstəbl] a.	impossible to resist; overpowering
literally [ˈlɪtərəlɪ] adj.	in a literal sense
lopsided [lɒpˈsaɪdɪd] adj.	turned or twisted toward one side
perception [pəˈsepʃn] n.	the representation of what is perceived; basic component in the formation of a concept
pinecone [[ˈpaɪnkəun] n.	the seed-producing cone of a pine tree
plea [pliː] n.	a humble request for help from someone in authority
preoccupy [prɪˈɒkjupaɪ] v.	to engage or engross the interest or attention of beforehand or occupy urgently or obsessively
preserve [prɪˈzɜːv] v.	keep or maintain in unaltered condition; cause to remain or last
n.	a reservation where animals are protected; fruit preserved by cooking with sugar
presuppose [prɪsəˈpəuz] v.	take for granted or as a given; suppose beforehand
principal [ˈprɪnsəpl] a.	most important element
project [ˈprɒdʒekt] v.	to communicate vividly; to extend out or project in space
n.	any piece of work that is undertaken or attempted
proposition [prpəˈzɪʃn] n.	a proposal offered for acceptance or rejection
self-respecting a.	having or showing self-esteem
sensory [ˈsensərɪ] a.	involving or derived from the senses
stumble [ˈstʌmbl] v.	walk unsteadily
subsequent [ˈsʌbsɪkwənt] a.	following in time or order
tangible [ˈtændʒəbl] a.	perceptible by the senses especially the sense of touch
tempting [ˈtemptɪŋ] a.	highly attractive and able to arouse hope or desire
treatise [ˈtriːtɪs] n.	a formal exposition
visualize [ˈvɪʒuəlaɪz] v.	imagine; conceive of; see in one's mind
whirl [wɜːl] n.	a twisting or spinning motion

Understanding the text

1. What's the possible relationship between Socrates and Plato?
2. Were Socrates' philosophical ideas passed on to his posterity from mouth to mouth?
3. What was taught at Plato's Academy?
4. What were the two problems concerned Plato most?
5. What was the world of ideas, according to Plato?

6. Where could true knowledge be derived, according to Plato?

Exercises

I Vocabulary

Section A Paraphrase the following sentences chosen from the text below.

1. She stood quite still for what seemed like an eternity, listening to him running farther and farther away. (Para. 4)
2. The fact that Athens could condemn its noblest citizen to death did more than make a profound impression on him. (Para. 6)
3. Plato's first deed as a philosopher was to publish Socrates' Apology, an account of his plea to the large jury. (Para. 7)
4. We are attempting to understand an extraordinary mind, a mind that was to have a profound influence on all subsequent European philosophy. (Para. 14)
5. Partly because one would hardly have time to study it in depth before it burst, and partly because it would probably be rather difficult to find a market for a philosophic treatise on something nobody has ever seen, and which only existed for five seconds. (Para. 28)

Section B There are ten sentences in this section. Beneath each sentence there are four words or phrases marked A, B, C and D. Choose one word or phrase that best completes the sentence.

1. The _____ cycle of life and death is a subject of interest to scientists and philosophers alike.
   A. incompatible B. exceeding   C. instantaneous D. eternal
2. The discovery of new oil-fields in various parts of the country filled the government with _____ hope.
   A. eternal   B. infinite   C. ceaseless   D. everlasting
3. Now a paper in Science argues that organic chemicals in the rock come mostly from _____ on earth rather than bacteria on Mars.
   A. configuration B. constitution C. condemnation D. contamination
4. Apart from philosophical and legal reasons for respecting patients' wishes, there are several practical reasons why doctors should _____ to involve patients in their own medical care decisions.
   A. enforce   B. enhance   C. endeavor   D. endow
5. The newly-built principal museum seems _____ enough to last a hundred years.
   A. steady   B. substantial   C. sophisticated   D. spacious
6. Would you please _____ a seat for this evening's concert?
   A. reserve   B. preserve   C. conserve   D. observe
7. The old building is in a good state of _____ except for the wooden floors.

A. observation   B. preservation   C. conservation   D. compensation
8. The doctors _____ the newly approved drug into the patient when he was critically ill.
   A. projected   B. injected   C. ejected   D. subjected
9. Most mathematicians trust their _____ in solving problems and readily admit they would not be able to function without it.
   A. conception   B. perception   C. cognition   D. intuition
10. The man to whom we handed the forms pointed out that they had not been _____ filled in.
    A. consequently   B. subsequently   C. comprehensively   D. properly

Section C Use the proper form of the following words given in the brackets to fill in the blanks.
1. We should _____ the market economy and planned economy. (disintegrate)
2. The stars twinkled in transparent _____. (clarify)
3. Your judgment of the case is based on the _____ that the witness is telling the truth. (presuppose)
4. The old building had an _____ air of sadness about it. (tangible)
5. He said he was a doctor, but it _____ emerged that he was an impostor. (subsequent)
6. We can _____ his sorrow by the looks on his face. (perception)
7. One should not _____ inexperience in excuse of his mistake. (plea)
8. The Chinese are unanimous in their _____. (condemn)
9. Although he was on a diet, the delicious food _____ him enormously. (tempting)
10. _____ that the demand for power continues to rise at the current rate, it will not be long before traditional sources become inadequate. (assume)

Section D Use the proper form of the following phrases to fill in the blanks.

of one's own accord	be identical to	be preoccupied with
get at	have the knowledge	in depth
may well be	fashion…into	

1. Swelled heads _____ the few things they know.
2. This knife _____ the one with which the murder was committed.
3. A typical cruiser or aircraft carrier _____ an easy target.
4. The symptoms will clear up _____ after a few days.
5. In today's lecture I'd like to interpret this problem broadly rather than _____.
6. He managed to _____ a piece of wood _____ a doll.
7. A translator himself should not only _____ as a scholar, but also have the inspiration as a writer.

8. It is no easy thing to _____ the meaning of every idiom.

II Grammar

Choose the best answer to complete the following sentences from the respective four choices.

1. After _____ seemed an endless wait, it was his turn to enter the personnel manager's office.
   A. that   B. it   C. what   D. there
2. Which of the following italicized parts is a subject clause (主语从句)?
   A. We are quite certain *that we will get there in time.*
   B. He has to face the fact *that there will be no pay rise this year.*
   C. She said *that she had seen the man earlier that morning.*
   D. It is sheer luck *that the miners are still alive after ten days.*
3. There is no doubt _____ the couple did the right thing in coming back home earlier than planned.
   A. whether   B. that   C. why   D. when
4. My boss ordered that the legal documents _____ to him before lunch.
   A. be sent   B. were sent
   C. were to be sent   D. must be sent
5. We consider _____ he should have left without telling anyone beforehand.
   A. strange why   B. it strange what
   C. it strange that   D. that strange
6. Men differ from animals _____ they can think and speak.
   A. for which   B. for that   C. in that   D. in which
7. Quality is _____ counts most.
   A. which   B. that   C. what   D. where
8. I am surprised _____ this city is a dull place to live in.
   A. that you should think   B. by what you are thinking
   C. that you would think   D. with what you were thinking
9. The government has promised to do _____ lies in its power to ease the hardships of the victims in the flood-stricken area.
   A. however   B. whichever   C. whatever   D. wherever
10. Intellect is to the mind _____ sight is to the body.
    A. what   B. as   C. that   D. like

III Cloze

Fill in the blanks with words from the following list. Use the words in their proper form. Pay attention each word is used only once.

appear	childhood	choose	comfort
darkness	despair	entrance	fault
flow	into	linger	mournful
painful	remorse	strike	stumble
sunny	surface	symbol	towards

It was New Year's Night. An aged man was standing at a window. He raised his (1) _____ eyes towards the deep blue sky, where the stars were floating like white lilies on the (2) _____ of a clear calm lake.

Then he cast them on the earth, where few more hopeless people than himself now moved towards their certain goal — the tomb. He had already passed sixty of the stages leading to it, and he had brought from his journey nothing but errors and (3) _____. Now his health was poor, his mind vacant, his heart sorrowful, and his old age short of (4) _____.

The days of his youth (5) _____ like dreams before him, and here called the serious moment when his father placed him at the (6) _____ of the two roads — one leading to a peaceful, sunny place, covered with flowers, fruits and resounding with soft, sweet songs; the other leading to a deep, dark cave, which was endless, where poison (7) _____ instead of water and where devils and poisonous snakes hissed and crawled.

He looked towards the sky and cried (8) _____, "O youth, return! O my father, place me once more at the entrance to life, and I'll (9) _____ the better way!" But both his father and the days of his youth had passed away.

He saw the lights flowing away in the (10) _____. These were the days of his wasted life; he saw a star fall down from the sky and disappeared, and this was the (11) _____ of himself. His remorse, which was like a sharp arrow, struck deeply (12) _____ his heart. Then he remembered his friends in his (13) _____, who entered on life together with him. But they had made their way to success and were now honored and happy on this New Year's Night.

The clock in the high church tower (14) _____ and the sound made him remember his parents' early love for him. They had taught him and prayed to God for his good. But he chose the wrong way. With shame and grief he dared no longer look (15) _____ that heaven where his father lived. His darkened eyes were full of tears, and with a (16) _____ effort, he burst out a cry: "Come back, my early days! Come back!"

And his youth did return, for all this was only a dream which he had on New Year's Night. He was still young though his (17) _____ were real; he had not yet entered the deep, dark cave, and he was still free to walk on the road which leads to the peaceful and (18) _____ land.

Those who still (19) _____ on the entrance of life, hesitating to choose the bright road, remember that when years are passed and your feet (20) _____ on the dark mountains, you will cry bitterly, but in vain: "O youth, return! Oh give me back my early days!"

IV Translation

Section A Translate the following Chinese sentences into English.
1. 正是这个优势赋予了核武器威慑力量。(deter)
2. 但对于爱着的人而言，时间是永恒。(eternity)
3. 她对别人对她行为的多方谴责一点也不在乎。(condemn)
4. 他的成功与其说是由于机遇，不如说是因为努力。(endeavor)
5. 我至为关心的是我一家的幸福。(principal)
6. 维护公共秩序是警察的职责。(preserve)
7. 话若投机嫌日短。[谚]（discourse）
8. 上帝并不受制于至上的、永恒的宇宙法则。(immutable)
9. 化石给了我们恐龙确实存在的确切证据。(tangible)
10. 他用尽全力在脸上装出一副坦然的表情来。(assume)

Section B Translate the following English paragraph into Chinese.

The average man who uses a telephone couldn't explain how a telephone works. He takes for granted the telephone, the railway train, the airplane, as our grandfathers took for granted the miracles of the gospels. He neither questions nor understands them. It is as though each of us investigated and made his own only a tiny circle of facts. Knowledge outside the day's work is regarded by most men as a gewgaw. Still we are usually in reaction against our ignorance. We excite ourselves sometimes and think deeply. We enjoy thinking about anything at all — about life after death or about such questions as is said to have puzzled Aristotle. "Why sneezing from noon to midnight was good, but from night to noon unlucky." One of the greatest joys known to man is to take such a flight into ignorance in search of knowledge. The great pleasure of ignorance is, after all, the pleasure of asking questions. The man who has lost this pleasure or exchanged it for the pleasure of dogma, which is the pleasure of answering, is already beginning to stiffen. One envies so inquisitive a man as Jewell, who sat down to the study of physiology in his sixties. Most of us have lost the sense of ignorance long before that age. We even become proud of our squirrel's store-house of knowledge and regard increasing age itself as a school of omniscience. We forget that Socrates was famous for wisdom not because he was Mr. know-all but because he realized at the age of seventy that he still knew nothing.

V Topic for Discussion

Discuss the following topic together with your classmates:

Plato believed the soul was eternal and indestructible. He also had a dual nature of reality. The realm of ideas was the real while the physical was a "receptacle" of those ideals.

The physical world was innately "bad" or defective compared to the ideal. In fact, the physical was seen as the "prison house" of the soul and kept us from understanding things as they really are.

The notion of innate ideas ties to Plato's belief that we all are connected to this ideal world and that we might be able to break out of the cave in which we don't see things as they really are but may be able to recollect things if we contemplate them enough.

What's your personal contribution to this topic?

VI Written Work

Write a short essay of about 150 words on the following topic.

Some people believe that the meaning of life consists in wealth one creates and the reputation one establishes; some other people claim that the meaning of life is best expressed in one's contribution to the community, the society, even the world. What's your opinion?

Text B

Who Was Socrates?

Jostein Gaarder

1 Socrates (470—399 B. C.) is possibly the most enigmatic figure in the entire history of philosophy. He never wrote a single line. Yet he is one of the philosophers who has had the greatest influence on European thought, not least because of the dramatic manner of his death.

2 Born in Athens, he spent most of his life in the city squares and marketplaces talking with the people he met there. "The trees in the countryside can teach me nothing," he said. He could also stand lost in thought for hours on end.

3 Even during his lifetime he was considered somewhat enigmatic, and fairly soon after his death he was held to be the founder of any number of different philosophical schools of thought. The very fact that he was so enigmatic and ambiguous

made it possible for widely differing schools of thought to claim him as their own.

4   It is known for a certainty that he was extremely ugly. He was potbellied, and had bulging eyes and a snub nose. But inside he was said to be "perfectly delightful." It was also said of him that "You can seek him in the present, you can seek him in the past, but you will never find his equal." Nevertheless he was sentenced to death for his philosophical activities.

5   The life of Socrates is mainly known to us through the writings of Plato, who was one of his pupils and who became one of the greatest philosophers of all time. Plato wrote a number of Dialogues, or dramatized discussions on philosophy, in which he uses Socrates as his principal character and mouthpiece.

6   Since Plato is putting his own philosophy in Socrates' mouth, we cannot be sure that the words he speaks in the dialogues were ever actually uttered by him. So it is no easy matter to distinguish between the teachings of Socrates and the philosophy of Plato. Exactly the same problem applies to many other historical persons who left no written accounts. The classic example, of course, is Jesus. We cannot be certain that the "historical" Jesus actually spoke the words that Matthew or Luke ascribed to him. Similarly, what the "historical" Socrates actually said will always be shrouded in mystery.

7   But who Socrates "really" was is relatively unimportant. It is Plato's portrait of Socrates that has inspired thinkers in the Western world for nearly 2,500 years.

The Art of Discourse

8   The essential nature of Socrates' art lay in the fact that he did not appear to want to instruct people. On the contrary he gave the impression of one desiring to learn from those he spoke with. So instead of lecturing like a traditional schoolmaster, he discussed.

9   Obviously he would not have become a famous philosopher had he confined himself purely to listening to others. Nor would he have been sentenced to death. But he just asked questions, especially to begin a conversation, as if he knew nothing. In the course of the discussion he would generally get his opponents to recognize the weakness of their arguments, and, forced into a corner, they would finally be obliged to realize what was right and what was wrong.

10   Socrates, whose mother was a midwife, used to say that his art was like the art of the midwife. She does not herself give birth to the child, but she is there to help during its delivery. Similarly, Socrates saw his task as helping people to "give birth" to the correct insight, since real understanding must come from within. It cannot be imparted by someone else. And only the understanding that comes from within can lead to true insight.

11   To put it more precisely: The ability to give birth is a natural characteristic. In the same way, everybody can grasp philosophical truths if they just use their innate

reason. Using your innate reason means reaching down inside yourself and using what is there.

12 By playing ignorant, Socrates forced the people he met to use their common sense. Socrates could feign ignorance — or pretend to be dumber than he was. We call this Socratic irony. This enabled him to continually expose the weaknesses in people's thinking. He was not averse to doing this in the middle of the city square. If you met Socrates, you thus might end up being made a fool of publicly.

13 So it is not surprising that, as time went by, people found him increasingly exasperating, especially people who had status in the community. "Athens is like a sluggish horse," he is reputed to have said, "and I am the gadfly trying to sting it into life."

A Divine Voice

14 It was not in order to torment his fellow beings that Socrates kept on stinging them. Something within him left him no choice. He always said that he had a "divine voice" inside him. Socrates protested, for example, against having any part in condemning people to death. He moreover refused to inform on his political enemies. This was eventually to cost him his life.

15 In the year 399 B. C. he was accused of "introducing new gods and corrupting the youth," as well as not believing in the accepted gods. With a slender majority, a jury of five hundred found him guilty.

16 He could very likely have appealed for leniency. At least he could have saved his life by agreeing to leave Athens. But had he done this he would not have been Socrates. He valued his conscience — and the truth — higher than life. He assured the jury that he had only acted in the best interests of the state. He was nevertheless condemned to drink hemlock. Shortly thereafter, he drank the poison in the presence of his friends, and died.

17 Why did Socrates have to die? People have been asking this question for 2,400 years. However, he was not the only person in history to have seen things through to the bitter end and suffered death for the sake of their convictions.

18 I have mentioned Jesus already, and in fact there are several striking parallels between them.

19 Both Jesus and Socrates were enigmatic personalities, also to their contemporaries. Neither of them wrote down their teachings, so we are forced to rely on the picture we have of them from their disciples. But we do know that they were both masters of the art of discourse. They both spoke with a characteristic self-assuredness that could fascinate as well as exasperate. And not least, they both believed that they spoke on behalf of something greater than themselves. They challenged the power of the community by criticizing all forms of injustice and corruption. And finally — their activities cost them their lives.

20 The trials of Jesus and Socrates also exhibit clear parallels.

21 They could certainly both have saved themselves by appealing for mercy, but they both felt they had a mission that would have been betrayed unless they kept faith to the bitter end. And by meeting their death so bravely they commanded an enormous following, also after they had died.

22 I do not mean to suggest that Jesus and Socrates were alike. I am merely drawing attention to the fact that they both had a message that was inseparably linked to their personal courage.

A Joker in Athens

23 Socrates, Sophie! We aren't done with him yet. We have talked about his method. But what was his philosophical project?

24 Socrates lived at the same time as the Sophists. Like them, he was more concerned with man and his place in society than with the forces of nature. As a Roman philosopher, Cicero, said of him a few hundred years later, Socrates "called philosophy down from the sky and established her in the towns and introduced her into homes and forced her to investigate life, ethics, good and evil."

25 But Socrates differed from the Sophists in one significant way. He did not consider himself to be a "sophist" — that is, a learned or wise person. Unlike the Sophists, he did not teach for money. No, Socrates called himself a philosopher in the true sense of the word. A "philosopher" really means "one who loves wisdom."

26 Are you sitting comfortably, Sophie? Because it is central to the rest of this course that you fully understand the difference between a sophist and a philosopher. The Sophists took money for their more or less hairsplitting expoundings, and sophists of this kind have come and gone from time immemorial. I am referring to all the schoolmasters and self-opinionated know-it-alls who are satisfied with what little they know, or who boast of knowing a whole lot about subjects they haven't the faintest notion of. You have probably come across a few of these sophists in your young life. A real philosopher, Sophie, is a completely different kettle of fish — the direct opposite, in fact. A philosopher knows that in reality he knows very little. That is why he constantly strives to achieve true insight. Socrates was one of these rare people. He knew that he knew nothing about life and about the world. And now comes the important part: it troubled him that he knew so little.

27 A philosopher is therefore someone who recognizes that there is a lot he does not understand, and is troubled by it. In that sense, he is still wiser than all those who brag about their knowledge of things they know nothing about. "Wisest is she who knows she does not know," I said previously. Socrates himself said, "One thing only I know, and that is that I know nothing."

28 Remember this statement, because it is an admission that is rare, even among philosophers. Moreover, it can be so dangerous to say it in public that it can cost you

your life. The most subversive people are those who ask questions. Giving answers is not nearly as threatening. Any one question can be more explosive than a thousand answers.

29 You remember the story of the emperor's new clothes? The emperor was actually stark naked but none of his subjects dared say so. Suddenly a child burst out, "But he's got nothing on!" That was a courageous child, Sophie. Like Socrates, who dared tell people how little we humans know. The similarity between children and philosophers is something we have already talked about.

30 To be precise: Mankind is faced with a number of difficult questions that we have no satisfactory answers to. So now two possibilities present themselves: We can either fool ourselves and the rest of the world by pretending that we know all there is to know, or we can shut our eyes to the central issues once and for all and abandon all progress. In this sense, humanity is divided. People are, generally speaking, either dead certain or totally indifferent. (Both types are crawling around deep down in the rabbit's fur!)

31 It is like dividing a deck of cards into two piles, Sophie. You lay the black cards in one pile and the red in the other. But from time to time a joker turns up that is neither heart nor club, neither diamond nor spade. Socrates was this joker in Athens. He was neither certain nor indifferent. All he knew was that he knew nothing — and it troubled him. So he became a philosopher — someone who does not give up but tirelessly pursues his quest for truth.

32 An Athenian is said to have asked the oracle at Delphi who the wisest man in Athens was. The oracle answered that Socrates of all mortals was the wisest. When Socrates heard this he was astounded, to put it mildly. (He must have laughed, Sophie!) He went straight to the person in the city whom he, and everyone else, thought was excessively wise. But when it turned out that this person was unable to give Socrates satisfactory answers to his questions, Socrates realized that the oracle had been right.

33 Socrates felt that it was necessary to establish a solid foundation for our knowledge. He believed that this foundation lay in man's reason. With his unshakable faith in human reason he was decidedly a rationalist.

Notes

1. He could also stand lost in thought for hours **on end.** (Para. 2)
   Here *on end* means "continuously".
2. You can seek him in the present, you can seek him in the past, but you will never find his equal. (Para. 5)
   Paraphrase: You searched the history but you cannot find another person who is

the same as or similar to Socrates.

3. He was not averse to doing this in the middle of the city square. If you met Socrates, you thus might end up being made a fool of publicly. (Para. 12)

Paraphrase: Socrates usually did so in the square and would always make someone's folly publicly known.

4. The trials of Jesus and Socrates also exhibit clear parallels. (Para. 20)

Paraphrase: There are many similarities between the fate and trial of Jesus and Socrates.

Questions for Discussion

We are encouraged to "look up into the starlit sky"; but why do think it's necessary to do so? And what do you think modern can get by doing so?

Memorable Quotes

1. If you would go up high, then use your own legs. Do not let yourselves carried aloft; do not seat yourselves on other people's backs and heads.

— F. W. Nietzsche

2. Light troubles speak; great troubles keep silent.

— Lucius Annaeus Seneneca

3. Optimists always picture themselves accomplishing their goals.

— Lucius Anaeus Seneca

Further Readings

1. Jostein Gaarder, *Sophie's World*
2. *Philosophical Magazine*
3. Bertrand Russell, *A History of Western Philosophy*

Phrase List

Unit 1
on the same page	在同一页上；进度相同；达成共识
deviate from	偏离，脱离
disabuse sb. of	使某人去除某个想法
accommodate sb. with	为某人提供
exert pressure on	施加压力
reflect off	反射，反映
commit oneself to	致力于；使自己承担
have aptitude for	有才能
be subject to	受支配，从属于
to put it in some perspective	说得更明白一点

Unit 2
confront … with.	使面临（问题、任务、困难等）
take hold	扎根，固定下来
on trial	在考验中；（人）在试验期间
bail out	摆脱困境
make for	促成，造就；导致
get away with	侥幸逃脱惩罚
strike a chord	打动心弦，引起共鸣
speculate on	推测，考虑
imbue… with	使灌输，使渗透
infuse… with	灌输，使充满
raise one's heckles	使某人生气
call sb. forth	唤起，使行动或存在
at all costs	无论如何，不惜任何代价
dredge… up	重提（不快往事）

Unit 3

in hopes of	希望能
be destined to	注定的
to the point	中肯
talk down to	用高人一等的口气说话
resign oneself to	顺从
hit a nerve	触及要害
stand up to	勇敢地面对；经得起
be adamant about	固执地
be in limbo	处于不稳定（或中间过渡）状态
squirrel away	贮存
hook up	有联系
have the presence of mind	镇定自若
loosen up	放松

Unit 4

be paralleled by	与之匹敌
be preceded by	在…前面
be presumed to	估计是，据推测
campaign for	争取
make room for	让给，腾出空间
switch over	转换到
tempt to	尝试
tune in	调频

Unit 5

account for	在数量、比例上占
put strains on	使紧张，施加压力
attempt to	试图做某事
reflect on	仔细想；回忆
in the midst of	在…中间
count on	依靠；指望
in exchange for	交换
be bound to	一定会

Unit 6

reduce to	降至；把…简化为
apart from	缺少；除…以外；且不说
resort to	诉诸于；求助于；凭借

result in	导致；结果是
reach out to	接触，联系；把手伸向
seek for	寻觅；寻找
embark on	上（船、飞机等）；从事
so as to	为的是，以便
be inclined to	倾向于；易于…的
adhered to	坚持；依附

Unit 7

in the status of	在…身份，地位下
at any rate	无论如何，至少
revolve around	围绕…转动；以…为中心
as such	同样地，本身；就其本身而论
be characterized by…	以…为特点
for decades	数十年
model on	模仿
on the premises that…	在…前提下

Unit 8

at its roots	从根本上说
reach one's fullest potential	发挥全部潜能
evolve into	发展成，进化成
make up	组成；补足；化妆；编造
in effect	实际上；生效
be grounded in	以…为基础；以…为根据
tailor to	定制；使适应；适用于
dream about	梦见；梦想
in a quest to	为了；寻求；以便
turn down	拒绝；调低；减轻
expose to	暴露于；使曝光；处于…影响之下
go through	参加；经受；仔细检查；被通过
in this respect	在这方面
as intended	根据预期

Unit 9

A… than any B other than C	除了 C 以外，A 比起 B 都要…
A be home to B	A 是 B 的家乡
in terms of	依据；按照；在…方面；以…措词
come in	出现；流行起来；起作用

in a range of	一定范围内；一系列的
emerged as	成为
(far) out of proportion to	（远）不成比例
be rooted in	深植于
come to realize	恍然；逐渐意识到
spill forth	泄漏出来；溢出
fuzzy around the edges	（某物）的意义甚为含糊；边缘模糊
nature and nurture	先天与后天；遗传与环境
excel in	在…方面胜过；在…方面很擅长
as a result of	因此，由于；作为…的结果
at a premium	高价；很受珍视；极为珍贵
hamper…from… (doing sth.)	阻碍…做…
It should come as no surprise that…	应该不足为奇
trace (…) to…	上溯；追查到
by way of	经由；途径；用…方法
in part	部分地；某种程度上
contribute to	有助于，促成
compete in	参加…比赛

Unit 10

be at play	起作用
figure in	包括进；列入
in pursuit of	追求
conform to	遵从，与…一致
press for	迫切要求
be crucial to	对…至关重要
square off	（打斗等时）摆好（架势）；准备好
arise out of	出自；源自
in that	因为

Unit 11

at best	充其量，至多
attribute to	归功于，归因于
clamber up	爬上，攀登
deprive of	剥夺，使失去…（权利）
in turn	轮流，依次
occur to	想到，意识到
on the defensive	取防守姿式，处于防御状态
pass muster	合格，符合要求

prop up	支撑，支持；给…撑腰；资助
split off	分裂，决裂
submit to	屈服；呈交
to the detriment of	有损于，对…有害

Unit 12

of one's own accord	主动地，自愿地
be identical to	与…相同，相当于
be preoccupied with	对…神贯注
get at	领会
have the knowledge	拥有知识；知道
in depth	深入地；详细地
may well be	很可能
fashion…into	制作，使成形；把…塑造成

Vocabulary List

A

abate	(10)	advocacy	(8)
aberration	(7)	aerobic	(9)
aboriginal	(9)	afflict	(9)
abortion	(10)	agile	(9)
absorbing	(12)	alienate	(7)
accommodating	(1)	alienated	(11)
accord	(12)	alleviate	(10)
accountability	(8)	ample	(6)
acquiescent	(10)	anaerobic	(9)
actuality	(6)	analog	(7)
address	(8)	anatomical	(9)
adrift	(11)	anatomy	(10)
advocacy	(8)	animalistic	(9)
aerobic	(9)	anthropological	(9)
afflict	(9)	anthropologist	(9)
abate	(10)	anticipate	(6)
aberration	(7)	appropriation	(10)
aboriginal	(9)	aptitude	(1)
abortion	(10)	arbitrary	(11)
absorbing	(12)	arrogance	(2)
accommodating	(1)	artifact	(7)
accord	(12)	assume	(12)
accountability	(8)	assumption	(6)
acquiescent	(10)	asymmetrical	(3)
actuality	(6)	at best	(11)
address	(8)	athenian	(11)
adrift	(11)	athleticism	(9)
		atomic	(6)

attorney	(3)	chrysanthemum	(3)
attribute	(1)	circulate	(6)
attribute	(11)	clamber	(11)
authoritative	(4)	clarify	(12)

B

		clearing	(12)
barb	(3)	cluster	(9)
barbell	(3)	cognitive disability	(8)
befall	(9)	cohort	(1)
Belarus	(8)	colonialism	(9)
Belorussian	(8)	commitment	(1)
benevolent	(6)	commonplace	(7)
biodiversity	(9)	comparatively	(5)
biomechanical	(9)	computer graphics	(7)
birthrate	(5)	condemn	(12)
blemish	(11)	confer	(9)
blemish	(2)	confront	(2)
blunt	(3)	connote	(4)
blur	(3)	constipated	(3)
blur	(7)	constraint	(4)
bravado	(2)	contemplate	(6)
brawny	(10)	contemporary	(4)
brim	(2)	controversial	(9)
bubble	(12)	convert	(7)
bulk	(9)	cosmetics	(10)
bulletin	(4)	counterpart	(5)
burgeon	(5)	coverage	(8)
butch-fem	(10)	crack	(2)
buttock	(9)	credential	(1)

C

		crude	(12)
cable	(4)	curriculum	(8)
caliber	(9)		

D

campaign	(4)	day-care	(5)
carnival	(5)	dearth	(5)
cascade	(9)	decimate	(6)
caveat	(9)	decline	(5)
censure	(11)	decompose	(12)
cerebral palsyn	(8)	decriminalization	(10)
chameleon	(2)	deference	(10)
childbearing	(5)	demeaning	(11)

depreciate	(6)	draw	(4)
depreciation	(11)	dropout	(2)
deprivation	(8)	**E**	
deprive	(11)	economics	(5)
deprived	(8)	economist	(5)
despairing	(11)	ego	(1)
despotism	(6)	egregious	(9)
deter	(12)	elevate	(8)
determinism	(9)	elite	(9)
detriment	(11)	élite	(1)
devastated	(8)	elope	(3)
deviate	(1)	embodiment	(10)
devilish	(7)	enchantment	(11)
devise	(3)	enchilada	(1)
diabolical	(6)	encode	(9)
dichotomy	(10)	encode	(7)
differentiate	(9)	endeavor	(9)
diffuse	(5)	endeavor	(12)
diminish	(5)	endorse	(10)
dire	(5)	endurance	(9)
disabuse	(1)	enrapture	(9)
disciple	(11)	entail	(7)
disciplinarian	(10)	entrench	(8)
disciplinary	(10)	environmentalist	(6)
discourse	(12)	enzyme	(9)
discretionary	(10)	epistle	(12)
disembowel	(3)	equation	(7)
disintegrate	(12)	equivalent	(1)
dismantle	(10)	equivocal	(4)
disparage	(11)	erode	(3)
disparaging	(3)	erode	(12)
disparate	(1)	erotic	(10)
disruption	(8)	eternity	(12)
dissect	(11)	Eurasian	(9)
dissolve	(7)	evacuation	(8)
dissolve	(12)	evolve	(8)
divine	(3)	exact	(10)
don	(10)	excel	(9)
donate	(8)	exertion	(1)

explicit	(3)	**H**	
exploitation	(8)	hackles	(2)
extension	(10)	hamper	(9)
extremity	(9)	harassment	(8)
exuberance	(5)	hemlock	(12)
F		heritable	(9)
facilitator	(8)	hoary	(5)
faculty	(12)	hotbed	(9)
fad	(3)	hotshot	(2)
famine	(5)	howl	(2)
fertility	(5)	huff	(3)
fetishism	(7)	humanity	(9)
fetus	(10)	humanity	(6)
fiscal	(5)	hydrogen	(6)
fixture	(9)	hygiene	(10)
flourish	(10)	hygiene kits	(8)
flung	(3)	hypotheses	(6)
-fold	(9)	**I**	
forego	(2)	identical	(12)
forte	(2)	illusion	(2)
forthcoming	(2)	imbue	(2)
forthcoming	(4)	immediacy	(4)
fortify	(2)	immutable	(12)
fraction	(9)	impartiality	(4)
frail	(9)	imposter	(2)
fretful	(11)	incandescent	(2)
fringe	(3)	incentive	(1)
funnel	(1)	inclusive	(10)
funnel	(9)	incorporate	(4)
G		incur	(4)
galvanizing	(2)	indignity	(9)
generalization	(9)	indisputable	(9)
genetic	(9)	inequality	(9)
genocidal	(9)	infatuation	(2)
grain	(1)	inflect	(10)
greasy	(3)	inform	(4)
grove	(12)	infrastructure	(10)
growl	(12)	inherent	(7)
		insinuation	(10)

institute	(10)	mink	(3)
institutional	(6)	minority	(9)
institutional	(10)	misconception	(8)
integrity	(8)	misperception	(8)
intellectual	(5)	mobilize	(8)
interface	(7)	modus operandi	(2)
interminable	(11)	monetize	(1)
intervention	(8)	moratorium	(2)
irresistible	(12)	mundane	(3)
irrevocable	(2)	muscularity	(9)

L

		muster	(11)
lag	(9)	mutable	(7)
lamely	(11)	mutations	(9)
legion	(10)	mutter	(3)
legitimate	(6)		

N

legitimate	(1)	narcissism	(11)
lesbian	(10)	necessitate	(10)
licentious	(10)	negate	(11)
liken	(10)	netball	(9)
literally	(12)	nimble	(10)
literate	(1)	normalcy	(8)
loafer	(3)	notably	(9)
loop	(9)	notion	(9)
lopsided	(12)	nuance	(8)
lossy	(7)	nudge	(3)
lukewarm	(3)	nurture	(9)

M

O

malevolent	(6)	objectify	(10)
malnutrition	(8)	obnoxious	(1)
manipulate	(7)	obstinate	(3)
marrow	(2)	obstinately	(2)
maternity	(10)	offset	(4)
mechanism	(1)	omnipotent	(2)
melanin	(10)	orphanage	(8)
mentor	(2)	orthodoxy	(9)
meritocracy	(1)	outgrow	(2)
mesomorphic	(9)	outnumber	(5)
metabolic	(9)	output	(5)
metaphor	(7)	outsized	(9)

Vocabulary List   253

overtone	(11)	pristine	(3)
overturn	(9)	problematic	(6)
		proclivity	(9)

P

pagan	(11)	productivity	(5)
paradoxical	(11)	progenitor	(7)
patron	(3)	project	(12)
pedagogical	(11)	pronounced	(7)
pejorative	(2)	prop	(7)
pensionable	(5)	prophecy	(5)
pensioner	(5)	proposition	(12)
perception	(12)	protract	(10)
perfectible	(6)	provisional	(2)
permanently	(3)	prowess	(9)
pernicious	(9)	prudent	(1)
perpetuate	(8)	pseudoscience	(9)
perversity	(6)	psychosocial	(8)
petition	(8)	putter	(6)
phrenology	(9)		

R

pigment	(10)	racism	(9)
pinch	(3)	racist	(9)
pinecone	(12)	radical	(3)
pixel	(7)	ravage	(9)
plea	(12)	ravaged	(8)
plight	(5)	recession	(5)
plummet	(5)	reconfigure	(7)
pogrom	(9)	rector	(8)
Polynesia	(9)	redress	(10)
pool	(8)	reflective	(1)
potency	(2)	reflex	(9)
preceding	(4)	reinforce	(1)
preen	(11)	renounce	(11)
pregnancy	(10)	replicable	(7)
premiership	(9)	resilient	(8)
premise	(6)	resolution	(7)
premonition	(6)	resource	(5)
preoccupy	(12)	resume	(8)
preserve	(12)	retain	(4)
presuppose	(12)	revealing	(10)
principal	(12)	reverence	(5)

reverse	(5)	stereotype	(9)
rigorous	(1)	sterilization	(10)
roulette	(9)	stewardship	(8)
S		stink	(3)
sanction	(10)	stopwatch	(1)
sanitation	(8)	straddle	(9)
scrutiny	(6)	straightforward	(4)
scrutiny	(11)	streak	(2)
scum	(3)	stumble	(12)
seductive	(11)	subject	(1)
seductress	(2)	subjugation	(10)
self-respecting	(12)	submit	(11)
sensory	(12)	sub-Saharan	(9)
session	(8)	subsequent	(4)
simulate	(7)	subsequent	(12)
singular	(10)	subsidize	(1)
skepticism	(6)	subvert	(7)
skittery	(3)	suffice	(1)
skull	(9)	surge	(9)
sloppy	(1)	surmise	(6)
smattering	(6)	susceptibility	(8)
smug	(6)	sustained	(8)
sneaky	(3)	symphony	(3)
sniff	(3)	symptom	(5)
snifter	(3)	synonymous	(7)
sociologist	(9)	**T**	
solidify	(7)	taboo	(9)
somatic	(10)	tactless	(3)
soother	(2)	tangible	(12)
sovereignty	(10)	Tarahumara	(9)
span	(5)	taxpayer	(5)
spatial	(7)	Tay-Sachs	(9)
speck	(3)	temperamental	(10)
split	(11)	tempt	(4)
sprint	(9)	tempting	(12)
sprinter	(9)	tentative	(2)
stance	(10)	terrestrial	(4)
startling	(5)	thigh	(9)
startlingly	(9)	thrall	(10)

thrive	(8)	unheralded	(5)
throes	(11)	unseat	(10)
thrust	(6)	unsupervised	(8)
thwart	(1)	uphold	(10)
timeslot	(4)	upsurge	(6)
tonal	(7)	utensil	(8)
torso	(9)	**V**	
trailer	(4)	variable	(9)
transgender	(10)	Venezuela	(5)
transient	(2)	vestiges	(11)
traumatic	(8)	visualize	(12)
treatise	(12)	vivacious	(2)
trepidation	(2)	vulnerability	(8)
trichotomy	(9)	**W**	
triumphant	(3)	warp	(1)
tug	(2)	watershed	(4)
tune	(4)	whirl	(12)
U		**Y**	
undergraduate	(1)	youthful	(5)
underhanded	(9)